John Griffiths has been an account planner for most of his career in agencies including JWT Manchester, FCB and CDP. He was one of the first planners to work outside a pure advertising environment in the 1990s as integrated communications came to the fore. He founded the consultancy Planning Above and Beyond, and regularly writes on the web about planning and research issues.

Tracey Follows has worked in advertising for over 20 years, both client and agency side. She was Chief Strategy Officer at J. Walter Thompson after VCCP, Lowe, McCann-Erickson and Cogent and has worked in marketing at BT, One2One and T-Mobile. She is now Chief Strategy and Innovation Officer at The Future Laboratory. She was Chair of the APG (Account Planning Group) 2014–2015.

98% Pure Potato

The origins of advertising account planning

JOHN GRIFFITHS
and
TRACEY FOLLOWS

unbound

unbound

This edition first published in 2016

Unbound
6th Floor Mutual House, 70 Conduit Street, London W1S 2GF
www.unbound.co.uk

Text Design by Ellipsis

A CIP record for this book is available from the British Library

ISBN 978-1-78352-228-6 (trade hbk)
ISBN 978-1-78352-229-3 (ebook)
ISBN 978-1-78352-291-0 (limited edition)

Printed in Great Britain by Clays Ltd, St Ives Plc.

1 3 5 7 9 8 6 4 2

For our families

Dear Reader,

The book you are holding came about in a rather different way to most others. It was funded directly by readers through a new website: Unbound. Unbound is the creation of three writers. We started the company because we believed there had to be a better deal for both writers and readers. On the Unbound website, authors share the ideas for the books they want to write directly with readers. If enough of you support the book by pledging for it in advance, we produce a beautifully bound special subscribers' edition and distribute a regular edition and e-book wherever books are sold, in shops and online.

This new way of publishing is actually a very old idea (Samuel Johnson funded his dictionary this way). We're just using the internet to build each writer a network of patrons. Here, at the back of this book, you'll find the names of all the people who made it happen.

Publishing in this way means readers are no longer just passive consumers of the books they buy, and authors are free to write the books they really want. They get a much fairer return too – half the profits their books generate, rather than a tiny percentage of the cover price.

If you're not yet a subscriber, we hope that you'll want to join our publishing revolution and have your name listed in one of our books in the future. To get you started, here is a £5 discount on your first pledge. Just visit unbound.com, make your pledge and type **purepotato** in the promo code box when you check out.

Thank you for your support,

Dan, Justin and John
Founders, Unbound

Contents

Chapter 4 – The professionalisation of planning

Chapter 5 – Where does account planning go from here?

Appendix

98% Pure Potato

Foreword

Contrary to what now so often gets said about the 1960s, I was there *and* I do remember it. The account planning bit anyway.

For me, in my 'callow youth' phase, the 'there', then, was Birmingham. Bournville and Cadbury to be precise. Early in my career, I was on the receiving end of – and a minor participant in – a quiet revolution (always the best sort, I think – you can still tinker): the emergence of 'account planners'.

In the latter half of the 1960s, out of one of our agencies, Pritchard Wood and Partners (PWP), was born a new agency, Boase Massimi Pollitt (BMP), featuring a new person in the familiar agency line-up, the account planner.

Conceived and shaped by Stanley Pollitt, and led from day one by Peter Jones, this made concrete and personified what had been bubbling under for some time at PWP: a better way to use research and other data in advertising development, for moving things forward not just measuring back, adding some subtlety and sensitivity, and an antidote to much that was then mechanistic, faddy and, often imported, mumbo jumbo.

A new approach and a new person to join others, centre stage, in agencies. Not one content to sit in the wings waiting for an occasional appearance.

Via BMP, one half of the birth of account planning.

We – the Cadbury Foods Group – moved some of our business to this new agency. We gave them their first business (Cadbury's Smash included). They gave us Martians (amongst other things), sales and awards. We got the better of the deal.

Meanwhile, at much the same time – spookily indeed for

this foreword – Stephen King came to Bournville to do a talk. Odd seeming, even at the time, since J. Walter Thompson (JWT) was not one of our agencies – Rowntree being rather important to them – but someone had met and invited him and he was not one to shrink from spreading the word. Wisdom-packed, of course, with his seminal thinking on the ad development process and its organisation, and his approach to account planning and the account planner.

Via JWT, the other half of the birth of account planning.

One birth: two fathers. And better for it in my view. Fathers as different as could be in most respects as, indeed, were their two agencies.

Pollitt and King are now rightly recognised and lauded, venerated almost – as is the creative leadership without which they couldn't have succeeded anything like as well (John Webster and Jeremy Bullmore: what a couple of planners they'd have been – correction, 'were', notwithstanding job titles).

What it was all about and why it came about is well enough known and has been well written about. This book will add to that. But what is much less well known, indeed little known, is how and by whom that thinking and leadership was turned into action, how it was put into practice, day by day, in the formative years.

This book serves, in particular, to put that right.

It is about the pioneers, the early account planners. It's about who they were, what they did and what they learned – many of the lessons as relevant today and still being learned. It's about how they moved things on and how foundations were laid upon which something substantial has since been built, standing the test of time.

That callow youth moved on too, just a few years later, joining the, by then, rather noisier revolution – helping start TBWA London, and starting account planning there. Not slavishly following, but certainly much influenced by the two agencies and the early account planners who kicked it all off.

Here then, a long time coming perhaps but, surely, better late than never, is a proper recognition of those early planners and what they started. Unsung then and still so, in many cases, today. Not any longer.

I, for one, am grateful to them and their efforts. And I am far from alone.

John Bartle

1965–73 Cadbury / Cadbury Schweppes
1973–82 TBWA London
1982–99 Bartle Bogle Hegarty

Introduction – how we came to write the book (and what it has to do with potatoes)

This book, like most, has several beginnings. My favourite was the Marketing Society annual conference in 2007. A chance meeting during a coffee break with a man with closely cropped grey hair and a steady look who handed over his card. It read *Forensics – Marketing Detective.* A dead giveaway for someone who had obviously been an account planner in a former life. Planners are archetypal problem-solvers and always present themselves as such. But what really caught the attention was his name. I knew who he was. Possibly the only person in the room who did. And he wasn't telling because he didn't know if it meant anything to anyone. David Cowan was named in Stanley Pollitt's paper 'How I started account planning in advertising agencies' as one of his first hires. This was one of the first planners ever. 001 or 002 to use Ian Fleming's parlance. And since Stanley Pollitt died in 1979 this was as close to the mother lode as anybody was going to get. The rest of our conversation is lost but I remember asking for an interview with him to talk about how he got started in planning. The year before I had heard of the death of Stephen King, the other father of planning, who started the planning department at J. Walter Thompson in 1976. And I couldn't believe it. I had had his email in my address book for a year, but never got around to mailing him to ask him to talk to me about why he started the function and what he thought about what had happened next. I promised myself that at some point I was going to try to talk to as many of the first generation as possible. It took another five years to keep that promise. But in the summer of 2012 with the help of Tracey Follows, at that point Chief Strategy Officer at J. Walter Thompson, the project finally got started and the names, numbers and email addresses started to roll in. Planners who had started working at Pritchard Wood, the forerunner of Boase Massimi Pollitt, and then from Boase Massimi Pollitt. And from J. Walter Thompson whose planning department opened in the same year. The first generation of planners told us how they did the job.

Oral history feels very different from papers and documents. Stephen King was a prolific writer of papers. He also designed processes and schematics to make the thinking about advertising and how it worked more explicit. Stanley Pollitt wrote relatively little. Both held court and that is what the planners told us about them. They revelled in informal meetings where planners argued about how advertising ideas worked and how people understood advertising ideas. And the most rigorous thinkers and the most persuasive debaters won. You get no sense of that reading the literature. But it's in these sessions that planning thinking was formed and tested and articulated. Planners didn't spend their time writing papers but producing advertising and demonstrating its commercial effectiveness.

This tiny band of intellectuals (because that is what they were) has swelled to cover not only the whole of the UK advertising industry, but across North America and most of the rest of the world as well. Planning has burst its banks and migrated to virtually every different kind of communications agency. Many companies, who once only had marketing departments, have planning departments as well. Planners have gone and started research agencies and new product development companies. Their fingerprints are everywhere. Planning is one of the greatest exports that Britain has produced in the last 50 years. And this is the story of how it came about. Why it matters and how planning as originally understood can revolutionise the way you think about marketing communications. Yes, there's a lot more advertising around these days. And a lot of it isn't very good. Yes, there's a lot of terrible research. But there was bad advertising and terrible research when planning had its beginnings. The purpose of planning was to fight back against dull advertising and meaningless research. And stupid or non-existent thinking. That is what planners are still doing.

So you're still wondering about the potato and that percentage aren't you? We called the book *98% Pure Potato* for several reasons. It is a line taken from one of the many famous Smash potato TV ads. The Smash ads featuring the Martians, consistently top the nation's list of favourite TV ads. It is the most enjoyable and seemingly the most memorable of the last 40 years or so. It was a Smash ad that led indirectly to the start of BMP's new planning approach of pretesting advertising creative with consumers. An unresearched Cadbury's Smash ad which failed in the market led to a new way of working where the voice of the consumer was put at the heart of the development of creative ideas. '98% pure potato' is a proposition, and therefore symbolic of what most planners spend most of their time doing – crafting clever propositions. But it's also a contradiction – a reminder that the way the best advertising works is through making a creative leap to something beyond words. Or are we overthinking this one? It's one of those quips that admirers put down to British humour. Account planning is a British invention after all.

We never set out to write a textbook or a history book but something rather different. To give you the chance to learn from the diverse group of individuals who first did the job and established its character. Who made it work and in so doing helped create some of the best and most effective advertising ever. Let's do it again.

John Griffiths and Tracey Follows

The gallery – an introduction to our interviewees

Here follows a list of the pioneering planners we interviewed. What makes this book special is that the story is drawn from interviews with all of those listed.

David Baker

Joined JWT's media department in 1968 with a degree in pure maths and discovered that negotiating skills were more highly prized there. So he moved into the new planning department. He then realised he could have more influence on strategic thinking by working as a senior account handler. But during the 1990s he was brought back into the planning department to manage it. He developed a system called Total Branding deployed by JWT worldwide to implement integrated brand communications.

James Best

Was brought into BMP as a graduate trainee in 1975. He was spotted by Martin Boase and moved across into account management and then a senior role in the agency. A former chair of DDB, he is current chair of the Code of Advertising Practice and the advertising think tank Credos.

John Bruce

Started his career in Masius as a media planner where he worked with mainframe computers, then moved across to J. Walter Thompson's media department. He was present at the meeting in August 1968 when Tony Stead suggested that the new role be called 'account planning'. And he was one of the first who moved from media into the new planning department. John eventually moved on to work at other agencies as an account handler. He has worked as a researcher with Peter Cooper at CRAM and as a lecturer of advertising.

Leslie Butterfield
Was hired as a graduate trainee into Boase Massimi Pollitt's planning department in 1975. He was headhunted to start the planning department at Abbott Mead Vickers when BMP was a top 20 agency and AMV a mere start-up. From there he founded his own agency Butterfield Day Devito Hockney. When we interviewed him he was Global Chief Strategy Officer for Interbrand.

David Clifford
Was brought to CDP from the London Press Exchange to start a planning department there in 1972 when Frank Lowe arrived to be the new MD. CDP was one of the first agencies after BMP and JWT to set up planning and they used it quite differently. (CDP is arguably the most creative agency the UK has ever produced so this warranted a closer investigation.) Five of those we interviewed had worked there. Jay Chiat, besotted with CDP, came over to discover their secret. It was David Clifford who explained how planning could be used to sell clients work they would otherwise be too nervous to run. Chiat returned to the US determined to bringing planning into his agency and found Jane Newman (see below) in New York. David went on to work at Lintas and McCann Erickson.

David Cowan
Cited by Stanley Pollitt as one of the first two planning hires (ever) in 1966 when he joined Pritchard Wood as a graduate trainee, to work in the experimental market planning depart-

ment. He joined J. Walter Thompson just in time for the start of their account planning department in 1968 and then joined the fledgling Boase Massimi Pollitt a couple of years later. He was Head of Planning during the 1970s.

Paul Feldwick

Joined Boase Massimi Pollitt in 1974 as an account management trainee then moved across to planning after a year. Paul is a former planning director of BMP, a former chair of the IPA Effectiveness Awards (twice) and arguably the most well known of those we interviewed. Often referred to as a planning guru, he is author of *What is Brand Equity, Anyway?* He co-authored with Robert Heath the paper, 'Fifty years of using the wrong model of advertising'. And in February of 2015 published *The Anatomy of Humbug – How to Think Differently about Advertising.*

Lee Godden

Was recruited by Stephen King into the J. Walter Thompson planning department in 1970. She had already worked in New York for five years in a variety of roles in advertising research. She describes herself as an intuitive who understands brands. Lee worked on Unilever for many years until she moved first into HR and then the training of planners around the world.

Christine Gray

Started as a qualitative researcher at BMRB but was recruited into the J. Walter Thompson planning department in 1970 and spent her whole planning career in the agency.

Ev Jenkins

Started as a Unilever marketing trainee from where she was headhunted into J. Walter Thompson's planning department in 1975. She acquired a reputation for being one of the most persuasive planners in the department. After JWT, she moved to be planning director at McCann Erickson.

Peter Jones

One of Stanley Pollitt's first hires, Peter Jones was a founder member of the market planning department at Pritchard Wood in 1965. He moved with the directors to Boase Massimi Pollitt when it was founded. Peter was instrumental in setting up and defining the planning department – he moved swiftly into senior management specifically negotiating acquisitions and the flotation. He eventually became a global board director of DDB in New York. Peter also managed a parallel career as an entrepreneur and trainer in horse racing, culminating with him becoming the chairman of the Tote.

Jack Krelle

Jack started his career as a creative at J. Walter Thompson. Jeremy Bullmore persuaded him to move across to the planning department in 1974. During the 1980s he moved to work as a planner at CDP, before moving to the market research agency SRU.

John Madell

One of the first three graduate trainees hired into the planning department at Boase Massimi Pollitt in 1969 a year after it opened. John was one of those who set the standard for what planners did at BMP. He founded his own agency Madell Wilmot Pringle and a research agency Drummond Madell. He also did a stint as chairman of EuroRSCG. He's the only former planner we interviewed with his own yacht and trout stream!

Tony Mortemore

Was working as a school-leaver at Glaxo when he decided to try to get into advertising. That was in 1964. Stanley Pollitt offered him a job at Pritchard Wood who had Glaxo as a client. Tony moved into the fledgling Market Planning department when it began. When the directors went off to start Boase Massimi Pollitt he had to find work elsewhere so he moved as a researcher to General Foods. From where David Cowan got him into J. Walter Thompson's planning department. He and John Siddall were headhunted a few years later to be planners at CDP where Tony was the planner who developed *that* Heineken campaign. The one that refreshes the parts that other beers don't reach.

Jane Newman

Was another of the three graduates hired into Boase Massimi Pollitt's planning department in 1969. She quickly established herself as a formidable planner, managing the next two graduate trainees, Ross Barr and Chris Cowpe. Jane moved to America to work first in Chicago and then in New York. Jay Chiat hired her to start planning in Chiat/Day. The first thing she worked on was Apple's '1984' campaign. Jane is generally regarded as the founding mother of North American planning. After a number of years she went off to travel the world and now lives in Kenya working on the Thorntree project improving education for Samburu girls from one of Kenya's nomadic tribes. She was inducted in the Advertising Hall of Fame in 2014.

Terry Prue

Started as an analyst at Southern TV before joining J. Walter Thompson in the media department and talking his way into the planning department in 1978. Terry was one of the last of the planners we interviewed who worked at J. Walter Thompson. A specialist in quantitative research and evaluation, he won four IPA Effectiveness Awards while at JWT and served on the judges panel a further four times. He moved to be a partner at the research agency Hudson Payne and Iddiols.

Doug Richardson

Started in the media department at J. Walter Thompson. The memo announcing the launch of the account planning department lists him as head of media research, but within a year he had moved into account planning and became a group head and then the first head of planning, succeeding Stephen King. Doug went on to work in New York at Ogilvy & Mather starting one of the first planning departments in the USA, and then working with Tim Bell in pioneering planning thinking in corporate branding. He died in 2013.

John Siddall

Started as a trainee at Dorlands then got a job at J. Walter Thompson in the planning department in 1970 as one of their youngest planners. From there he was headhunted to work as one of the first planners at CDP before moving to work in BMP's planning department as a group head in 1974. John is one of the rare planners who has a critical perspective that goes across these key agencies. He went on to set up Reflexions, the advertising research agency. He currently runs the Fine Cheese Company and Artisan Biscuits with his partner Anne Marie Dyas, a former account handler from BMP.

Cathy Simmonds

Started as a marketing trainee at Unilever. From where she moved to Vernons as a quantitative researcher and then moved to CDP in the mid 1970s. She was strongly influenced by the arrival and spread of qualitative research which helped you answer the question 'Why?' in a way that quantitative research could not. After CDP she moved to Saatchis and then ran her own communications consultancy.

Roderick White

Joined J. Walter Thompson's marketing department in 1962. When in 1968 half of the department were co-opted, with the media planners, by Stephen King to become the new planning department, Roderick stayed in marketing to work on consultancy projects. He became head of planning at the JWT subsidiary Lansdowne Euro 10 years later. Much later he became editor of *Admap* magazine.

Jim Williams

Was the last of the three graduates hired into Boase Massimi Pollitt's planning department in 1969. A postgraduate physicist with a passion for the theatre, he worked on Courage and established himself as the planner who knew more about beer drinkers than any one else in the country – including the client – because he talked to more of them (several times a week). Jim went on to be planning director first at SJIP and then at Young & Rubicam. He was commissioned to develop the Brand Asset Valuator system based on the theory of archetypes, a system that was deployed by Y&R all over the world.

Jan Zajac

Started as a researcher in the research agency NOP before being recruited into BMP in 1974. He has worked across a number of agencies including J. Walter Thompson and CDP, giving him a unique perspective across the agencies.

Other people we talked to:

John Bartle who was the first ever client who worked with planners while at Bournville – first with Pritchard Wood and then at BMP. John moved into planning himself in 1974 when he was asked to set up planning at TBWA. Ten years later he was a founder of Bartle Bogle Hegarty.

Martin Boase who was a director at Pritchard Wood and a founder of Boase Massimi Pollitt – one of the first 'suits' to see the value of account planning.

Jeremy Bullmore joined J. Walter Thompson in 1954 and persuaded Stephen King to join a few years later. They were at school and university together. Jeremy became head of TV in 1964. His partnership with Stephen King as creative and planning thinker is the stuff of legend. The two of them persuaded JWT's clients of the long-term value of advertising in building brands.

Louise Cook who worked at BMP as one of the first econometric modellers.

Peter Dart who was a product manager for Persil and one of the earliest clients working with planners. He went on to found Added Value, one of the first brand consultancies to actively work to take brand consultancy back from planners in ad agencies!

Roddy Glen who was hired by David Cowan to manage the qualitative research function in BMP in the mid-seventies.

Geoff Howard-Spink who was hired to work at Boase Massimi Pollitt as an account handler and moved to CDP to work with Frank Lowe. In 1981 they set up their own agency Lowe Howard-Spink at which point he became the head of planning.

Dave Trott started his career as a creative in New York. He was the first BMP hire when John Webster took over as creative director from Gabe Massimi, so experienced planning at BMP first hand. He went on to start his own agency Gold Greenlees Trott with a planning director taken from BMP, Barry Pritchard.

Judie Lannon who was recruited by Stephen King to set up a creative research department at J. Walter Thompson prior to the launch of the planning department in 1968.

Creenagh Lodge who was hugely influential in researching advertising at Pritchard Wood, and in the way advertising was pretested at BMP though she never worked there. She set up her own new product development consultancy Craton Lodge and Knight.

Adam Lury joined BMP as a planner in 1980, too late to be included in the core list of interviewees for this book. But he is fiercely critical of BMP planning and went on to develop a different model when he started his own agency Howell Henry Chaldecott Lury, which pioneered interactive advertising in the UK.

Tess and Katy Pollitt – Stanley Pollitt's daughters.

Jon Steel also falls outside the 1980 cut off point, joining BMP as a planner after that. But he then went on to set up planning in the West Coast agency Goodby Silverstein, and as such is hugely competent to comment on the development of planning in the USA. He is currently Group Planning Director at WPP.

Chapter 1

The context

Account planning nears 50 – pause for thought

As account planning approaches its fiftieth year it would be wise to take a breather to consider where the role has got to. Middle age can leave you short of breath. It can trigger a midlife crisis. There is a moment where you notice that you have been doing the job longer than those who taught you how to do the job. In the case of one of the authors, he realised that he had been doing the job longer than those who taught him could have been called account planners! Account planning is a craft which is passed on from the senior planners to the junior. As are most skills in advertising. The name is still problematic reflecting the high status of planning – aka town planning, corporate planning, scenario planning – in the energetic 1960s when the past was being demolished and the future was being built. The 1970s oil shock brought that optimism to an abrupt end.

So where have we got to?

Well, global domination, if job titles are anything to go by. There are planners in every advertising agency around the world, although some may have rebranded themselves as strategists. There are debates about whether strategy is different from planning and more high-end. Planners are no longer to be found only in ad agencies. They have also started popping up in almost every other kind of agency. Inevitably their job description varies depending on what that agency does and how it earns its money. Agencies who publically repudiated planning usually quietly reintroduced it some time later. But that is probably because marketers expect a strategic contribution from their agency and like there to be an alternative point of view to that of the account handler, who represents their interests, and the creative, who have work to sell. Nearly 50 years on, the account planning role is the most recent substantial role to be introduced into agencies since visualisers – better known as art directors – were recruited to support copywriters and then partner with them in creative teams. Planning is an interesting role since the function has to be charged directly these days by billing planners' hours to clients, and planners are not essential to the process of making communications. Someone is perfectly capable of collecting a brief from the client to create advertising and to present it back to them. There are craftspeople to make the work and to place it in the media. Recently there has been some attempt to reposition planners as a subset among creative people who borrow, re-appropriate or possibly even create branded content. The strategist becomes an executioner. But the planner's output today is part social, part conceptual. Planners still don't make 'stuff'.

The mention of the 'brand' word is also another cue, since the scope of brands today is truly vast. From packaging, to relationships with producers, distributors, retailers and, of course, customers, brands have sprawled in all directions. There is an army of caretakers who ensure that communications is kept 'on brand' and fits with everything else. A generation ago those policing the frontiers of brand identity were flippantly nicknamed 'logocops'! Today with programmes of social listening in place, what customers are saying and whether or not they actually name brands when they post on social media platforms, has to be engaged with and incorporated into the marketing team's overall narrative. An advertising museum showing work from the 1950s could point at packaging, shelf labels and, of course, advertisements. Today that would be only a subset of the branded material in use today. So the work of agencies has become more cerebral and there is a need to co-ordinate all this content. So more work for planners – some of whom have taken to calling themselves brand planners.

Then there is what has come to be known as 'big data.' Organisations have found that the generation of data about products and customer behaviour and usage has broken all boundaries. Most of the analytics deployed to make sense of this is automated. There is an emerging function of data scientists creating dashboards and monitoring data streams because there is far too much to be easily summarised. But a client has to be very bold before they turn their backs on the 'data tsunami,' opting to concentrate on the core business. Who is to say that the next market leader doesn't leapfrog their way to the top because they have found an algorithm for reimagining the market in a totally different way? So marketers hire more data analysts and grimly play the zero-sum game. Just in case. Planners within agencies have a vested interest in looking at this data even if their time and attention is limited. They likewise need to keep up with what the analysts are studying.

That is hard to do because the planning function has become stretched. Planners can work across numerous pieces of agency business. They may be the only planner in their agency or the one assigned to work on a particular range of business, so rarely work with other planners. This casts them into the role of representing *the* strategic point of view. It may be difficult if not impossible to get a wider perspective. Even in agencies with a sizable department of planners, there can be little overlap – so others don't know what you are doing, and are able to make little contribution to it, even where there time to do so. So although most of the work is team-based, the planner is relatively isolated from their peer group. The proxy has often been professional bodies like the Account Planning Group. Planners have also been very communicative with each other online. It's an ideas business and however proprietary the ideas in their clients' businesses, there seems nothing proprietary about planning ideas which circulate over and over.

Then there is the nature of the planning task, which has expanded. Planning can take on everything from market analysis in a pitch situation, to market sizing and segmentation, to customer understanding, to customer journeys, to media touchpoints, and to managing experiential architecture. And let's not forget evaluation and return on investment. In reality planners may only deal with a subset of these, but they are often expected to be able to contribute at all of these levels even if they are not expected to deliver them. Where there is anxiety about the number of hours to be used, the planner is nudged towards execution – demonstrating that they are able to support the rest of the team in delivering the volume of communications across the variety of platforms which the client now routinely expects.

As if all of this weren't enough, campaigns solicit customer feedback. And commentary and criticism need to be countered and incorporated. Real time has become the way to operate. There are campaigns where the marketing team sets up a 'war room' and buys space and repurposes content within hours, depending on what feedback has been received. There is a need to make active choices about what serves the needs of the brand best, where further investment needs to be made – or an unhelpful avenue discouraged. This requires thought – often with minimal time for reflection. So planners have found themselves on the front line, supporting tactical decision-making to such an extent that tactics can seem to be more productive than the original one or two strategic choices before the campaign was commissioned.

We mentioned the relative isolation of the planner. That is only part of the story. Often the planner finds themselves in competition with other planners from other agencies. If the client has put all of their work into a single agency, well and good. But more often than not, the client is using a range of different types of agency. Each with their own planner. Each of whom has a separate point of view. The planner in the ad agency at the top of the food chain can bang the table and shout with the loudest voice. But not always. And on international campaigns there may be planners whose expertise relates to geographical areas, or particular segments of the business. So planners have to become adept around the strategy table as diplomats herding cats. Woe betide the planner who is caught representing the client's interest above that of their own agency.

And this represents the last challenge: which is of being pushed towards a sales role where planners are under pressure as advocates of their agency's output, working in their agency's interest whether or not that work has been properly thought through or is likely to be effective. It is difficult if not impossible for planners to represent the agency's conscience in tension with the account handers and creatives under these sorts of pressures.

Has planning always been this way?

Has planning always been this way? Is this a sign of the adaptability and power of the function that, with the arrival of multiple channels, there is still a way of organising communications that is more than pragmatic, and gives the agency involved and the client a strategic advantage? Or has the pressure on planning become so relentless that the job has become something else entirely? In which case planning would need to be radically reinvented or retired.

The question 'Has planning always been this way?' can be answered, but not for very much longer. The founders of planning, Stanley Pollitt and Stephen King, died in 1979 and 2005 respectively. So we can't ask them. Those they hired as planners for the most part have left the advertising industry and gone on to do other things. Some are retired but not all of them. So there is a shrinking window of opportunity to sit them down and to find out how they did the job. Why they did the job? What would have happened if they hadn't been there to do the job they did?

That's why we have written this book. Because that is what we have done. We have interviewed 10 planners from each of the agencies where account planning began. And spoken to interested and expert bystanders who worked in creative departments with the first planners or as agency managers, as researchers, or indeed as clients. So we are in a unique position to be able to answer the question: was it always like this?

No it wasn't. Planners spent a lot of their time in their agencies but they did different things. They worked on far fewer accounts for a start. The most we ever found at one time was three. They found time to take long lunches. Liquid lunches. Alcohol figured largely and not just after hours. They worked more intensely because they were addressing a simple set of fundamental questions. And once those questions were answered, the job was basically done. It is hard today to grasp that the job was finite. Because with the choice of hundreds of different channels, the work today is never done.

Another difference is the relative lack of processes. It may surprise you – it certainly surprised us – but the creative brief didn't become standardised until nearly 10 years after planning had been started. That is hard to credit now that communications has become so process driven and now that productivity is defined by how much has been produced and how well it has performed. Productivity for the first planners was defined in terms of how good the advertising was. Before it was made. Before it left the agency, the work could be redone or reshaped many times. Because if the work was right then its efficacy would be such that making more variations of it would not lead to better results. And if the work was wrong or only halfway there, then planners were encouraged to say so – sometimes to go back to the start, or at least to consider how the communication might be improved. Planning was just as cerebral as today but the questions were simpler and related to the job the advertising had to do. Planners could be called the conscience of the agency because they could stand up to the others and were encouraged to. And they could stand up to clients as well. It sounds like a simpler world because it was – there were many fewer channels and many fewer planners. But that made the departments relatively more important – where planners talked to each other about what they were doing and compared notes.

Paradoxically planners didn't deal with less data. They dealt with a lot of data but it came in reports and printouts. They didn't have desktop computers or calculators to analyse it – that had to be done by hand. So written reports and summaries of data reports were the norm. They had to be effective in communicating face-to-face and arguing their corner. As well as on the typed page. That's right – no word processing – every document handwritten then typed by a departmental secretary. It took a couple of days for each meeting to be summarised in a contact report and the summaries circulated by post.

They didn't talk about brands a lot – not to start off with. That was one of the great innovations of planning, that it shifted the focus from immediate results to the long-term effects of advertising, which were reckoned to be so powerful that they beggared the immediate short-term result. That was also a surprising finding. Since the received wisdom of the time was also short-term – sales often driven by long copy and direct response. The currency was the campaign. An idea which was refreshed periodically with new advertising but which evolved slowly. And which created long-term value. Some of the most well-known campaigns had been running for decades. No self-respecting junior product manager would have dared to throw the campaign out and start from scratch. So the discussion was about how to keep the story fresh and new, while keeping elements which were familiar and reinforced what people already believed about the product. Inevitably in that environment, brands and advertising were treated as synonymous. Today as branding sprawls in all directions, we make a clear separation between communications and brands. But that responsibility for keeping the brand on track made agencies, and the planners in them, responsible and reflective. They would often be drawn into deep discussions about the best next step because the future of the whole business depended on it. That kind of decision-making couldn't and shouldn't be made overnight. And the case for change – or staying the same – needed to be supported with hard numeric evidence. But also with intuition.

There is enough commonality between communications now and then to warrant our going back to see how the job was originally done. For several reasons. Yes, advertising was simpler, but it was, on the whole, better liked and remembered. This was actually measured on Target Group Index (TGI) – the BMRB survey that started in 1968 – the same year that Boase Massimi Pollitt and J. Walter Thompson employed planners. One attitudinal measure ('The ads are as good as the programmes') rose to a peak in 1991 but by 2004 it had halved. Advertising was at the centre of the culture to be discussed, mocked and vilified whether you were a customer or not. Captains of industry took an interest in the campaigns their agencies were running. Often they made the decisions to run particular campaigns themselves, rather than leaving it to the marketing manager or the brand manager. Some of the best advertising was enjoyed by the public for celebrating the British way of life in a way that is hard to imagine now. Planning had a lot to do with that – because striking the right note with customers meant getting close to them. And clients had to be convinced that advertising which wasn't overtly hard-selling would actually deliver the numbers. It often fell to planners to make that case. And planners had to keep brands on track because the values portrayed in the advertising mattered to customers whose identity was tied up with the way those brands performed. The 1960s and 1970s propelled British agencies to be a world force in advertising – widely admired and imitated. Account planning can take its share of credit for this as it was exported everywhere else. In this book we want to explore how account planning came about and to see it through the eyes of those who first did the job. You can still read the papers of Stephen King and Stanley Pollitt. This book gives you a whole new group of practitioners to learn from.

Dear reader: what you need to know before venturing further

This book is an exploration of the rise of account planning in London in the 1960s, as seen through the eyes of those who did the job and the perspectives of a selective few who watched them do it. It is not a history book nor is it a textbook. Otherwise you might have lost interest already. Advertising is something almost everybody has an opinion about. Something people will discuss animatedly with each other given the opportunity. Most people can tell you about an ad they like, usually a TV commercial. And they can tell you about advertising they dislike. And complain that there is too much of the stuff. Very occasionally advertising moves into the centre stream of culture, so commentators leap on it, programme makers parody it, and it becomes a regular topic of discussion in pubs and at parties. The 1960s was such a time. But today mostly advertising is tolerated and filtered out. What has changed since the 1960s is that marketing has become so widespread that you can hear people explain what the 'brand' is doing and how they think the advertising works. But they will still tell you that they themselves aren't influenced by advertising even if other people are.

So let us begin with a little ground clearing – assuming that you are not an expert who spends all of your waking hours making advertising and thinking about it, or that you know nothing about it. To put you in the picture about how account planning came to start in London of all places.

The first point to make is that modern advertising is an American invention. Yes, we can find graffiti in Pompeii and handbills are mentioned by Dr Samuel Johnson – but it was the size and scale of America which turned advertising into a business which would help businesses reach their customers at distances of hundreds, if not thousands, of miles. It was the size of the USA which gave advertising its power.

It was an American who got the idea of buying space in newspapers and selling it to businesses and offering to write the advertisements that filled it – hooking the media on advertising as part of the revenue model ever since.[1] It was another American who negotiated a flat-rate media discount in return for buying the space, using the commission to remunerate himself. This system of payment became embedded for more than a century, only disappearing in the 1980s. While it was in place the most successful advertising agents became wealthy because a flat discount goes a long way. The more media space is sold the richer the agent becomes.

The commission was negotiated for newspapers, magazines, outdoor advertising, and then commercial radio and then commercial TV stations. An agent would have to satisfy the media owners that they were working on behalf of a group of clients. A client would be encouraged to give their advertising business to that agent on an ongoing basis and the arrangement became known as an account. Agencies accumulated accounts by pitching for new business by presenting campaign plans and advertising ideas. And they tried to grow the amount that each client spent because they benefitted directly from the volume of spend.

Advertising is a trade, not a profession – don't let anybody tell you otherwise. Which is why all sorts of people have moved into advertising and a few have made fortunes out of it.

---

1 Much of this comes from Winston Fletcher's excellent overview of the history of UK advertising *Powers of Persuasion: The Inside Story of British Advertising 1951–2000*, Oxford University Press (2008).

You need no qualifications and there is no agreement about how advertising works. Except that it does[2].

By the middle of the twentieth century you would find a handful of roles in an advertising agency. There was the rep who persuaded the client to buy the space. There were media buyers who picked the spaces and booked them. Both were courted assiduously by the media with lunches and all sorts of incentives. To persuade agencies to book space in their publications they included media research which told you all about the lifestyles of those who read the publications and saw the advertising. Originally the reps wrote their own ads but soon the copywriting function began, where specialists wrote ads and were paid small fortunes because they could generate huge direct response and sales. Ads were word heavy but this didn't stop them being effective. And then the visualisers arrived who would add pictures to the advertising under the direction of copywriters. These designers worked in different offices and sometimes on different floors. The production line would lead with the client and end with the media owner.

All of this originated in America and because of the scale of the country even though advertising agencies had a regional presence, inevitably hubs sprang up in the biggest conurbations. On the West Coast in San Francisco, in Chicago in the Midwest and in New York on the East Coast. Agencies needed to coordinate the placing of advertisements in every publication. When cinema, radio and TV were added on top of the press, they experimented with mass surveys to measure the impact of network advertising. Much as advertisers like to measure the effectiveness of advertising in sales, other factors

---

2 Though we would commend Paul Feldwick's *Anatomy of Humbug: How to Think Differently about Advertising*, Troubador Publishing (January 2015). It is an masterful overview of the various theories of how advertising works. No single theory covers all advertising.

influence sales. And advertising can do more than persuade people to purchase a product once. At one stage TV audiences were measured on the calibrations of changing pressure in the water supply and spikes on the power grid as the audience flushed their toilets and put on kettles during commercial breaks. And in many countries there were few limits on the minutes per broadcasting hour when commercial spots could be shown. And companies were able to sponsor the programmes themselves (this is where the term 'soap opera' comes from as the detergent companies sponsored kitchen sink dramas) and have live presenters endorse products to camera close to programme breaks. The soap companies became notorious for the volume of spending. At one stage they even agreed to restrict their advertising spend so the new TV channels were not overwhelmed with exhortations to use product X or product Y.

It should be obvious by now that advertising was conceived as selling, pure and simple. John E. Kennedy at the beginning of the century had defined press advertising as 'salesmanship in print'. Four individuals are worth mentioning for the influence they wielded through the middle years of the twentieth century in explaining how advertising worked. All four had their heyday in the 1950s which meant their influence on advertising ideas was still flowing strongly in American advertising for the next decade.

The first[3] is Rosser Reeves of Ted Bates who formulated the Unique Selling Proposition (USP). He claimed that advertising worked on immutable principles, which needed to be applied ruthlessly. His theory in a nutshell was that there was a limited

---

3 For these very abbreviated introductions we are indebted to *The Art of Writing Advertising,* Advertising Age NTC (1965) which features interviews with these legendary creatives. So we have been able to distil their ideas from what they said rather than what third parties wrote about them.

number of benefits from which a product could be advertised. One of the benefits was chosen because it was different from or superior to those of competitive products and was then hammered endlessly. It might be unpopular with the audience but through sheer power of repetition it would get noticed, get remembered, and would change people's purchasing preferences. Eventually customers would believe whatever was said about the product benefits – it was the equivalent of carpet-bombing. Reeves would use any medium but his technique was most visible on the then new medium of television. Where a limited set of brands fought it out with each other making competitive claims – striving to carve out unique territory for themselves. Much of the language of today's advertising borrows heavily from Reeves's ideas though he is rarely read today.

The second was David Ogilvy, a British expatriate who moved to New York and started his own agency at the age of 35, which became eventually Ogilvy & Mather. Ogilvy's famous maxim was, 'The consumer is not a moron, she is your wife'. His approach was to use long copy to charm his audience and persuade them with the facts. Before Ogilvy worked in advertising he spent some time working for George Gallup so he used quantitative research[4] and the techniques of direct response to calibrate the effects of his advertising. 'My ideas about what constitutes good copy almost all derive from research not personal opinion.' The form this subsequently took was rules of thumb about how many times the consumer was to be referenced in every hundred words of copy, how many words should be in the headline, why a question mark

4 Quantitative research uses surveys of statistically significant numbers of respondents to draw conclusions about the size and opinions of the population. Researchers are external to the research process and use questions structured to derive standard responses which are deemed objective and repeatable. Though depending on the size of the sample, findings are subject to degrees of error.

should never be used, and so on. He was also brother-in-law to Rosser Reeves, so the two of them claimed to agree with each other more than a cursory overview of their work might otherwise indicate.

The third was Leo Burnett from Chicago who also started his own agency. Burnett's approach was to dramatise the product. 'We stress the inherent drama of things because there is always something about that product that keeps it in the marketplace. Something that makes that thing arresting and keeps people buying it.' One of his campaigns for the Jolly Green Giant became so famous that the client, the Minnesota Canning Company, renamed itself after the advertising. Tony the Tiger for Kellogg's Frosties and The Marlboro Man, were other examples of iconic campaigns which have lasted for decades. Burnett is important because his creation of advertising properties suggested that advertising could create long-term effects and that these effects were ultimately more valuable than driving short-term sales. Even if he spoke more of campaigns than brands.

The fourth was Bill Bernbach, the creative director of Doyle Dane Bernbach in New York. He brought together copywriters and art directors and expected the interplay between the two to provide something new and unexpected. He held that advertising was not selling but persuasion, and therefore not a science but an art. Bernbach wanted to provoke and persuade the consumer. His understated work for the Volkswagen Beetle, Avis Rent a Car, and Levy's Bagels became legendary. It wasn't just what was said – it was how beautiful the ads looked with acres of white space where the convention had been to fill every square inch with product claims and testimonials. He didn't like research because it blunted differences. 'One of the disadvantages of doing everything mathematically by research and by mandate, is that after a while everybody does it in the same way. Because you go out and find the same things. If you think when you have found out what to say, your job is done then you're saying it the same way everybody else is saying it, and you lose your impact completely.' The trick was to be different. Bernbach hired writers and art directors because they were individuals – he attempted no system. It was Bernbach's approach, idolised by writers and art directors alike, that triggered a creative revolution. DDB advertising was witty – it was popular with ordinary people whether or not they were in the market for the product. Bernbach's approach suggested a different way for advertising to work. And his thinking has been compelling for creatives ever since.

In the late 1950s, with the Cold War in full flow, Vance Packard published an incendiary book, *Hidden Persuaders*,[5] in which he revealed the dangers of subliminal advertising and the motivational research which lay behind it. Motivational research comes from psychotherapy and explains consumer behaviour in terms of drivers and associations, which are beyond the individual's understanding, but are all the more powerful because they are hidden. Only the analyst can spot them and draw them to the surface. Contrary to the direct approach of Reeves, Ogilvy and Gallup, the 'hidden persuaders' – for which read advertising agencies – made a single frame saying 'Coca Cola' flicker on a cinema screen giving audiences a sudden inexplicable thirst. It didn't matter that the experiment referred to turned out to be a complete fabrication. America in the throes of McCarthyism and spooked by Russia taking the lead in the space race with *Sputnik*, swallowed a magical theory of advertising that made you do things you didn't even know you were doing. It made advertising sound sexy and dangerous at the same time. Motivation research made small fortunes for consultants like Ernst Dichter, who had moved from Vienna to New York to ply his trade as a

5 *Hidden Persuaders*, Vance Packard (1957).

psychotherapist working for business; but agencies became wary of being seen to undermine consumer choice.

The real issue was the volume of advertising that people were being exposed to. There were few advertising channels but they were crammed with advertising and it wasn't popular. The consumerisation of America did not go unchallenged. Ralph Nader spent the 1960s challenging the US automotive industry on the safety of its cars and arguing that manufacturers like General Motors were not behaving in their customers' interests. Consumerism cut both ways – a way to self-define using products and services but also a way to kick back at brand owners who did what they wanted – and kept an army of lawyers in case of a very public product failure.

The creative revolution was all the more powerful because of the way advertising, with its repeated claims or its attempt to get underneath the radar into the subconscious, had forfeited public goodwill. Creative advertising might get the advertising talked about and it might be liked. The drawback with creative advertising was that, just because it was witty or humorous, it was no guarantee of effectiveness.

On the West Coast the ad man Howard Gossage[6] railed against the 'billion dollar hammer on the 30 cent tack' and argued that advertising broke the First Amendment, tipping the balance of power too far towards advertisers and away from the public. He argued that almost all advertising was trivial and banal. The only advertising that could be morally justified needed to be utterly interesting and diverting. Gossage's methods were unorthodox to say the least. His 'pink air' campaign for Fina gas stations is an apt illustration. Each press advertisement was placed once only. Gossage argued that the succession of ads

6 *The Book of Gossage*, a collection of Gossage's advertising, published articles and homages by his admirers, Copy Workshop (2006).

was a conversation with the audience, so he shouldn't need to repeat himself. He took marginal features and made them central – pink air being put into car tyres at Fina gas stations. Giveaway pink balloons inside another transparent balloon so you can see what pink air looks like. A competition to win 15 yards of pink asphalt. Why pink air? No reason but it makes what would otherwise be an identical suite of gas stations services seem more interesting.

But it isn't just the off-the-wall nature of his creative ideas. In Gossage's book *Is There Any Hope for Advertising?* he proposed using *The New York Times* as the best place to launch a campaign. With advertising men as the primary audience because they talk to clients for nothing, with the client's own competitors as the secondary audience and with the consumers as a distant third. 'When advertisers speak of consumers they think they mean "people" but they don't. A consumer is a functional being designed to use whatever it is you have to sell. He will therefore be a grotesque on the order of Hieronymus Bosch, all mouth or belly . . . consumers are non-existent except in the manufacturers' imagination.'

Gossage saw advertising campaigns as interventions that create cultural change. Which is why he didn't need to worry too much about selling products to real people. He wanted to be interesting and engaging and claimed that he could deliver commercial results by being the outstanding brand communicator in a given category. There was no point in reaching everyone and speaking to them multiple times. You will only succeed in boring them. Another of his metrics was not using up the client's advertising budget. Or getting paid for telling the advertiser not to advertise at all. That's what he told Volkswagen. Doyle Dane Bernbach gave different advice and produced one of the greatest advertising campaigns of all time.

According to Gossage advertising VW Beetles was unnecessary. The product was quite distinctive enough.

We mention Gossage because the idea of the intellectual creative impresario was influential, even if his methods weren't followed. The concept of the creative genius beloved of artists and designers moved effortlessly into advertising where great copywriters had long been lionised for writing advertisements that created huge response. These iconoclasts didn't actually have to meet real people, any more than bestselling novelists do, to demonstrate that their writing reflected the attitudes and aspirations of real people. Research, particularly quantitative research, was dismissed as vague and self-serving of the organisation – usually a media company – paying for it. Gossage has strong views that the medium chosen needed to be integral to the advertising idea. He introduced Marshall McLuhan to the United States, organising a lecture tour for the Canadian academic. He used the ideas of Norbert Wiener, the father of cybernetics and systems thinking, to define communications effectiveness by consumer response which was why he put multiple coupons in his ads to test the water. Gossage gathered a coterie of other intellectuals, including Buckminster Fuller and the writers Tom Wolfe and John Steinbeck. This fad for creativity out-of-the-box and off-the-wall spread across the advertising industry through the 1960s, wherever there were clients who were fighting overwhelming odds being outspent by corporations with the firepower to pound audiences into submission. It was a significant movement in the UK too.[7] As we shall see.

---

7 A conversation with Steve Harrison, author of *Changing the World Is the Only Fit Work for a Grown Man* – a book about Gossage, Adworld Press (2012) – produced this gem. We asked about how influential Gossage really was, to which Harrison replied by quoting Rory Sutherland: 'Gossage was The Velvet Underground to Ogilvy's Beatles and Bernbach's Rolling Stones.

By the end of the 1950s US corporations were expanding around the world and taking advertising ideas with them. And for the most part clients in other parts of the world and their agencies knuckled down and adopted the practices and theories which had come out of America in the first place. The one contrary exception was the account planning movement which started in the UK. In the next section we will look at how these advertising ideas played in the UK, and how they came to incite a revolt called account planning. The creative revolution may have started in the USA in line with all the other innovations you might expect from a business superpower. But account planning is the only advertising innovation that began not in the USA, but in London.

Hardly anybody saw them play but they influenced more people, more start-up bands than any other.' In 1972 at CDP John Salmon told John O'Donnell to study Gossage's Irish Distillery ads to learn how to use the press medium in an original way.

The UK advertising scene at the start of the 1960s

The launch of ITV in 1955 marked a sea change in UK advertising. Commercial television was by no means an instant success, but when advertisers started to use it in volume, it very quickly became the largest advertising medium and centralised the way in which mass audiences could be reached. Although it was possible to place advertising to run in a particular region, a national campaign soon reached far more people than read any individual daily newspaper. There was only one commercial TV channel. That made television advertising prestigious and newsworthy. It also meant that mistakes or missteps were very visible. So an immediate consequence of the arrival of commercial television was the apparatus of measurement – watching television viewers. It brought pressure on the ad agencies to test commercials before they ran on network TV or at least very quickly after the campaign began. Television advertising cost a lot of money. In parallel with this, research became more sophisticated, because for the first time surveys into product purchase and consumption began to be linked to surveys about TV viewing and readership. And you no longer had to take the research respondents' word for it. Black boxes appeared in television sets testing to see what percentage of all households were watching each TV channel. Remotes linked to the television told you who in the household had switched channel. By the middle of the 1960s dustbins were collected from a panel of households in AGB's household audit. So you knew what people were throwing away even if it didn't match the diaries they also kept. This kind of data was accurate enough to be analysed down to individual households in individual weeks – so you could correlate household purchasing with advertising campaigns. You could actually drill down to see which households had switched brand in the days following the start of a TV advertising campaign. You could find out what was selling in the supermarket (if they gave permission for the data to be collected – not every retailer did), down to the pack size; and measure pipeline stock by seeing how much stock was still held in store stockrooms. And linking together the surveys allows you to connect what people bought, to the advertising they had seen.

Agencies employed researchers to keep track of these new data forms.[8] This was because advertising agencies were already locked into providing marketing services as part of the work they did for clients. In the absence of strong client marketing departments, it was the agencies who delivered marketing and sales plans. Some agencies even wrote the annual business plan for their clients and met with them to write the quarterly promotional plan. This had come to be taken for granted because of the business model prevalent at the time the commission system, which had proved so profitable to agencies. So agencies increased their investment in researchers. They didn't have just one research department but three or four: one for marketing, one for media research, one for advertising and perhaps one for new product development. Agency researchers were on hand to answer all client enquiries from clients or framed by the agency supervisors. The arrival of commercial television dramatically increased the amount of research being commissioned because the stakes were higher.

Simultaneously the arrival of mass marketing was making it more necessary for clients to manage their own destiny and

8 *Sampling the Universe: The growth, development and influence of market research in Britain since 1945*, Colin MacDonald, Stephen King, NTC (1996).

take their marketing and their research in-house. The largest clients not only set up research departments but created teams of hundreds of interviewers.[9] This created an issue for advertising agencies. How were they to justify the amount of income they were generating from commission if there was no need for their marketing services? And how were they to keep their influence with clients if research and marketing moved into client companies?

Changes in how market research was run were of direct concern to UK agencies. Not least because it was advertising agencies who had introduced market research to the UK in the first place. J. Walter Thompson set up its BMRB subsidiary in the 1920s. World War II saw governments turn to research as a way to track the morale of the population suffering under the bombing of British cities and needing to ensure that people were able to feed themselves. Those who were employed by the government to set up the annual Social Attitudes Survey[10] and the Family Food Panel came from an agency background and many then returned to it. Tom Corlett, who helped the first generation of planners at J. Walter Thompson assess the effectiveness of advertising campaigns, had been a leading light in pioneering the mathematics of mass social sampling in the 1950s and he had also run the National Readership Survey, which for the first time analysed who was reading newspapers and magazines.

When the Market Research Society organised its first event in 1946, the lunch attracted 23 members, half of whom came

9 The agency Research International started as the in-house research division of Unilever.

10 Social survey interviewers did more than complete questionnaires. They were also briefed to collect urine and saliva samples from particular subgroups, for example to monitor the effects of passive smoking.

from advertising agencies.[11] Significantly two were from BMRB and one from Pritchard Wood, the agency in which Stanley Pollitt 20 years later would start his first account planning experiment. So advertising agencies continued to lead the thinking on how market research should be used.

We should also make honourable mention of the Mass-Observation experiment started just before the Second World War, which collected daily diaries of the experience of ordinary people, along with studies featuring interviewers, who not only asked questions but also sat in public places and listened to and recorded topics of conversation.[12] Mass-Observation was a remarkable example of trying to achieve with pen and paper what the internet allows us to do effortlessly today. It proved too advanced and costly an approach. It generated far too much data to be analysed. But what it did achieve was the planting of the idea that the experience of ordinary people was accessible and immensely useful.

The reason why advertising agencies needed to use research, was that their clients depended on them to understand these new mass audiences so far removed from their operations. Client companies ran huge sales forces – but that was in order to ensure that their products were sold into the supply chain and successfully found their way onto the shelves. But what ordinary people thought and felt about these products – that was the province of the agencies.

Not classified as research as such, was the way in which

---

11 At the time it was conjectured that the total membership of the MRS would never rise above 25 members in total, which shows the expectation that advertising agencies would continue to play a central role. By the 1970s the membership of the MRS was expanding so rapidly that it was projected that if the rate of expansion continued that by 2011 the entire UK population would be members. Alas that trend was not to continue!

12 One of the most famous Mass stories was the attempt to measure the volume of sexual activity by observing Blackpool beach after dark!

creatives were expected to go and meet and talk to ordinary people about their lives and their use of products. In 1962 Tom Rayfield, within days of being offered his first job in J. Walter Thompson as a copywriter by a youthful Jeremy Bullmore, was sent the following week to Northern Ireland to ask housewives why they get headaches. Weeks would pass before he was deemed well informed enough to write a press advertisement on how a headache pill would transform their lives. As a copywriter he was expected to immerse himself in the experiences of ordinary people.

What was happening during the 1950s and early 1960s was a wholesale transformation in the economy from supplier-led – where customers had no choice and no access to credit – to a consumer-driven economy where your brand choices showed your social standing and your levels of aspiration. Rationing in Britain finished only just over a year before the launch of ITV. Retail price maintenance was only abolished in 1964. Before that date, a tin of beans cost the same in every shop in the land. It is hard for us today – bamboozled by decades of price promotions, deal advertising and price comparison websites – to imagine a society where prices are fixed.

The switch to a consumer-led economy fuelled a bonanza in advertising spend because there were relatively few media where advertising could be placed. Newspapers and magazines boomed once the rationing of newsprint stopped. Newspapers were still only in black and white, though magazines were printed in colour. The first colour Sunday supplements came out in the early 1960s, creating new opportunities for advertisers. There was outdoor advertising and cinema advertising – the latter fed by the still powerful British film industry who supplied directors and cinematographers. There was limited commercial radio and much of that was product placement.[13]

---

13 J. Walter Thompson wrote a weekly 15-minute episode of *Dan Dare* for

Just one channel of commercial television and that was in black and white. The golden age of TV advertising began at the end of the 1960s when commercial television went colour and the production values of cinema could be experimented with on the small screen.

The birth of commercial television had been a struggle through the 1950s. The BBC (nicknamed 'Aunty' because she knew best) had created an expectation that publicly-owned media channels should be educational and improving. The public weren't given a say. Ever since the founding of the BBC and its radio services, each household was required to pay an annual licence fee to fund first the BBC's radio channels and then television. So there was censorship and a programming ethos of what was good for society.

For example the BBC kept dance music at arm's length on radio, insisting on playing light music from 20 years before, abetted by the Musician's Union who claimed that too much popular music would take away the livelihoods of working musicians. As an alternative they started to broadcast documentaries about blues music as sung by segregated black musicians in the deep south of the United States. The inadvertent effect of this paternalistic approach to culture inspired a generation of musicians who idolised blues and jazz – musical genres which the segregated white audience in America almost never encountered. Bands like The Beatles, The Rolling Stones and Fleetwood Mac invaded the US with a sound which was American, but not a slavish copy of Elvis and the other rock and rollers. Britain was on a path to becoming a cultural centre that itself was influencing the US as it was being influenced.[14]

Radio Luxembourg sponsored by the bedtime drink Horlicks – so copywriters wrote cliffhanging science fiction to order.

14 This is from *Ta-ra-ra-boom-de-ay – the dodgy business of popular music* by Simon Napier-Bell, Unbound (2014).

There was a lot of censorship on television. Press advertising didn't need to be cleared to run in the newspapers, but television ads had to be approved at the script stage, and as a finished ad, before they were allowed to run. It is not surprising that television filmlets (as they were sometimes called) were not very interesting. They usually involved presenters lecturing the audience, or demonstrating two products side by side to demonstrate the superiority of one. Experts (male) in white coats told housewives why the product they favoured was scientifically superior. Television advertising was fulfilling the warnings of the anti-commercial TV lobby, who had opposed any TV advertising at all. The silver lining was that at least the BBC hadn't been made to carry advertising. Advertisers were not allowed to sponsor TV programmes as they were allowed to do in the USA. For every hour of broadcasting on commercial television no more than six minutes could be devoted to advertising. But much of the advertising looked as bad as the American advertising which the critics deplored. The issue was the hard sell, which looked and felt American because it was. And overly salesy advertising was disliked by the British – labelled as American. Not British.

Towards the end of the 1950s pressure was growing in the creative industry to do something about their dire output. Pearl & Dean spun off the Cannes Advertising Festival from the Cannes Film Festival to promote the directors, and cinematographers who were getting work in advertising. Often the only way a young director could find their way to their first feature film was to make advertising commercials. Initially it was confined to cinema advertising, but under pressure it was opened to TV advertising as well. Cannes Advertising – a UK invention – has become a global phenomenon, garnering thousands of entries from all over the world. But it became something of an embarrassment that British advertising, at the start, rarely won any awards. But since very often the ads were made by film-makers who were also making Oscar-winning features, there was much soul searching about creative standards.

The D&AD (and its annual awards and annual), was founded in the early 1960s as a not-for-profit organisation to improve creative standards. Dominated at the outset by art directors, after a few years they allowed copywriters to join too. This became yet another UK powerhouse which extended around the world, raising the UK's advertising profile and also creating expectations that UK creative standards would be at least as high as the submissions that came in from around the world.

One response to the critiques of hard-sell advertising was to make advertising that was clearly made in Britain and about British daily life – in the subject matter, humour, and the wit that was displayed. In 1959 J. Walter Thompson won the Oxo account and launched the Oxo Family campaign where family members had names and roles and the product emerged from the life of the family as they sat down and ate together. Dad wiping up the gravy with a piece of bread triggered a bag of letters of complaint for his bad table manners. There was still an expectation that advertising should set standards for polite behaviour. The BBC cast a long shadow.

We have mentioned the growing influence of research in advertising. For many agencies this was simply part of marketing services which agencies provided free because of the amount of agency commission they were receiving from the media they booked. But some advertising agencies such as Bensons made it central to how they made advertising. They would pretest television advertising showing a reel of finished ads to a cinema full of people and ask them questions about it. There were hall tests where TV advertisements could be shown and questionnaires administered in a few minutes to housewives brought in off the high street. The weakness in these methods is that, although the sample was supposedly randomised, there was no guarantee that the people brought into these sessions bought and used the products featuring in the advertising. Whether the sample are customers, prospective customers or even have any interest in buying the product, makes a huge difference to how people respond to advertising.

The revolt against American approaches to making advertising and research methods which constrained advertising, began in 1960 with an agency start-up called Collett Dickenson & Pearce. They made a virtue of the fact that they wanted to make the best advertising possible – the provision of free marketing services wasn't a priority. The creative department would take however long it took to come up with the right solution. And they would show the client only one creative idea. Which the client would be under strong pressure to run.[15] CDP's first creative director was a Yorkshireman by the name of Colin Millward, a tyrant who bullied and coaxed the best out of his creatives. He expected world-class ideas and the best craftsmen in the world to make the work. CDP prized its creatives above everything. Over the years Millward assembled the best creative people in the country. Following the lead set by Bill Bernbach in New York, the creatives were put into creative teams: a copywriter with an art director – which made it easier to come up with great television ideas where words and pictures working together were so crucial.[16] But CDP became famous first for the quality of its press advertisements. They set a very British tone: Cockburn's port, Benson & Hedges Gold cigarettes, Hamlet cigars, Parker Pens. These made advertising interesting and newsworthy whether you were in the market or not.

---

15 Much of our information comes from *Inside Collett Dickenson Pearce*, John Salmon and John Ritchie, a 40th anniversary edition (2001).

16 Dave Trott makes the point in our interview with him that the 'judging brain' is different from the 'doing brain'. You need a spotter, hence the value of working in pairs or at least not alone.

CDP had an ambivalent attitude towards research. John Pearce hired John Wood, a market researcher from RSL because he saw him debrief some groups about cigarettes in which he calmly directed the audience to ignore what most of the respondents had said because it didn't reflect what they really did, but to pay attention to the minority expressing a different point of view. CDP used research for its own purposes, to find out what customers thought about the products and to define the product benefit. But they refused point-blank to allow their advertising ideas to be tested. As far as they were concerned consumers simply weren't competent to talk knowledgeably or helpfully about advertising. So what got made was clever, funny and famous. It wasn't always successful in selling the products for whom it was made. But it always got noticed. Colin Millward saw to that. CDP won creative awards every year. They weren't the only ones – other agencies took the cue and started to make advertising that was also funny and which was distinctively British in tone. But CDP was far in front.

CDP was also a radical user of media. When Sunday supplements were launched they were filled with CDP ads taking advantage of the high resolution colour production values. Television was still black and white and wouldn't be completely colour until 1969. Newspapers wouldn't print in colour for another 20 years. So magazine supplements and cinema advertising were where the production values could be shown off. CDP employed Alan Parker as a writer, David Puttnam as an account handler, Hugh Hudson as a producer, and Ridley and Tony Scott among their film directors. All went on to have distinguished film careers of their own.

CDP's flaw was that they appealed to certain kinds of clients in certain categories: booze, fags, and cars. Packaged goods companies needed to secure steady sales by making product claims that connected with everybody. Unsurprisingly, they preferred to use the Unique Sales Proposition route championed by Rosser Reeves, backed up by research. Being asked to approve a single idea which the agency would refuse to research was anathema. So despite their fame CDP became the agency of choice for brands who were third or fourth in their marketplace. And who were desperate enough to use advertising which made them even more famous than the market leaders.

The cultural revolution that was Britain in the 1960s transformed music, fashion, photography, and film. All these changes affected advertising as they affected everything else. But the transformation from a supplier economy to a consumer economy and the pressures this placed on media, meant that agencies were having to learn how to use what were, for them, new media for which there was no precedent. They had to grapple with new data sources to make sense of this brave new world. Every agency wanted to make creative work as visible and alternative as CDP. But the majority of packaged goods companies needed stability and so wanted evidence (for which read 'research') based advertising and marketing strategies on which to build their growth. But before we turn to two individuals from whom the breakthrough came, we want to answer the question: 'but why did planning start in the UK rather than the USA?.'

Why did account planning start in the UK?

This is an attempt to explain why the UK context was different enough to spark an intellectual movement to hypothesise how advertising worked, and to apply that to make the advertising better.

The first factor was the resistance of the British to hard sell. Pressure selling was distrusted, just as the US at the height of the Cold War distrusted advertising after they were told in Vance Packard's *Hidden Persuaders* that it contained subliminal messages. Advertising which used humour or charm was far more likely to be appreciated (whether or not it was effective). David Ogilvy, himself a Scotsman, told American clients that nobody buys from a clown. But here in the UK he was pointedly ignored.

The second factor was education and the drivers for social and personal betterment through self-education. The mass market development of the paperback in the 1930s had led to the general population reading the classics and more widely. There was a familiarity with what in other parts of the world would have been seen as high culture and a love of linguistic play which again advertisers (and broadcasters) took advantage of and, as we have seen in the previous chapter, public broadcasting was pervasive and influential.

Soldiers returning from the Second World War were given the opportunity to go to university and bright children from right across the social spectrum were given the opportunity to go to university for free, paid for by national grants. Even though universities represented a minority of the national population (barely five per cent), the mix of students widened. The result was an increase in bright graduates who came from a wider range of the population but represented a tiny proportion of it. Only 25,000 in 1960s and 50,000 in 1970, with men outnumbering women three to one.[17] There were still questions being asked as to why women needed tertiary education beyond teacher training college. The handful of graduates may not have known a lot about advertising but they knew how to think, how to argue.

In advertising agencies the copywriters may have come from the universities with English degrees (and tried to write novels in their spare time), but the phenomenon of the northern art director emerging from art school, paralleled the arrival of northern actors in the drama schools displacing the received pronunciation of actors reared on Shakespeare. Creative departments weren't hiring women but they were hiring across a social divide. The creative palette was broadening. But the quality and diversity of graduates had broadened too. And the new arrivals didn't feel deferential towards those who had gone before. There was an egalitarianism emerging from the creative agencies in strong contrast to the agencies which had gone before, with their directors' dining rooms.

Thirdly the marked increase in the volume of research being carried out was not leading to a lack of confidence in research itself. It was suggesting that advertising wasn't working as advertised. The linking of media research to purchase and consumption was raising much deeper questions about what advertising could potentially achieve for a client. Not all agencies wanted to acknowledge this. But the advertising scene after the arrival of Collett Dickenson Pearce was ripe for change. Which brings us to the point when our interviewees come into the story. They haven't all been to university, though

17 House of Commons Library education report , Paul Bolton (2012).

most of them have. They don't come from upper-class backgrounds, though a few do. They aren't all men, though most are. They buy into the creativity which is moving British advertising centre stage, getting advertising written about in the papers, and British company bosses directly involved in selecting the ad campaigns. But they worry that many of the wildest creative ideas are, to put it bluntly, indulgent – and don't connect with ordinary people. They complain that the wall of quantitative research which every agency has to contend with, kills most interesting ideas so that what advertising gets made ticks the boxes but is invisible to most people.

Just a few get the idea that advertising is being massively undersold. That advertising is not just a way to empty supermarket shelves the following day, but can be shown to have long-term effects which make the intangible associations around a company more valuable than the manufacturing plants it owns. Time then to stop talking about long-running campaigns and to start talking about advertising that builds brands.

There is a wider ferment[18] which took hold at the end of the 1960s and broke in 1968 when these account planning departments were set up. The counter culture wave finally broke in anti-Vietnam demonstrations across the USA, student demonstrations in Berlin, Paris and London. The response to the assassination of Martin Luther King and Bobby Kennedy. The uprising which led to the Russian invasion of Prague. The second wave of feminism dates from this year. Everywhere the younger generation announced that the older generation could not be trusted. In *Planet of the Apes,* which came out in the same year, Charlton Heston instructs a chimpanzee not to trust anyone over the age of 30. While there is no direct evidence

18 Taken from *1968: The Year that Rocked the World* by Mark Kurlansky, Vintage Digital (2010).

that counterculture was driving King and Pollitt, the *zeitgeist* was suspicious of received wisdom and no longer deferential towards authority and the establishment.

This is an attempt to explain why it was in London, and not in New York, that the account planning revolution started. All agencies use research, always have. All agencies depend on creative thinking. But two agencies in London rejected the either/or of research or uncontrolled creativity and combined them into a more powerful force.

Chapter 2

Beginnings

From research to response

'You have to look at the greater context of what was happening then. British advertising was getting away from the ghastliness of American advertising thought and American advertising. Bright people got an idea about how to make advertising better by simplifying it.'

Tony Mortemore.

'Most advertising aims to intensify or lessen people's existing predispositions. It is not trying to drive something new into their brains.'

Stephen King introducing the 'T-Plan'[19]

In this chapter we tell the story of how a small group of people in two agencies set out a very different way of thinking about advertising and making it. Advertising thinking was spreading out from the USA as a global force to be reckoned with. Rosser Reeves and David Ogilvy were public figures because of the books they had written about their methods. Bill Bernbach might not have written a book but his ads were in advertising annuals everywhere, revered by art directors and copywriters alike.

But none of those we interviewed mentioned these names.

19 Stephen King interviewed in *Fifty in 40: The Unofficial History of JWT London, 1945–1995*, Tom Rayfield (1996).

The frustration they describe came from the mechanical application of mass communication methods. The London advertising scene at that time was broadly divided into American-owned agencies whose largest accounts were American multinational advertisers, and British-owned agencies whose work was self-consciously different from that coming from America. As global businesses and advertising campaigns rolled out of America using Britain as a bridgehead into Europe, the planners described the frustration of having advertising, and advertising measurement conventions, imposed upon them by executives who might have notional authority to make decisions, but were frequently applying rules and norms which reduced advertising to a formula.

Globalisation expanded as fast as it did because of the combination of process and pragmatism – factors that have driven the expansion of many empires. Several of those we spoke to had worked in the USA. They spoke admiringly of the brilliance of the American researchers and marketers they worked with and their flexibility, willing to ignore rogue results that didn't make sense. One talking about working with Proctor & Gamble: 'They would say – "no, we don't know a better way so it's the one we've got," so we get on with it. Their research people were wonderful, very smart and constructive.'[20]

But this was not how it was in London. For example there was the Schwerin[21] preference test in which people were asked to say what products they were aware of, and whether their desire for the product had changed after they had been shown advertising – with the quantified results being used as a gauge of success. We have already mentioned the advertising pretests in cinemas where TV commercials were shown and scored.

20 Interview with Lee Godden.

21 There is an extensive explanation of Horace Schwerin and the Schwerin test in *Madison Avenue USA*, Martin Mayer, Bodley Head (1958.

Methods which made little, if any, attempt to determine whether those they recruited to watch the ads bought or used the product in the first place, or how they had used the product in the past. Day-after recall was another *bête noire* – deciding the worth of the campaign based on what percentage of the audience could describe it without being prompted, 24 hours after a single showing of the ad. London agencies were required to submit their advertising ideas to these tests and to throw out the creative ideas which didn't pass the benchmarks. When J. Walter Thompson set up their advertising research unit in 1964, they struggled to deter clients from off-the-peg quantitative evaluation methods from America. And the unit's purpose was to find methods subtle enough to show what an ad was capable of – perhaps even improve it.

Advertising agencies were changing. They were losing control of the marketing services which clients were progressively taking in-house. Like banking, advertising has always been a trade, not a profession, a set of skills that practitioners have to learn on the job. But as advertising moved centre stage in the culture, it attracted more graduates from universities, attracted by the glamour and the money. Communications was also becoming more complicated, requiring analytical skills. And so although agencies continued to sell their work using their judgement and experience on what advertising approaches would be effective, increasingly they started to hypothesise how advertising worked, and test those hypotheses to challenge existing orthodoxies. Universities were beginning to develop business departments and academics who studied the way business was being done. Business was becoming smarter.

The prevailing orthodoxy for how communications worked then, is now called the 'persuasion model' which follows a linear sequence. First you obtain the consumer's **attention**. You had to **interest** them, you had to create **desire** and you had to stir them to **action**. This model became known as AIDA for short. If the customer didn't buy the product, it was because one of the stages had failed or been ambiguous. If the recipient couldn't immediately buy the product (which was of course most of the time) then a message which lodged a unique truth linked to a brand name needed to be lodged in the memory to influence their behaviour for when the customer was next buying. Linear processing lent itself to linear forms of testing which could measure standout, understanding of rational messages, and evidence emotional involvement – persuasion to action. And this was how the marketplace filled with sure-fire ways of testing advertising. Response wasn't the starting point. It was the goal. So all of the attention fixed on what you needed to say in order to obtain a predictable result.

Agencies resented the methodologies imposed upon them. One initiative included the increased use of a new discipline – qualitative research[22] – that did not rely upon surveys but listening carefully to what real buyers said about products and the advertising. John Treasure, chairman of the research agency BMRB and the head of J. Walter Thompson's marketing department, travelled to Chicago in 1965 where he watched what was then called a creative workshop – a group discussion with consumers of a particular brand, though it also took the form of serial depth interviews. The facilitator would have been a qualified psychologist and the participants would have been given a number of creative tasks or enabling exercises to carry out to help them answer the questions. The quality of the output was far more insightful than the mechanical measures being used to test and to evaluate advertising at the time. Treasure came back asking himself how qualitative research

22 Qualitative research is so called because it uses semi-structured or unstructured interviewing where the interviewer as part of the process draws out the research participants' opinions and feelings and interprets the data drawn from a sample of interviewees or research groups.

could be used as a supplement – on top of the quantitative research to reveal things that quantitative research simply couldn't.

This took some nerve. In the middle of the 1960s, qualitative research was used to find out the language that customers used so that survey questionnaires could be written with appropriate language. Nobody had thought of running discussion groups as a stand-alone. Motivational research was known to agencies and was suspect. It too relied on the use of psychologists who interviewed customers and who conducted sophisticated analyses of products and advertisements. To a motivational psychologist nothing was what it seemed. Everything had an occult explanation. Qualitative research was much simpler. It relied upon customer response. Listening to what they said in their own words. Not taking the surface of what was said but also not being in thrall to an expert. So interviews were conducted with buyers and users. And then interviewers started to talk to whole groups at a time. This was familiar territory to researchers, many of whom had trained in psychology. And therapists used the one-to-one interview and also the therapy group as a way to work. But what was done was much simpler than the theories applied by the motivational psychologists. These methods were called testing, just as much as the surveys which companies continued to run in large quantities. But what emerged from this qualitative testing was much more subtle than what emerged from surveys. It matched the way ordinary people thought and felt. And the advertising that seemed to be most effective connected with these thoughts and feelings.

Models of thinking were also being developed which forced consumer-centric thinking to the fore. One such was the Target Plan or 'T-Plan' for short.[23] We mention it here

23 This account is drawn from *Fifty in 40* previously cited.

because the shift in thinking was so foundational to what follows and shapes not only J. Walter Thompson but other agencies as well.

Stephen King, working in the marketing department at J. Walter Thompson, went to Harvard in 1962 to study the prevailing theories of how advertising worked. He realised that all of the current theories were based on input – that is to say what the advertiser is setting out to say rather than what the receiver takes out. Both Judie Lannon and Jeremy Bullmore emphasised how critical this trip was to the development of King's thinking, with Jeremy remarking, 'He came back clearer in his antagonism of the prevailing advertising and marketing models of communication, and in his determination to do something about it.' The opportunity came shortly afterwards. Unilever developed UPGA (The Unilever Plan for Good Advertising) which was based firmly on the persuasion input model. King was appalled. A wag who had left Unilever's employ, claimed it stood for Use Proctor & Gamble Advertising! J. Walter Thompson and Lintas, both Unilever agencies, responded. Lintas produced the 4D model – one which was also based on input.

King consulted Jeremy Bullmore, then a recently promoted creative group head. Bullmore was by this time giving a presentation within the creative department called 'Stimulus and Response.'[24] The simplest articulation of the response argument is that you announce that you are modest, and the audience conclude not that you are modest but the very opposite. A communication based on inputs will produce a diverse number of outputs with no guarantee that these bear any relation to the original input. King reshuffled the whole process

24 A truncated version of this presentation can be found – minus the copious examples – in the paper 'The consumer has a mind as well as a stomach' in the published collection of Bullmore's papers *Behind the Scenes in Advertising*, Admap (1991).

to put the emphasis on what produced the desired output. So he replaced message as the input with stimulus. The creative task was to provide the stimulus, whatever form that might take, to provide the output we have agreed is the objective of the communication.

The output was defined in three ways – in terms of the target *beliefs* he wanted the receivers to have; in terms of the target *feelings* he wanted the receivers to have; and whether there was brand character, or satisfaction in using the product. The last was most radical: the target perceptions the recipient should have in terms of the physical characteristics and sensory experience of the product. This was a bold move since J. Walter Thompson had its own system called the T-Square – also based on input rather than outputs, so this was also to challenge the way his own agency approached the creation of advertising.

The first converts were the creative department. No longer saddled with the responsibility of delivering a proposition like a missile warhead into the consumer camp, they were liberated to create anything they wanted as long as it delivered the desired outputs – even a hot-air balloon might fit the brief. Designing for outputs simultaneously freed and focused the creative task. Evaluation was much easier since it was measuring tangible changes in the consumers.

Unilever was eventually won over. There were a series of shootouts between Lintas and J. Walter Thompson where the 4D plan and the T-Plan were tested on a brief. Lintas won the early contests, no doubt because they aligned more naturally with the design of UPGA.

Having crossed the Rubicon to outputs, the new model could be applied to a client of any size, not just a major advertiser such as Unilever. Here's one of the first Thompson planners talking about its application to Campbell's Soup: 'It required you define the responses you wanted from the advertising which, of course, was a new thought. It wasn't what you put in, it was what they took out. It was what you wanted them to notice, its physical characteristics. How you served it. What you could do with it. How you wanted them to see it. What you wanted them to believe about the brand, the quality of the ingredients, the size of the portions, the incredible reasonableness of the price. And what you wanted them to feel about the brand. Campbell's was a great big mother figure of a soup. It required you to know a lot of adjectives otherwise you found yourself writing the same thing for every brand. Traditional but curiously modern. It used to drive Stephen mad: the up-to-date but harking back to its heritage. It was a single side of A4 paper and that was it.'

The T-Plan became a central piece of thinking for J. Walter Thompson for the rest of the 1960s. It's the first example of the famous collaboration of Stephen King and Jeremy Bullmore but by Bullmore's account it was something which they, in their spheres, came up with separately but discovered that their thinking was very congruent. Bullmore in his focus on the way he wanted creatives to work, and King within the marketing department persuading clients. Which made the resulting model even more formidable.

We have taken the time to unpack the T-Plan here because the shift in thinking towards outputs is foundational to early planning thinking. The date of the T-Plan's inception is also significant: four years before the launch of J. Walter Thompson's planning department in 1968. But without the T-Plan the setting up of the department would have made no sense.

The people we spoke to not only mentioned Stephen King but Andrew Ehrenberg of the London Business School who was pioneering evidence-based marketing. Ehrenberg found out that advertising is a lot better at reinforcing the beliefs of existing customers than persuading new people to try something they have never heard of before. That people don't necessarily become more loyal the more they use a product – sometimes they become less loyal because they have acquired the confidence to shop around. Ehrenberg, like King, developed theories about what advertising did best and what it didn't do as well.[25]

If these findings are startling to you it is because since that time, the forces of the input-driven persuasion model have proved overwhelming. At the start of the twenty-first century the agency world is dominated by rules of thumb and norms that nobody has the time or talent to challenge. But in the 1960s there were a handful of people who did more than ridicule the orthodoxy coming over from America. They set out to challenge it and to make advertising that worked because it connected with real people and which could be shown to work. They did their best to avoid clumsy quantitative research methodologies based on flawed or failed theories of advertising and consumption.

The core idea which drove all of the people we spoke to, is that how people respond to advertising is much more important and interesting than what the advertiser wishes to tell them. To make advertising that is effective you can't just measure sales or awareness. You have to understand how people are decoding it and how they are making use of it. As the thinking became more sophisticated it evolved into the concept of the active consumer – who consumes and shapes their understanding of advertising – not the passive blank surface the advertiser writes on.

Once you have determined the outputs you want, the next task is to define the role of the advertising – how it does its job. There is no single way that advertising works and each campaign will work in a different way because of the differences

25 For more on Ehrenberg's thinking *How Brands Grow*, Byron Sharp, OUP (2010) is perhaps the most accessible introduction.

between brands and the differences between the customers drawn to those brands. An ad which brings about a change in belief works very differently from an advertisement based on emotion or likeability. A single model for how advertising works is bound to fail. So each communication needs a model building for it to understand how well it does its job and if possible to improve what it does.

If there was a single tool which defined how advertising worked then it would have been automated years ago. There would be a grand unified theory of advertising and endless normative case studies backing up the theory. But having opted to understand each campaign on its own merits, a tiny group of thinkers set out to understand and optimise each one, and in doing so assisted in the creation of some of the most successful advertising ever made.

Account planning's power has been its ability to disrupt the norms of business communications by asking simple and awkward questions. And going on swiftly to find answers that work for individual brands and advertising campaigns. Advertising agencies were already full of researchers and the occasional motivational psychologist, who sat in service departments waiting to be called as a component within marketing services. The breakthrough was to have a group of individuals who worked on the advertising all the time not waiting to be summoned. They met regularly with the client. They worked alongside the creatives and the media planners and buyers. They took the idea of customer response and the role of advertising and used it all day, every day. This is the simple and central idea which came to be known as account planning.

Stephen King and Stanley Pollitt are reckoned to be the fathers of account planning. What they both had in common was an Oxbridge education – Stephen King in Oxford and Stanley Pollitt at Cambridge. And central to their methods is the tutorial. Oxford and Cambridge use a collegiate system where the teaching staff live in college with the students – they usually eat together as well. The tutorial format requires that every week a student should present a paper to his tutor at his lodgings, often one-to-one or with another student in attendance, and the paper is discussed and critiqued during the tutorial. The way in which Stephen King and Stanley Pollitt set up their respective planning department in each agency was different, but what they shared was the basic format of the Oxford or Cambridge university tutorial – with Stephen and Stanley as the tutor or college don who would initiate discussion, ask testing questions and use wit to skewer lazy or illogical thinking. Account planners were the students who had to reason, infer and persuade, to have a chance of their argument surviving. Planning was collegiate in its organisation, intellectual and discursive in how theories were formulated. And the goal was not winning the argument but coming to a truer understanding of how an advertisement or a brand was supposed to work.

The spark then for account planning was born neither from an innovation in process or from pragmatism but from evidence – born of deduction, imaginative jumps and a lot of arguing.

This model was so deeply embedded in the first decade that when account planning was exported to the USA at the start of the 1990s it was seriously proposed that Americans were not capable of becoming planners because their educational system did not furnish them with the formal intellectual training to think and debate![26] While this earnest discussion continued, UK planners were imported on vast salaries to make up the deficit. Happily we have discovered that an Oxbridge education is not a prerequisite to being a good account planner. But even if the role has mutated into many

26 Interview with Jon Steel.

different ways of working, it is still worth noting account planning's social beginnings. Being set apart from the day-to-day production line of the advertising production process, enabled a small group of individuals to be disproportionately effective – without needing a formalised method, a filing cabinet of tools, or a single theory by which they operated. And by dint of being argumentative and contrarian.

It would be naïve in the extreme to think that before planners arrived, no market analysis took place in agencies or that there had never been discussion about how advertising worked. But what is true is that before the planning 'great leap forward', the focus was more on marketing and market understanding. The regrouping into the planning function put the emphasis firmly on advertising, on customer response and what makes advertising persuasive and effective.

In 1965 Stanley Pollitt, an account director at Pritchard Wood, took over responsibility for research and media. In 1966 he began an experiment.

The Pritchard Wood experiment

> *'It was about making sure that research was central to how all decisions about advertising were taken. Planners were the practical, pragmatic people taking up this central role. More concerned with solving problems than selling techniques.'* Stanley Pollitt[27]

This is the earliest prototype of a planning department at Pritchard Wood in 1966. Stanley was a board director with responsibility for media research. In his paper 'How I Started Account Planning in Agencies,' Stanley describes it as an experiment with mixed results. He explains the context: the research function as a profit centre in agencies was winding down as clients increased their own marketing capability. There wasn't enough paid work for researchers to do. At the same time the amount of data relevant to professionally planned advertising was increasing, and the facilities for analysis were becoming more accessible. Somehow there had to be a way to keep the people with the skills to do this work gainfully employed inside the agency.

It is worth noting that this data was primarily quantitative research and company statistics. And those with the skills to make use of it were found in the media research department. But these were far too removed from the day-to-day development of advertising. So Stanley co-opted the media research department analysts, together with a general researcher and a

27 *Pollitt on Planning,* Collected papers by Stanley Pollitt.

creative researcher. Significantly he also decided he needed to train this new breed from scratch. 'I found the existing researchers had grown cosy in their backrooms. They did not want mainstream agency activity. They had grown too familiar with relying on techniques as a crutch, rather than thinking out more direct ways of solving problems themselves. Too academic to know how to be practical and pragmatic. They mostly disappeared into research agencies.'[28]

In the paper Stanley mentions three names: Bob Jones who managed the department, Peter Jones who was the first recruit, and David Cowan who joined as a graduate trainee. Bob Jones died in 2002. We spoke to Peter Jones, David Cowan and also Tony Mortemore, whom Stanley had brought in from his client Glaxo, about their memories of the Pritchard Wood experiment.

They were very different people. Bob Jones the departmental manager, a quiet thoughtful man, was from a media research background. Peter Jones was the showman – before he joined Pritchard Wood's media research department he had graduated from LSE in statistics and was familiar with social statistics and qualitative research as well. Peter was also an inveterate follower of horse racing and a gambler. As he said, 'Stanley took a punt on me.'

David Cowan was the intense one. He had studied maths and theoretical physics at University College London and had opted for a job at Pritchard Wood over a predictable post as a government scientist at the Farnborough Aircraft Establishment.

Tony Mortemore was the boy who left school and got a job in London because, as he put it, he was too lazy to go to college. He worked at Glaxo and then applied for a job in the Pritchard Wood media department. They decided he must be

28 *Pollitt on Planning*, Collected papers by Stanley Pollitt.

all right because Glaxo was a client of theirs. And he knew statistics. Tony identified himself as lower middle class. 'So I aspire. I collect stuff – Michael Caine titbits.'

This group of media researchers and statisticians was an odd bunch of people. They sat together in two offices. It worked, explains Tony Mortemore, because they were all 'just bright people. It was the interaction between them. It works. Being in the same office makes such a difference.' In those days everyone smoked so there would be regular pauses to talk and smoke. 'They thought about how advertising could be better if we understand your business, but by amalgamating all that is known and simplifying it. It was to get away from the ghastliness of American advertising research.'

The department was called the research department, its members, researchers. They called what they did market planning.[29] It wasn't entirely clear what it was. David Cowan observed, 'Reading Stanley's papers it was clearer what he was against, than clear in words. Though he was very clear in thought.' Peter Jones adds, 'Stanley just loved advertising and what advertising could do in a practical sense. He was dismayed by how far the research function at Pritchard Wood had been divorced from the problems the agency was trying to solve.'

Stanley Pollitt had an arm's length relationship with the department – Bob Jones actually reported to the media director. Tony Mortemore describes Stanley as being notionally in

29 In *Madison Avenue USA,* Martin Meyer mentions that in the mid-fifties McCann Erickson had a wholly owned subsidiary called the Market Planning corporation whose role was to help the agency's clients to do a total marketing job in controlling the market from innovation lab to distribution, even if the agency didn't have ultimate responsibility. This is the earliest reference to planning we have been able to find. Perhaps Pollitt knew of it, perhaps not. But market planning was a term that was in use and agencies were willing to use it.

charge. David Cowan is characteristically more blunt. 'Stanley was an account man. He wasn't a planner as such. He stayed as an account director and then went on to be joint founder at BMP.'

A lot of what they were challenging, was ways of deploying research and researchers that weren't effective. There was more than one research department at Pritchard Wood. As well as media research there was advertising research and also a new product development research unit. Not all of these were incorporated in the rebranded research department. There was some turnover in the department as researchers either adapted to their new proactive role, or didn't and were moved out.

The departmental function was different and new and ultimately those in it would need to be trained from scratch. There was a bit of jostling at the time about who was the first account planner, but Peter Jones and David Cowan can at least claim that Stanley identified them as the first of this new breed – though this may be because it was these two who made the transition when Boase Massimi Pollitt started up. David Cowan: 'The others were retreads of something else and we were completely new. We had a science base, not something we were aware of at the time. So I suppose we were the new men.' Later as planning director at BMP he would recruit researchers as planners but never rated them. 'Planners have different mindsets. Trying to understand causes and effects rather than describing things. Market researchers are descriptive and the technique is what they focus on.'

So at Pritchard Wood the department's basic activity was analysis – applying common sense to the process of advertising and understanding data. David Cowan comments, 'That was one of the big motivations that Stanley had. We had those repertory grids and principal component analyses and segmentation studies; things that we had been sold or were in possession of. All of which, large fast-moving consumer goods (FMCG) businesses had. Pritchard Wood had a lot of that kind of client, including Unilever. Part of our motivation was that a lot of this stuff was of limited use in developing better advertising or demonstrating effectiveness. But there was also recognition that data and research and information was pretty important. So we had better get a handle on it, otherwise we would be swamped by it.'

Tony gleefully recounts the Porridge Model as developed by David Cowan. 'It was for Beechams – correlating sales with the weather. It sounds rather naïve now but was wonderful at the time. We had to wait every month for the meteorological figures to come in to see if it was working. But then there were quite important people at the client watching this and it kept the account in the agency.'

We asked David Cowan how much their role involved selling advertising to clients and persuading them to buy work. He disagreed. 'Was it a persuasive function rather than an analytical one? No, not at all. But no, the whole thing was how do you create effective outstanding advertising? It was about understanding relevance, cause and effect. Why is it when someone looks at it that their take-out is what it is? What someone brings to the advertising is a key part of what they take out and see and hear. But why should that influence their behaviour in the way that it does? It's about that, I think.'

There were meetings with the client – the media researchers never used to do that. And the meetings led to more opportunities to sell in thinking or more research projects which weren't always about advertising. Working on Boots No7 they were commissioned to come up with genuinely new products. They made a graph of product sectors which Boots might consider entering. Tony Mortemore: 'Bob Jones said we'll sit down and have a think about that. Generating silly ideas, chopping them up and re-forming them. It was the first time I had come across brainstorming though we didn't call it that then. '

Everyone mentions Creenagh Lodge and her significance in shaping how they used research to think about advertising. She joined Pritchard Wood and was trained to be a researcher there. Peter Jones describes how she led the evolution of qualitative research to test advertising ideas: 'Creenagh developed the notion of sound tracks: an audio tape description played back to accompany key frames of a commercial. This approach was used to present rough materials in advance of showing them a finished full commercial.' Creenagh used to present the material to individual respondents in hour-long depth interviews. Qualitative discussion groups came later. David Cowan has no recollection of groups being used to creatively develop advertising at Pritchard Wood. Creenagh went on to be a founder of the seminal new product development agency Craton Lodge and Knight, creator of Wispa – the only successful chocolate brand launched in the UK in the last 50 years – and a pioneering thinker in applying brand thinking to the promotion of nation brands.

Where the Pritchard Wood researchers also innovated was getting the sample of respondents right. So much research was run in the same places and close to London with a similar set of people, who were neither the target buyers nor users of the products. Peter Jones comments, 'Interviewing eight people at random talking about a product they don't buy, or haven't thought about, is a pretty useless exercise.'

They also started working towards the ratio of a researcher for every client supervisor. In other words, getting the work right was as important as selling it to the client and keeping the client involved. Peter Jones: 'Towards the end of my time at Pritchard Wood, planning was actually working to the extent that one of the people who was from the then research department, would work on a one-to-one basis with an account handler.' What they never formalised was assigning a researcher to each account. They still functioned as a pool of analysts and thinkers.

What began as a rebranded media research department did some research studies that went well and even won awards. And gave them new opportunities to meet with clients. Peter Jones describes himself as the practical implementer of this new form of research. 'We were given more and more client access as a result. So we began integrating those functions and we became a one-stop shop, if you like, for research. And people who understood research decided what sort of research was necessary and, at the same time, started suggesting techniques which helped with the advertising.' The point of the research was never to sell ancillary services but to make better advertising.

So this is what the first planning experiment looked like – a grab bag of media researchers with statistical and media research skills, who were involved daily in the creation of better advertising. Though there is no mention of involvement with the creative teams. The impetus came from Stanley Pollitt, so it is to Stanley we turn next.

Stanley Pollitt

> *'Stanley was a philosopher. We were sort of called into his office to have daily tutorials. Actually we weren't called into his office. We had to go out with him to lunch and drink a lot of wine for tutorials. His stamina with alcohol was amazing and he was brilliant. He was always highly intellectual when he was drunk so it was good.'*
>
> Jane Newman

So at Pritchard Wood, the first planning department, there was an eclectic group of bright people, very different from one another; the brainchild of an account director who is notionally in charge. We need to understand what Stanley brought to the mix. Stanley Pollitt was the son of a portrait painter who was trained by the pre-Raphaelite artist Holman Hunt.[30] There is still a Pollitt collection of Holman Hunt sketches and paintings. Stanley had a thorough grounding in fine arts and music, though he wasn't a painter or musician himself. And he went to Cambridge to study law. He had a brilliant mind and wide ranging interests.

In his youth Stanley was a boxer who boxed for his school and for his college at Cambridge. In his younger years he was not averse to having a punch up as part of an enjoyable night out. Paul Feldwick talks of Friday evenings when Stanley would walk past Soho pubs with drinkers filling all the surrounding pavements and push past in the hope of jostling a drinker

30 Interview with Tessa and Katy Pollitt.

or two into spilling their beer and squaring up to him. And Stanley's daughter, Katy, confirmed that her father sometimes came home with cuts and bruises after a night out. Dave Trott recounts an incident when Pollitt knocked an art director – a taller, younger man – to the floor after an altercation and chased him out of the pub. This explains Stanley's comment that planners find themselves in a contest with creatives and account men and need to 'fight their corner'. It shows that he thought of the planning role as being one of influence, not a tick box in the process of assembling advertising. And that influence was expected right the way through the development process. There was a lot more to planning than intellectual exchanges – there was supposed to be conflict and passion – human exchange not process and deduction.

Most descriptions of Stanley describe him shambling around in a tweed jacket out of which he would pull a packet of cigarettes and a lighter – he smoked constantly and was reputed to have set fire to himself more than once, forgetting his lit cigarette in the heat of debate. He also had a reputation for mumbling – he wasn't easy to follow – and sometimes he was impossible to understand. This meant that however brilliant a thinker or controversialist, he wasn't a natural presenter. Clients adored him as an eccentric professorial figure who was passionate about their advertising and who thought deeply about how it drove their business. But when it came to big presentations Stanley might write the presentation, but it would be given by someone else who was easier to follow.

Stanley was a fervent Catholic who made sure he got his children baptised even though, being a divorcee, the Catholic church gave him short shrift. He loved discussing the work of the mystic Jesuit priest Teilhard de Chardin who was exiled to China by the Vatican for his radicalism. 'He wholly believed there was a life hereafter so he wasn't bothered that he might die in a year or two because he was going somewhere else quicker!' says Jan Zajac.

His daughters recount the writing process because Stanley didn't much enjoy writing either. He would rather talk. He would go into the living room, put classical music on the stereo and crank it up loudly. The girls were under strict instructions not to interrupt him while he was writing. Compared with the prodigious output of Stephen King, the other father of account planning at J. Walter Thompson who was a prolific writer of papers, we have only a handful of papers written by Stanley.

He wasn't a practical person – and he found this immensely frustrating – he held conventional views of the gender roles and he wanted to be able to fix a broken-down car or turn his hand to home 'handymanship' but, although he had a talent for gardening, this didn't extend to repairing machines.

Stanley's natural habitat was the dinner table. With an open bottle of claret and cigarette in hand the debate could get under way, and he would argue about anything and everything. His daughters recall him explaining the need for account planning to them over the dinner table, with them trying to understand him, when Katy, the older, was not yet 10 years of age! And an evening, when a client came round, that was devoted to the articulating the benefits of a particular brand of toilet paper. Translated into the workplace this meant that any opportunity to have dinner with Stanley was highly prized. Because if he had an early morning meeting then there would not be time to catch the train in from his home in Sussex, so he would be staying in London overnight and would need at least one person to have dinner with. Dinner with Stanley was a provocation and an education.

Jim Williams, one of Stanley's first trainees at BMP, comments: 'He was wonderfully perceptive about things. One of his favourite sayings was "Things that are around", which was his idea of market research. It wasn't all precise or putting things into boxes. He was a sensitive teacher of the broader view and that was ideal, because that was the way I felt when writing a strategy – you are not trying to answer specific questions. What you are trying to do is understand the consumer and their reaction to the product and build on that.' It was difficult for Stanley to be precise. He kept the focus on intuitive understanding rather than an analytical understanding, forcing his people who had strong analytical skills to be more intuitive in how they solved communication problems.

Perhaps if Stanley had been a better presenter or writer, then he would not have developed his market planning idea in the way he did, and seeded it so effectively to those whom he gathered around him. It grew out of the lunch and dinner conversations where his researcher/planners were expected to think and to fight their corner on any subject under discussion. But particularly advertising and how it worked. It is probably inevitable that in such an environment it was easier to be negative about what didn't work, but it meant that those who worked with him continually developed their critical thinking. Even if their skill sets were different. The Pritchard Wood experiment was of relatively short duration. The directors planned a management buyout. The American owners had other ideas. Events came to a dramatic head when the board went across to New York to buy the agency. The sale was agreed in principle. The Jewish accountant wouldn't work at the weekend so they flew on the Monday, by which time Interpublic had found some more finance and refused to sell. The directors were abruptly removed from their desks and escorted out. There was no alternative now. They had to start their own agency. There were various meetings, one at Bob Jones's house, and a meeting at Cadbury's in the office of their research manager. That research manager was John Bartle who went on to found an agency himself – Bartle Bogle Hegarty – and to be one of the finest planners of the next generation. When the directors were removed Peter Jones had been in a meeting with John and told him after a phone message that he had just left Pritchard Wood so couldn't do any more work for them. So the two of them went to the pub instead. Back in the agency, Peter told Tony it was time to stand up and be counted. Only in a start-up there is no budget to pay junior researchers whether you stand up or not. The new agency started with a single solitary client: Cadbury, who had stuck with the departing directors. Bob Jones and Peter Jones followed Stanley to the new agency. Stanley telephoned Stephen King at J. Walter Thompson to ask if he would give David Cowan a job. Stephen King was on the verge of starting a planning department himself and agreed to take him. Martin Boase commented that at J. Walter Thompson, King would have struggled to find enough planners to work across everything. David Cowan didn't officially start until January 1969. He took himself off on a holiday to France. But before he did so, he had to come into the JWT office for a couple of days at the start of November when the JWT planning department was officially launched.

Tony Mortemore was another refugee – he went off on holiday to Scotland, during which time Bob Jones cabled him to tell him that they had found him a job with Simon Broadbent, 'though he wasn't famous then.' Broadbent, a brilliant media analyst, went on to be one of the creators of the IPA Effectiveness Awards designed to isolate and demonstrate the commercial contribution of advertising. It was the only job on offer. Feeling abandoned, Tony Mortemore turned it down. And got a job with the enemy: an American multinational in Banbury.

And that is how Stanley's first planning experiment ended. When you talk to the earliest members of the Boase Massimi Pollitt planning department – Stanley is central as a Socratic mentor. Whether or not he performed the role of an account planner (and there are those who argue that he didn't), the way in which Stanley Pollitt conceived of planning and the way he selected, gathered and coached planners was grounded in debate, conflict even, and being able to develop an informed opinion and carry everyone else with you. That is Stanley Pollitt's legacy.

Although Stephen King launched the JWT planning department on 1 November 1968, the start-up Boase Massimi Pollitt set up shop a few days before, with planning baked into the structure from Day 1. So, for the time being, we will follow the BMP strand of the story.

Boase Massimi Pollitt

'The prevailing culture in ad agencies was very "Madmen" – account man driven. No one was really interested in doing work that was effective. Relevant plus distinctive equals more effective, was BMP's mantra so that's where planning came in; and there was no other agency at that time that was questioning the relevance and therefore the effectiveness of the work they were doing.' Jane Newman

When Boase Massimi Pollitt opened its doors in October 1968 they announced that the new agency was going to use researchers (still not called account planners yet). On every single client. For every single ad. And that there would always be a 1:1 ratio between research and account supervisors. The most radical experiment yet attempted. But it was a start-up. Stanley Pollitt had brought Bob Jones with him. And Peter Jones too. But they had had to break up the team. Peter still regrets not fighting harder to have got David Cowan into the new agency sooner. Their priority was to win new clients. There would be no further hirings until they had done that. What everyone associates with Boase Massimi Pollitt is creative pretesting, but that came almost by accident out of calamity. The agency opened its doors with a single client, Cadbury. They made a new TV commercial for Smash instant potato. And the ad was a disaster.

Jane Newman joined BMP as a planning trainee two years later and from one remove she describes the trauma and the way it shaped planning: 'They had shot a TV commercial for Cadbury's Smash. Their first one had been spectacular. It was the one with the potato being peeled. It was iconic for the sixties and really just the kind of advertising that they wanted to do because they were admiring what was going on in America. So they shot this second commercial and I only ever saw a glimpse of it once, and it was basically never brought out and never mentioned. It was called "Christmas Day at the Workhouse". So basically what had happened was that they had taken what they thought was the idea in the Potato ad and produced another commercial on it, but it just did not work. The directors had to remortgage their houses and everything for this new agency, and they had to eat the cost of that spot which was just a huge amount of money for them. Planning became an insurance policy against this ever happening again.'[31]

The agency's future was hanging by a thread. So the founders made a very simple commitment. They would never ever run an advertisement or commercial without pretesting it with real consumers of the product to be advertised. At first sight this might seem to be a massive concession to pretesting ads the way every other agency in London was wont to pretest ads, by putting them in front of people completing questionnaires and counting heads. But Stanley Pollitt didn't believe in that kind of pretesting. So they went back to the pioneering work

31 There is an amusing postscript to this story. It isn't true! John Bartle, who was working at Cadbury at the time, took us to task over this. Cadbury paid for the remake of the advertising. The directors didn't have to remortgage their houses. But it is a measure of how traumatic the event was that the trainees were told that pretesting was the only way to prevent the sky falling on their heads. We have opted to leave the story in because it shows the power of myth in forming cultural practices – planners researched hundreds of ads and spent thousands of hours travelling to groups and back. They were convinced that there was no alternative, although at the time they were the only agency in the world doing this.

of Creenagh Lodge. An audio recording was made which describing the commercial idea. While this was played back during the research, some simple sketched images showed how it might look as if one were briefing the film director on how to shoot the commercial. Right down to the viewing angles. The planner assigned to the account would recruit a customer outside of London, who had never ever been researched before. The interview would be carried out in the customer's home. The planner would ask them to talk about their understanding of the advertising idea. What was happening? What was the message? What did it say about the product and the company who made that product? They also watched the way the person talked about it, to see if they were confused, bored, engaged. In other words, how they responded.

The planner would take notes on what was said and bring the feedback back to the agency. There the results would be discussed with the creative team and the account manager on the account. If the ad could be improved, or elements moved around, then it was. If not, the creative team began again. The altered or new commercial concept would be taken back and shown to a new group of customers. Conducting individual interviews was too work intensive, so they started to gather the interviews together in groups to save time. And again this feedback would be brought back to the agency. This cycle could continue as many as five times until the advertising was seen to be connecting, and its message was being fully understood.

This may seem a hugely arduous and costly way to develop advertising. And it was. But clients were expected to pay for the costs of running the pretesting. That meant the cost of randomly recruiting customers, the incentives for those who participated, and the time of the planner. The process was entirely transparent. The client was allowed to attend any of the groups. After all, they were paying for them. But there was a simple rule: no client was allowed to come to only one group. It was too easy for a client to form a strong opinion from a single comment from a solitary respondent. So clients were expected to come out for at least a couple of evenings.

James Best talks about an early triumph with the marketing director of St Ivel when they were developing a campaign for Gold Spinner cheese triangles. 'He was naturally rather uncertain, not convinced about this strange approach, and he came to the groups in Trowbridge and saw first-hand two or three bunches of housewives talking enthusiastically about the treatment. That was an unusual event for us, seeing a senior client converted to the approach, and a bit black and white because it gave us the authority of first-hand access to the consumer.'

This was one of the first times marketers actually got to see and listen to their customers talking about their products and the advertising ideas. Marketing departments were full of data but they rarely sat in the same room as real customers. The research they read was mostly surveys with highly structured questions. This was a golden opportunity for marketers to enter the lives of those who bought and used their products, and to see it all first-hand. The advertising ideas weren't always successful. But the agency usually learned something. And the marketers almost always learned something.

No other agency was doing this. It required a huge commitment in terms of people. In his paper 'How I Started Account Planning', Stanley Pollitt calculates that BMP ran something like 1,200 groups a year: that's around 25 a week. This volume of research would have been attained much later as the agency won more clients, but what it meant was that, quite aside from its core business of advertising, BMP was functioning as a major research company. At one point they employed three qualitative researchers full-time, as a supplement to the planners to cope with the pressure, because the research workload was too great for the planners to do alone.[32] However, the norm tended to be for the planner assigned to a particular advertising account to do most of the groups themselves after a day in the office.

Doing qualitative pretesting proved to be a winner in pitches too. Other agencies went in with data and creative ideas. BMP was able to tell you what real people had said about your products and about rough ideas. One of the strengths of qualitative research was the way it enabled you to get detailed feedback with very simple sketches called keyframes which didn't look at all like finished advertising. Fairly soon after starting these pretesting groups, they moved from using the audio tape with crudely animated sketches to filming the sketches and placing this with a soundtrack on a piece of video tape. Video players were heavy and unwieldy but these new experimental films were called 'animatics' because they could do simple movements that suggested the camera movements tracking across or zooming in. There was enough detail for the planners to give feedback on shooting angles and executional guidelines. These helped to establish BMP as a pre-eminent television agency when it was still very small.

The content of the advertising reflected the discussions that were had in people's houses. Not prioritising key messages or key moments, demonstrating benefits or consumers' appreciation (as the big packaged goods brands liked to develop advertising) – but characters, storylines and visual gags. An ad which had successfully come through this treatment was often funny or moving. It made those who saw it animated. It got them talking. So the research method produced a different

32 The interview with Roddy Glenn, a qualitative researcher, illuminates when and how researchers were used instead of planners for particular situations. Usually it was because there was an issue of perceived independence. So the qualitative researchers had to be much tougher than the planners. That was the job.

kind of advertising to the kind which tested propositions and was focused on *message* delivery.

BMP became famous very quickly as the agency who qualitatively pretested their advertising. They were regarded as rather eccentric and doctrinaire for insisting on carrying out the process. What had driven it initially had been self-preservation, but then it rather started to become the way things were done. This didn't impress everybody. Judie Lannon who had been hired by Stephen King to found a qualitative research unit in J. Walter Thompson earlier in 1968, didn't approve. 'I thought it was extremely unprofessional and likely to be biased and not a very good idea.' How could planners researching their agency's own work possibly be objective? To research properly there needed to be a distance between researcher and the creative work.

Later creative research development became more formalised – 'industrialised' as Paul Feldwick put it, referring to the setting up of the Research Business by Wendy Gordon and Colleen Ryan. Qualitative agencies sprang up all over London to service the demand, as agencies tried to match what BMP was doing. They used qualitative researchers, not their own planners (nobody knew how to do the magic themselves). And the industry formalised a process of distillation that, without deconstructing the advertising, allowed you to collect first reactions, an understanding of the creative idea, the message of the ad, the product benefit, how it made people feel, and at whom they thought the ad was aimed. One could also test recognition or recall of the company behind the ad. From this time the convention began of removing all brand references on the creative materials, so that people were forced to guess who might be behind it. And when they were told who it really was, the shifts in perception could be very insightful, and were duly noted. Perhaps the most important change was the way in which the advertising idea could now be separated from the execution. It meant a strong creative *idea* could produce many different *executions*: and an execution which failed didn't mean the underlying creative idea was wrong. This meant the ad could be tweaked and re-researched. Many great campaigns came into being this way and gained new energy.

Honey Monster was a campaign referred to by several of the BMP planners which showed how a campaign, which didn't work in research, could become successful when it was modified to change one critical executional element. Paul Feldwick explains that the Honey Monster 'was simply not right the first time around. It was a sort of small irritating creature that all mums hated because it reminded them of naughty children. John Webster had never thought of it as being like a child. He thought of him as a monster. So that gave him the idea, let's make him more like a child but let's make him really big. That came out of that. So he got the cap, and he became like a big baby eight feet tall. By turning the Honey Monster into a shambling giant towering over mums and children in the roughs he became a lovable scamp. His behaviour was detached from the bad behaviour of children and became part of the playfulness that the brand was trying to communicate with the cereal. For me, the process of ad development is to start with something tangible and then mess around with it, rather than get into this intellectual headspace where you can spend 18 months arguing about: Is this nutritious and delicious? Or delicious and nutritious? Forgetting that this whole thing is going to really be about the Honey Monster and whether it's three feet tall or six feet tall.'

The language of pretesting now seems over the top referencing what was a qualitative process. James Best, another trainee, protests: 'You could literally test how an ad would work if you did it in a form that people could understand, before it was too late to make an execution better. Whether the idea had wings. Whether the execution that clothed the idea was appropriate and would be successful, and you could give it a yes or a no. You came back with a diagnosis and understanding and some suggestions for making it better. It *was* a test.' For him the fault line lies between understanding and selling. Agencies who used research themselves deployed it as a selling tool. And that corrupted the way they used the research. 'Frank Lowe adopted planning as a sales tool. CDP didn't do it to understand but to sell.'

BMP unintentionally spawned an entire qualitative research industry. But even when planners in other agencies learned how to do their own groups, nothing matched the purity of the original leap into pretesting: the same planner going back to core customer groups over and over, night after night. One of the anecdotes oft repeated is that of the BMP planner knowing more about the customer than anybody else including the client marketing team. Jon Steel, one of BMP's most famous alumni – one of those who many years later took planning to the West Coast of America as planning director of Goodby Silverstein – talks about how his deep knowledge of Courage beers came about: 'I worked on the Courage account, but I spent six months working in the marketing department at Courage as an element of my training, and effectively remained part of Courage's marketing department for all the time that I was a planner at BMP. And I was involved in developing new products, I was involved in packaging design, I was involved in pretty much every aspect of their business, so I knew it back to front. I always had that in the back of my mind in any conversation I might have been having with beer drinkers in York or down in Bristol, because I knew what the business objectives were, and I knew what the business strategy was, and I could make connections between that and things that people in the real world were saying.' It has become a cliché that the planner is the consumer representative in the agency. What Steel describes is much deeper than an ombudsman-like role but an embodying of the client's strategy, and the totality of the customer experience being internalised. This is not a strategy document but a strategy person.

Focus groups have become a debased coinage for many reasons. The original impulse was the purest form of marketing – customer-centric communications development. Whether or not you believe in focus groups, using them propelled BMP from being a start-up to being a top 20 agency within 10 years of opening its doors. And BMP's creative output was one of the best in the country, garnering creative awards and public accolades in equal measure. The walls of John Webster's office were covered in half-finished sketches, as were those of many other creatives. But also on his walls were letters from children and customers who loved the advertising and wrote to the agency to tell them about it. John treasured these and would read them out to visitors. The growing pile of creative awards by contrast was pushed into the backs of cupboards.

The qualitative group idea is so dominant in the BMP legend that it might appear as if the planning role was no more than bouncing backwards and forwards between briefings and focus groups. When we examine the craft skills of planning you will see that – just as at Pritchard Wood – the planning department did very much more than qualitative research, so the analysis of data and product statistics continued in much the same way. They also planned the media space even if they didn't book it. Peter Jones explains that media planning was part of the planning process. 'More so at BMP than anywhere else, so working out the best media structures with the statistical data to back it up. We would put a presentation together for a client that would be as much about the hard data as it was about the soft data. In fact you had to get the client to accept the hard data before embarking on any other soft data and sometimes that would require research work in its own right.'

The use of pretesting using group discussions led to the

BMP planners being labelled, rather disparagingly, as 'ad-tweakers' by Stephen King. This was in contrast to the 'grand strategists' of J. Walter Thompson, of course. The early BMP planners are still sensitive to this slur which implied, incorrectly, that they never looked at data or thought strategically.[33] So now let's turn to J. Walter Thompson and the factors which led to the creation in November 1968 of what was called from the outset a *planning department*.

33 Though Jeremy Bullmore points out rather gleefully that Stephen King never called BMP planners 'ad tweakers'. King set up a scale and they obediently positioned themselves on it, adding that he had counselled King to call the other end 'advert tweakers' because it is even more disparaging.

Stephen King

> *'Thompson's was a very different kind of agency from BMP; it was a lot bigger for one thing and much more organised. Planning had come about in a different way and it had a different focus, a different emphasis.'*
>
> Paul Feldwick

Stephen King was arguably the greatest advertising theorist of his generation. It is tempting to retrofit his thinking into his biggest idea: that of the planning department. But even if J. Walter Thompson had never set up a planning department, Stephen King's thinking would still be peerless. He joined J. Walter Thompson in 1957 – 11 years before the founding of the planning department, and he never worked anywhere else after that. He worked in the marketing department because J. Walter Thompson's clients needed marketing and many of them didn't have marketing departments of their own. None, aside from Unilever, would have matched the power of their own marketing department which was capable of conceiving and launching products, as well as building marketing programmes and fitting advertising into the other components of the marketing mix.

During Stephen King's time at J. Walter Thompson he produced a steady stream of papers and books that were seminal. If they are hard to read now, it is not because of the way they are written but because of the concentration of his thinking. Some of his papers were intended for the marketing department of J. Walter Thompson and then latterly the planning department. But much of his output was published and presented at Market Research Society events or other industry gatherings relating to marketing and advertising. He was an early exponent of the modern concept that if you have a good idea then you should give it away – partly to make your idea more successful, but also to test it so as to apply it properly, and then establish a lead that others cannot catch. At the time thinkers in London advertising agencies feasted on Stephen King's ideas.

Here's a brief list of them:

1. The Target Plan which we have already covered in some detail. Stephen introduced this to the marketing department in 1964. The premise of the T-Plan was radical because it shifted the focus away from what advertisers *say* to what consumers *take in,* specifically listing three kinds of desired response. It was brand rather than execution specific, so changed very slowly. Over time the T-Plan proved too cumbersome (at least one of the planners we spoke to described it as unworkable).

By the early 1970s it had been incorporated into the Planning Cycle:

- where are we?
- how did we get here?
- where do we want to go?
- how do we get there?
- how will we know when we've got there?

Once again Jeremy Bullmore deserves some credit. King attributes the Planning Cycle to Jeremy Bullmore. Bullmore claims that he was using the questions with the creative department and King appropriated them as headlines for a thinking process he had already designed, which added strategy – How do we get there? and evaluation – How will we know we have got there?

When David Cowan moved from J. Walter Thompson to BMP in 1971, he took a copy of the T-Plan with him. And it is clear from Jan Zajac the planners at BMP knew what the Planning Cycle was. The legacy of the T-Plan can still be found in the question in the Thompson's creative brief: *What do you want the consumer to do, think, or feel as a response to this communication?*

2. A theory of advertising which stated that advertising rarely affects action directly but, more so, indirectly. The paper presenting this theory goes on to list a variety of different indirect effects which advertising can have and provides examples of advertising campaigns which do so – the aim being to identify which indirect effect you would like your advertising to have. This shifted advertising strategy into a territory of communications objectives like 'to remind customers not to run out of brand x' and away from simplistic marketing objectives, like 'to increase sales'.[34]

An extension of this idea was The Consumer Buying System, which broke down a purchase decision into its component parts, and articulated the role advertising could play at each stage.[35]

3. He also had the notion that an advertisement was a whole and needed to be understood as such. So if you were constructing, or measuring, by breaking it down into constituent pieces

34 See Stephen King's paper 'Practical Progress from a theory of advertisements' in *A Master Class in Brand Planning: The Timeless Works of Stephen King*, Wiley (2007).

35 The consumer buying system can be found in *The JWT Account Planners Toolkit* (unpublished).

you would have destroyed something that was essential to the way that advertising worked. He saw this as being one of the most powerful reasons for deploying qualitative research alongside quantitative techniques, because quantitative techniques used alone, necessarily broke up the communications and made the respondent evaluate it piece by piece (often using scales: 1: for not at all likely – 5: for very likely, and so on).

4. He had the idea that advertising could create emotional responses which were more powerful than changes in belief. This effectively liberated advertising from a vicious cycle of picking from a small subset of claims about product performance, and supported the idea that advertising could be funny, moving, shocking, astonishing. Bill Bernbach started a creative revolution in New York, but until Stephen King nobody had demonstrated how advertising that was liked, could also be more effective.

Extending this idea into new product development, famously with Andrex toilet tissue and Mr Kipling cakes, Stephen King proceeded to measure the price premium which emotional advertising campaigns had created – including measuring how many of the most loyal customers would actually go to another store rather than buy an alternative. He could demonstrate how much more money the emotional-driven brand returned as a result.

5. The last idea was perhaps the biggest: that the most powerful advertising is not about driving or influencing sales but creating long-term beliefs about the product, which would continue to influence purchase and consumption long after the advertising was off-air. As a result, J. Walter Thompson stopped talking about long-running advertising campaigns – though they had several of those going back as far as the 1930s (classics such as 'Guinness is Good for You'). They spoke instead of *brand-building* advertising. J. Walter Thompson clients were quietly locked into a cycle of creating brand value through advertising. This made it more difficult to move their accounts elsewhere and justified the budgets they were already spending: justification which other advertising agencies didn't have, given that their advertising testing promoted the recall of particular executions and end lines. But the round of quantitative testing was in effect a closed ecosystem to find the best execution for the next phase of the campaign. Stephen King broke the cycle by suggesting that advertising could achieve long-term effects. So it was more important to identify executions that build the core brand values for years to come, than to get a high persuasion score which might spike sales for just a couple of months.

That is the briefest of overview of Stephen King's thinking. Account planners are employed to make advertising better rather to theorise about advertising, but Stephen King's thinking fed J. Walter Thompson's success for decades. And because his thinking was widely available, others used it too.

Boase Massimi Pollitt weren't at all interested in planning and research departments in other agencies. They weren't particularly impressed with the output of J. Walter Thompson's creative department. But they swallowed Stephen King's thinking whole.

To Stephen King's thinking must be added his wit and gift with language. This made him a wonderful conversationalist and a devastating controversialist. He could out-think and out-talk anyone, by disarming them. One of his great creations was the hapless and fictional 'Colin Thrust' – the marketing director who did all the right things by marketing convention but whose decisions were utterly generic and cliché-driven if you asked why he was doing them. With clients and within J. Walter Thompson, King followed a similar model to the one Stanley Pollitt was following. The tutorial model where the tutor listens, challenges, provokes and shapes was his forte.

Roderick White describes what he gained most from working with Stephen King. 'It was about not accepting received wisdom because it was usually wrong. Question everything. But if it turns out to be right accept it.' But not being tempted to speculate if the logic didn't warrant it. 'He would say things like "I don't know, I think we should just put that in a box called 'too difficult'",' says Lee Godden with a chuckle.

This way of working is critical because, by comparison with Pritchard Wood and BMP, Stephen King's work can appear doctrinaire if all you have is his written output as an example of his thinking. As if he sat in his office checking T-Plans or Planning Cycles all day and summoning in miscreants for making errors. But King's tools are conceptual tools to encourage people to think, and to make it easier to identify and correct flawed thinking before expensive mistakes have been made. What Stephen King achieved was a way to push brilliant thinking down deeply in the J. Walter Thompson organisation, so that bright youngsters could deliver it with only light supervision from planning group heads. He democratised strategic thinking, which until then had been the province of experienced practitioners and agency managers.

Stephen King is a tough act to follow. If J. Walter Thompson is the university of advertising, it differs from conventional universities in not continually publishing its thinking. A generation after Stephen King, the most prolific writer from the agency on advertising topics is his long-time colleague and contemporary Jeremy Bullmore. Though honourable mention should be given to Merry Baskin and Judie Lannon, who have continued to write and publish collections of papers by reminding us of the fundamental tenets of Stephen's thinking. As Bullmore observed wryly, 'There is only one King.'

It is ironic by contrast that so many thinkers and writers have emerged from Boase Massimi Pollitt alumni. Paul Feldwick has published books on advertising evaluation, and theories of advertising. Adam Morgan who created the language of the 'challenger brand' in *Eat the Big Fish*. John Grant of the *Manifesto* series: 'New Marketing', 'Brand Innovation' and 'Green Marketing'. Leslie Butterfield writing about *Excellence in Advertising* for the IPA. Mark Earls, the author of *Herd* and *Copy, Copy, Copy*. And Jon Steel with *Truth, Lies and Advertising*, the best-selling introductory planning text in recent times.

So we turn now to J. Walter Thompson at the point when Stephen King joined it to work in the marketing department and the changes he brought about.

J. Walter Thompson

> *'J. Walter Thompson had class and history and it had people like Derek Causton who was in charge of business development. There were polished, assured people with education and with breeding: John Lindesay-Bethune, Derek Higham. In the 1960s everyone wanted to work at JWT unless you were more of a client person in which case it was Masius.'*
> John Siddall

The contrast between J. Walter Thompson and Pritchard Wood was considerable (and the contrast with the upstart BMP was even greater). Though both agencies were subsidiaries of large American agencies, J. Walter Thompson London was the biggest agency in the UK. It was vast – its offices in Berkeley Square held 900 people and that didn't include other subsidiaries around London. Descriptions of J. Walter Thompson make it sound like a cross between a cruise ship and Claridges – it had its own choir and orchestra. Several MPs worked there so meetings with clients would be scheduled for the mornings before the House of Commons went into session. In the Hill Street side, behind the main Berkeley Square offices, clients might be invited to lunch with the Chancellor of the Exchequer. The Duke of Edinburgh even lunched there once. If you were fortunate enough to get a job there you could stay for life – there was a star system of pay grades that recognised performance and length of tenure. Stephen King joined J. Walter Thompson from a small agency called Mond Nickel in 1957, his first job after university and he stayed at

J. Walter Thompson for the rest of his career. Many others did the same.

The way to the top often began the post room, where you worked from the age of 16 as a runner and learned how the whole agency worked. Graduates started at a higher level. Peter Mead was interviewed for a job in the post room during which he asked if there was a canteen. It was explained that his wages wouldn't allow him to afford to eat there, but that if he made up his sandwiches he could always eat them in Berkeley Square. He didn't take the job. When years later his agency, Abbott Mead Vickers, became the largest agency in the UK, Peter Mead made up a Tupperware box of sandwiches and instructed his chauffeur to drive him to Berkeley Square where he sat and ate on a bench looking up at the J. Walter Thompson offices. Revenge is a sandwich best served cold![36]

J. Walter Thompson was an agency that took client service to the highest level. The account representatives often sported double-barrelled names – they had come through the public school system: well-dressed, well-mannered and well-spoken. Almost certainly better bred than the clients they served. So when a client commissioned a new advertising campaign a representative would come to collect the brief, and would go and brief the creative team (art director and copywriter) permanently assigned to work on the account. The representative would bring rough sketches of the creative ideas to the client and present them in the client's offices. If the work was approved it ran. If the client wanted changes there might be some discussion, but the representative would return to the agency to get the work amended or to get more creative ideas. The agency couldn't do this endlessly despite the considerable padding of a 15% deduction in media commission. So part of

36 Story told by Dave Trott.

the value of the marketing department was in providing the understanding of the market, so that the advertising campaign could be shown to achieve the marketing and communication goals. But a lot depended on the charm and persuasion of the account representatives, backed up by solid creative work and sound market thinking.

The coming of the 1960s had brought a sea change with it – an influx of bright graduates alongside the well-bred client supervisors. There are various stories about this. One was Jeremy Bullmore – asked how much money he had, he answered £63 before he realised he was being asked if he had a private income. That was the assumption.[37] He didn't! The first graduate trainee not to have graduated from Oxford or Cambridge (but Newcastle university) had to run the gauntlet as a junior account exec by being made to select the wine for a client lunch.[38] He chose a lukewarm claret on a day so hot that only a chilled Chablis would have fit the bill. He was banned from subsequent lunches until he knew enough to make himself useful. And the agency was wont to empty out on Friday afternoons as the staff returned to their country houses in the shires.

Since the 1930s J. Walter Thompson had been known as the university of advertising, a term which described the New York agency but came increasingly during the 1960s and 1970s to be attached to J. Walter Thompson London. The culture was positively intellectual – clients expected the agency to tell them how the advertising worked and to draw on whatever expertise was necessary. The marketing department was the hub of this, but during the 1960s as clients' own marketing

37 There is another anecdote to parallel this from Dave Trott who asks for 'seventeen fifty' when he joins BMP. And is astonished to find he is paid double: £35 a week. It turns out that what he had asked for, and received, was an annual salary of £1,750, when as a working class boy from the East End he thought he was asking for a weekly wage!

38 This from a conversation with Chris Davies.

departments became stronger, the agency opened new departments: an advertising research unit and a media research unit; and in 1965, a new product development unit, and an operations research unit close to the marketing department, but separate from it. The agency had a huge commitment to market research which it had pioneered in the 1930s. Not only were world-class research pioneers like Tom Corlett employed there, but both John Treasure, who went on to be chairman of J. Walter Thompson London, and Tom Sutton, who was managing director of the London agency before going on to global management in New York, began their careers as researchers. Research was key to how the agency serviced its clients.

As clients' marketing departments grew in scale and power, the days of a separate marketing department which was all part of the service, looked numbered. Adding on specialist units was an initial response to this. But the invention of the T-Plan by Stephen King had moved the role of the analyst away from marketing towards a single-minded focus on the role of advertising. The T-Plan, simply put, required the analyst to summarise the response framed from the other end – what the customer took out rather than what the advertiser wanted to put in. The Rosser Reeves Unique Selling Proposition method argued that if the advertising carried on banging the consumer over the head by repeating ads endlessly (and backed up its claims with facts), then eventually the consumer would come to hold the belief you wanted them to. The T-Plan allowed for assent and belief in the claims being made. But it also allowed for irritation, boredom and simple incredulity.

Advertising works in different ways – it wasn't likely that sensory, emotional and rational response were going to be equally important. But people respond to advertising in different ways. Stephen King posited an immediacy scale, because advertising as he said 'rarely affects action directly'. So the marketing analyst needs to think about what type of response the campaign was aiming for. And to build this into the target response plan.

Building on the idea of customer response was the related idea that accumulated usage of products and exposure to advertising reinforced beliefs and emotions. These impressions were put under the heading of the brand. J. Walter Thompson didn't invent brand theory but what it did espouse was the idea that the long-term effect of advertising was to build brand awareness and brand loyalty. And that this was as emotional as it was rational. In a marketplace which was much more crowded with brands than it had been in the 1950s, there were limits to the number of unique performance claims that could be made by different brands. But by building relevance through emotional claims, there were many more ways to make a brand distinctive. Brands sat in consumers' heads and were used by them to choose products. The more desirable a brand the more likely it was that the user would stick with it or even pay more for it.

The last piece of the jigsaw is the way in which the media channels worked. Within the media department there were buyers, who negotiated for the spaces with the media owners – starting with the rate card and bargaining them down. There were also media planners, who put together media schedules. These used audience statistics to calculate the best mix of advertising exposure to reach the audience most effectively, and to ensure that a significant proportion of the total audience saw the advertising a minimum number of times. The number of media channels where the commission system operated was relatively limited, but allowed advertisers to reach most of the population more cheaply than through any other medium. These channels were newspapers and magazines, outdoor posters, cinema, radio and, the most recent, television. Much of the media planner's time was to calculate the most cost-effective way to spend the media budget, but inevitably questions were asked about the context in which advertising was consumed. Across the Atlantic Marshall McLuhan had recently coined the phrase 'the medium is the message'. The idea that how media was consumed would influence consumers' purchasing and consumption habits.

By April 1968 Stephen King had conceived a plan to create a new department focusing on advertising by bringing together analysts from the marketing department and all the planners from the media department, which was left with buyers only.[39] It is interesting reading Stephen King's papers from this time, how his proposal of creating a planning department was seen as not particularly radical. Those affected by the move expected that they would be doing more of the same. Judie Lannon comments that the move was more popular with the media planners than the members of the marketing department who were being sent into the trenches – the day-to-day development of advertising – and away from longer standing project work. But the move also meant that the newly created planners were put together in a single location in the agency and that each group of planners would have daily responsibility for working on particular accounts, just as the account representatives and creatives did.

The setting up of the account planning function wasn't as inevitable as it looks in retrospect. The two departments from where the new planners came had very different attitudes to the launch. For some of the marketing people it was a demotion but also a move up to the front line of advertising production. Many of them were more confident working in a

---

39 In *Fifty in 40* (previously cited) King recounts having lunch with Stanley Pollitt in January 1968 'to discuss the possibilities. Planning evolved from Stanley's idea of the researcher at the elbow of the account man, assigning a researcher/planner to each account.' So it would seem that, despite the very different contexts of J. Walter Thompson and Pritchard Wood, King and Pollitt were pooling their ideas.

back-room capacity. The new department had access to the client in a way that made some of the account handlers nervous and feel threatened. Those joining from the media department looked forward to that increased exposure with relish, but the media director was seeing his department significantly reduced by the departure of the media planners who henceforth would be building schedules in the planning department.

It was perceived that moving this group towards the advertising would, as Jeremy Elliot put it, 'steal the thunder of the reps' – the account handlers. King's laconic response is 'Reps always feel threatened – it's part of their job description.' The real challenge for account handlers was that the most interesting part of the job had been taken away from them. Management was in favour – the chairman and MD of the agency were from a research background and they understood exactly what King was trying to do. Creatives were positive about it. Getting the planners themselves to work together and settle down was the biggest issue. And King reports the request of one client, 'Stop talking about your internal reorganisation but be sure to bring Ev Jenkins to the next meeting!'[40]

During the summer there were arguments over what to call the new department. A web search for planning will reference financial planning and town planning rather than the marketing variety. The term has different connotations now, but during the 1960s town planning was in the ascendant. Corporate planning and market planning were also in the ascendancy as the 1960s boom went on – consumers and markets grew richer and more acquisitive – so any organised attempt to do business and make money seemed destined for success.

They would have known that the Pritchard Wood experiment had been called 'market planning'. They tried **target planning** and **campaign planning**. Neither felt right. **Brand**

40 Taken from *Fifty in 40.*

planning interestingly seemed too restrictive suggesting that it only related to grocery categories, which shows how narrowly branding thinking was focused at that time. Tony Stead, one of the first group heads in the new department, came up with the term **account planning.**[41] And the name has stuck.

Aside from Stanley Pollitt busy setting up his next planning experiment as Boase Massimi Pollitt opened its doors; it is hard to see how anyone else outside of J. Walter Thompson would have paid much attention to the launch of the account planning department. But Stanley immediately borrowed the term account planning to rebrand his fledgling research department. None of the planners we spoke to remembered much of the transition. Some meetings, some announcements. So a step change rather than a sea change.

41 See John Treasure's paper 'The Origins of Account Planning' in *A Master Class in Brand Planning: The Timeless Works of Stephen King,* Wiley (2007) Tony Stead was a key figure at the launch of account planning at J. Walter Thompson. He came up with the name account planning, he became one of the first three group heads and many years later became the head of department. Tony suffers from dementia so it was not practical to interview him for the book.

The end of the beginning

> *'We just saw it as the obvious way to produce advertising. It was as simple as that. There was no sense that it had to justify its existence. It came out of a clear conviction that we wanted to produce advertising that was effective. We thought the best way to do that was to be very closely in touch with the consumer at every stage of development. And beyond. And it was for the planners to make sure that that happened. All that stuff about being the consumer's voice in the agency I think was very central.'*
>
> Paul Feldwick

So what have we learned? That the planning function wasn't necessarily a sea change but a way of concentrating the thinking about how people consumed advertising, and therefore what role the advertising needed to play. There was not one way of planning – it operated in different ways, and there was no agreement about how planning created the value it did. Significantly, planning wasn't a process. It wasn't a component in a modular sequence for making advertising. In some situations it would thoroughly disrupt the development process and planners needed a measure of protection.

It is also important to recognise that the form planning took was tailored to the situation and strategy of the agency using it. It enabled the agency to continue to do what it did best: whether J. Walter Thompson kept longstanding clients; Pritchard Wood held on to clients by thinking about how advertising affected sales; or BMP won new business by demonstrating that its advertising connected with ordinary people. None of the agencies consciously imitated each other – it was Stephen King's thinking which Stanley Pollitt borrowed, not the way he ran the planning department.

Boase Massimi Pollitt and J. Walter Thompson London were poles apart, the one a start-up and the other the most successful and powerful advertising agency in the UK. They used planning differently because as agencies they had different clients and different goals as businesses. Planning made it possible for each agency to develop advertising which was not remotely generic, but was often recognisably British in the situations depicted and the humour that was so often used. It gave permission for creatives to make more adventurous advertising because it made it easier for clients to buy it. Planning was an essential part in developing, for a while, a British tone of voice. Advertising looked and sounded as if it came from London. It wasn't simply American advertising adapted for the UK market.

Very soon the planning idea was adopted by other agencies, but BMP and J. Walter Thompson's distinctive models were the starting point for most of them. It is also significant that both agencies created *departments* – they weren't using senior consultancy figures to sell advertising work. Planning is a function which requires that someone stays involved in the everyday work the agency does to develop advertising for a particular client. So they recruited bright young people who could stay involved.

So in our next chapter we meet the first generation of planners who were hired by Stanley Pollitt and Stephen King. Whatever the theory, it was these people who made planning work on the ground.

Chapter 3

In which we introduce the cast

The first hires at BMP ('Stanley's Strawberries')

> *'It was so difficult with Stanley to be precise because he kept talking about "things that are around". It was an intuitive understanding rather than an analytical one.'*
>
> Jim Williams

Stanley had come to the conclusion that he needed to train his planners his way from the very start.[42] So he recruited them from university. His first three hires were nicknamed 'Stanley's Strawberries': John, Jane and Jim.[43] The year was 1969, a year after Boase Massimi Pollitt had been founded. These first planning hires were not from the same mould. Their personalities were quite different from one another. John Madell was inclined to be flamboyant, not unlike Peter Jones. Jim Williams was quiet. Jane Newman was intense. Geoff Howard-Spink had joined as an account man when the three were hired. He observes: 'BMP recruited planners that they could train and shape into their way of doing things, because there wasn't a great pool of talent. And they got account handlers like me, who they felt would fit culturally.' He comments that when he

42 *Pollitt on Planning*, previously cited.

43 A quotation from Anne Marie Dyas, a board account director from BMP. In fairness Jane Newman had never heard the nickname.

joined the planners didn't seem that different from researchers who worked in other agencies. 'It was only later that the role of planners developed: taking out animatics and doing focus groups and coming back with, as Peter used to call it, "the voice of a thousand housewives".'

John had studied chemistry at Oxford for four years. He missed the 'milkround' where undergraduates get fixed up with employment, so went to the University Appointments Bureau to see what was still available. He managed an interview at J. Walter Thompson even though they weren't hiring that year. Stephen King interviewed him. He remembers the receptionist with the triple-barrelled name but nothing about what Stephen King said about planning. He also went to an interview at Benton Bowles which he hated. 'I was forced to go into this thing where they get 10 of you to sit around a table and discuss a problem and you think, "What is the strategy here? Should I be quiet or should I try to get my view across?" By contrast BMP was intellectual and friendly. Stanley had some very interesting ideas and then he took me down the pub in Goodge Street and got me drunk and beat me down to £1,250 a year. I was terribly impressed by that. So I took the job and never went to any more interviews with JWT.' What Stanley sold John was the basic principles he had laid down about advertising research from the experiment at Pritchard Wood; his prejudice against day-after recall testing, and how advertising research should be used 'for good and not for evil' by testing advertising qualitatively. And to do this planning needed to be put into the heart of the account team. Planning was so important it couldn't be compromised. This turned out to be a double-edged sword in terms of responsibility. Even junior planners had a lot of power because of what they recommended – based on the groups they had run.

Jane Newman was the next hire. She was finishing a master's degree in marketing at Lancaster University. She speaks about the frustration of going to interviews at advertising agencies and having to camouflage her interest in marketing and her passion for advertising after the first few interviews, when nobody seemed interested in the quality of the advertising in their agencies. Meeting Stanley was a delight because he was so interested in how advertising worked. They talked, among other things, about cognitive dissonance and Stanley's ideas about how advertising worked. There were only two vacancies and Jane assumes the reason why she was hired was because she was a girl and 'they were trying to be ahead of the curve.' There was only budget for two hires and she was hired along with John Madell. The third 'strawberry' had to wait until the Courage pitch was won before there was budget to pay him too. His name was Jim Williams.

Jim had been a doctoral research student in Oxford studying the electric velocity and analysis of thin metal crystals and it wasn't going well. He was having problems with his supervisor, and he was spending too much time in the Oxford Playhouse as an actor. He decided he needed to apply for a job, took an occupational analysis test, and was told he could do just about anything but should focus on the scientific civil service, the military, or the church. Advertising was substituted for the military and he began to apply for jobs in advertising. There were no vacancies but BMP liked him and told him they would hire him when they won more business. Three months later they had enough money and Jim was in. 'They employed me and I was eternally grateful.'

Jane had been told not to accept less than £1,500 as a graduate with a master's degree, 'so I got them their first salary increase from £1,250 to £1,500 a year!'

Jane talks about the daily tutorials which took place over a liquid lunch. 'I think it was very much made up as we went along, but Stanley's notion was that there should be somebody on the team that would stand up for the target audience.'

Jim talks also about dinners with Stanley. 'He was one of my mentors and I spent quite a lot of time with Stanley, when he was looking for someone to have dinner with because he had a meeting early the next morning and was staying in London.' All of them struggle to articulate what exactly Stanley was teaching them, because it was about intuitive understanding, not analytical training. Jim Williams again: 'The only official training I had was a presentation skills workshop where we had to make a presentation to the group about anything we wanted. That was the only training. I was also sent out to do some fieldwork with NOP and I ended up on a real sink estate in Croydon to see what the real world was like.

'Stanley was a wonderful man in himself and he was actually very amusing. He was easy to poke fun at, which was a bit cruel, and I know he didn't particularly like it. One day he was pitching for the anti-smoking campaign. The presentation included some frightfully important person from the Department of Health. Stanley came in late and spent the rest of the meeting addressing his comments to someone else, who turned out to be his secretary.'[44]

Stanley had a clear idea about how he wanted his planners to function. The job of the planner was to bring all that was known about the business together, to ensure that the thinking about advertising was always factually based. Jane gives the example of the New Zealand Wool Board. 'Stanley had all these different clients who were all sheep farmers in New Zealand, plus the creative people and their entire PR team, and he wanted someone in the room who would ground the discussion and

44 There are several mistaken identity stories involving Stanley presenting to someone who turned out to be the technician who was waiting to mend the projector, and mistaking the producer for an obstructive client and taking him to see a finished film to clear supposed objections. Which, unsurprisingly, he didn't have.

provide relevant facts about who they were supposed to be talking to: which was the consumer.'

They spent a lot of time on analysis. Jane lists the sources they were expected to work through; Nielsen sales data and the AGB 'dustbin surveys' – where all the used product packages dropped in a dustbin were listed. 'We used to get the actual printouts and analyse them and that's what I did when I arrived, for about six months. I was working on a competitor to Smash and we were looking to see if they were taking share from Smash. So I just want to explain: it was all the elements that would help you understand the strategy; all the behaviour of the staff, the audience; the attitude at the time; the product itself; the elements that resonated with the target audience.' But analysis went hand in hand with research. 'Before it went to production it was always researched amongst the consumer. It might seem strange for a creative agency but it sat in their back pocket as a kind of insurance policy.'

All of them mention research groups – which they ran incessantly. The numbers ran into thousands for each of them. Jane talks about how Peter Jones, using his experience at Pritchard Wood, constructed the new research process: 'What Peter Jones had done was to take this advertising out to the consumer – so he basically invented focus groups from scratch. He had to call up the women himself and organise somebody's living room. We had to carry those huge reel-to-reel video machines and show it on a television. Through that, he gained incredible insight into that Smash campaign. Basically its benefit was that it was a convenience food – which historically had been tinned peas versus fresh or whatever – so what it did was to emphasise the simplicity and at the same time undermine the natural item, the potato.'

John Madell had an unusual research tool – his Ferrari. 'It was easier because you didn't have to write reports. But it was stressful because you also had a daytime job. You do "qual", you have to get up to Birmingham. Many a time a meeting has dragged on and finishes at five o'clock and I have a group starting at seven in Birmingham. I had a Ferrari so that was quite useful. You could go up the M1 at 140 those days!'

Jim Williams talks about the minimalist style David Cowan used when he ran groups. 'David was unique, he used to come in with his tape recorder, switch it on and then said one phrase "Instant mashed potato" then he would put his hands on his stomach and listen, and people said what they thought was important, and if they mentioned some aspect that hadn't been pursued, David would go back and probe that. When I have seen some American groups, it's like an interrogation. What I learnt from David was that I wasn't interrogating people, I was listening to people, and that gives you a much better idea of what is going on and how that ad is going to work. The interesting thing about that is that other agencies I went to, didn't have the time, or the people, to do that kind of in-depth analysis, so they would to ask simplistic questions which are not necessarily the most important.'

The next morning they would return to the agency to deliver the insights from the previous evening. John Madell: 'The next morning you might be allowed in as late as 10am. You would be driving back with your eyes held open by matchsticks, working out in your mind why it didn't quite get the reaction it should have done. Or otherwise. When you came back in, there would be this pregnant expectation not just with the creative team. In the early days everyone would want to know. I never got leaned on. No, you leaned on yourself to be quite honest. I'd rather kill myself than be shot.'

On one occasion Jim Williams found the creative team hovering about the front door to find out what had happened. 'Because they wanted to know as soon as possible. And I gave the debrief and checked off all the things in the strategy and said they did this very well, but I said I still don't think it's good enough. They said why and I said "because people were bored with it". They didn't respond positively to that so John Webster (the creative director) said "We've got to do it again and I'll do it myself".

The planners got involved in pitches right from the beginning. John Madell talks about his first pitch experience. 'I was there a couple of months before Jane Newman and the first thing I was put on was for a pitch for Baxter's soup. Geoff Howard-Spink was running it and I was doing the planning. And it was an absolute disaster for two reasons. Firstly, the day before the pitch we won the Courage account and Stanley took the entire agency out and we ended up at a restaurant very much the worse for wear. And it was unfortunate because Mr and Mrs Baxter had come down to London the night before and were in the restaurant. You can imagine the creative department, and you can imagine poor Stanley three sheets to the wind, and the creatives saying "How's your Cock-a-Leekie, Mrs Baxter?" So it wasn't an ideal situation. And in the pitch, the only thing I had to do was to turn on the animatic and in those days it was reel-to-reel. There was a lever and – at my bit in the pitch – it went BAM! All the tape went up in smoke. I survived, but we didn't get the account!'

What these snapshots show is how these trainees were thrown into the deep end and were expected to swim. They grew up fast because they had to learn to negotiate the political currents of the agency. What was interesting was how management backed them up.

John Madell, who later founded his own ad agency and then a research agency, says wryly. 'As a relatively junior person I got rid of a client once. I was an account director for a while and Armstrong kept changing their mind every three weeks. They were an appalling client. So I fired them. I came back and Martin Boase backed me up. Absolutely fantastic. If it had been a member of staff in one of my own agencies I would have gone bonkers!'

This way of working shows a level playing field: a meritocracy where all members of the account team have equal power and no one function can shout the others down.

The second wave of planning hires at BMP

> *'BMP was an open environment when a 22-year-old planner can say the emperor has no clothes. That doesn't work in big organisations or in American ones, or a corporate one with a Frank Lowe at the top, or a dominant creative director, but it can do in a strange Paddington democracy.'*
>
> James Best

The work of 'Stanley's Strawberries' – John, Jane and Jim – and the vast numbers of groups they ran, set the tone for how Boase Massimi Pollitt operated. The next pair of hires were Chris Cowpe and Ross Barr. They were set to work for Jane. During this time David Cowan was retrieved from J. Walter Thompson and was set to run the department in this small but growing agency.

Then Paul Feldwick arrived. Paul who, from his subsequent work as one of the early chairs of the Advertising Effectiveness Awards, and his books and papers, is now regarded as one of the very best planners. Ever. But it didn't start that way. He began at BMP as an account supervisor trainee in 1974. Planning wasn't an option partly because he didn't think he would find it interesting, but mainly because planners were supposed to have a maths A-level. 'It was presented as a kind of technical research job and they had a requirement of A-level maths which I didn't have. Well, it tells you something about what was in David Cowan's mind about the sorts of research skills that they thought were needed.' Account handling was not Paul's strong suit and so six months into the job Stanley called him into his office and suggested he might like to try planning. 'So I said fine. I thought I would do it because I wanted to have a job. I clicked with it very much more quickly and in fact I managed to busk the fact that I didn't have A-level maths, because I discovered that when it came down to it I did have a certain sort of brute numeracy which was all that was really needed and that has served me well ever since.'

After six months in the agency he noticed that while planners did do analysis, they did a lot of qualitative research that didn't require numeracy skills. And he is one of the first to claim how much more enjoyable the life of a junior planner is than that of a junior account manager. 'As a junior account man it was very much logistics, even bag carrying, filling in forms in triplicate and getting press ads done and getting moaned at by clients when things were late – none of which suited me particularly well or allowed me to shine. I was quite a callow youth in those days. So I didn't know a great deal about planning but I got the idea that this was closer to the action, but I think I was quite naïve when I got into it. And it was very much a case of Stanley saying "Would you like to try it?"'

Paul's perceptions of what planning was are very much rooted in the way Stanley talked about it. 'It was very much the way we do things here – and there was also a strong sense at BMP that the way we do things here isn't like the way they do things anywhere else. We felt very self-sufficient, very confident in our own path. Planning was a very visible part of the BMP way.'

Jan Zajac started in the planning department at the same time. He had had misgivings about advertising when he graduated because he was into left-wing politics and film-making, so he went first to the research agency NOP, joining their graduate scheme. But he started hunting for jobs again after he had been through it. 'I thought it was going to be a kind of applied sociology business, only to find out it was a glorified number crunching.' He wrote to BMP and made the most of what advertising research experience he had managed to acquire at NOP. 'I didn't know what account planning was at all. I was interviewed by Pete Jones, Jane Newman and David Cowan. In the interview with David Cowan I said I wasn't quite sure what the job is. He was silent for about a minute and then he said planning is to define the role of advertising. And I went away still not knowing.'

Once he joined, Jan Zajac realised he had fallen on his feet. It wasn't so much the job as being 'in the hottest agency in town (apart from CDP). You meet creative people, these funny people get huge salaries, these other people were account men who were handsome and sweet-talking and there are fantastic secretaries everywhere. It's paradise, which is the first impression you get.' He defines his training very simply: learning what makes a good ad and forming an artistic judgement about advertising. 'I hadn't really thought about it before. Very soon I got into knowing what BMP advertising was about and why it was better than anyone else's.'

The second thing to learn about was how to do qualitative research. In this he at least had the advantage of having done depth interviews before at NOP. 'You had to do your own groups and that was the rule. To begin with, you go along with your senior planner and watch them do it, and after that, you go and do your own. Bridget Shirley was kind of teaching and giving you guidance on how to get insight, and I think that was a huge job you learnt at BMP as a planner.'

The following year Leslie Butterfield and James Best were hired in the next cohort of planning trainees. James remembers awkwardly sitting on the sofa next to Leslie in reception on the first day.

Leslie Butterfield came from Lancaster University, the same route by which Jane Newman had come. Like her, he had done a masters in marketing after doing a business degree. And his professor, Mark Thomas, had invited Stanley Pollitt and Jim Williams to come to the university to talk about the Smash case study. 'I remember sitting there being completely riveted by this conversation and this presentation, having not really had a clear idea about what I was going to do next. Mark Thomas put me in touch with Stanley Pollitt. I went there for an interview. The interview consisted of having lunch with Stanley in a restaurant called Canaletto in Maida Vale. He consumed a bottle of red wine over lunch, I consumed a one glass of white wine and at the end of the lunch he offered me a job. The only negotiation that took place was that he said we will pay you £2,500, and I said could you stretch to £2,750 a year, and he said OK then. So I started there in October 1975.'

David Cowan was away from the agency on a period of extended sick leave. Leslie remembers a conversation when David returned to the agency and Leslie began to work for him. 'I talked about the degrees I had done – the first degree and the master's degree and how that had featured consumer research, statistics and stuff like that. And he said, "That is all very well, but we feel that we get a better class of person from Oxford and Cambridge," and I didn't know whether to feel mortified or who knows what, by that particular comment. We actually got on extremely well, but I hadn't had any formal quantitative research training. I learned very fast because, the statistics that I had done before about managing and understanding business data, became as much a necessary part of my job as the qualitative side.'

These trainee planners were expected to develop quickly. Here's Leslie Butterfield talking about an early triumph. 'I was most proud of Tic Tac the cartoon detective because I worked on it very early on. It was such great fun. The client was very small in the UK. They had Tic Tac and Kinder Eggs and they were very adventurous and very imaginative, and sales were kind of going crazy. It was just exciting to be involved. Working with people like John Webster, which was, you know, a privilege and a joy. I didn't know then how big or important he was. Just seeing somebody create something – not from nothing, but just the leap that was involved – you know you could do great groundwork and that created a small mound. He could take that small mound and turn it into something gigantic and pointed and witty. It was a wonderful transformation.'

James Best's interview was rather different. He had studied history at Oxford. He wanted to get into advertising and describes the process as him choosing the agency and them choosing him. 'I sat in the cinema and watched funny clever ads and there had been that life force coming out of the work itself. But it was a tiny agency. No one had heard of Boase Massimi Pollitt. It was a refreshing change from the rest of the agencies who all wrote the same things about themselves.'

After one or two interviews David Cowan told him they wanted him to think about being a planner. 'I thought, do I want to be one of those? Tell me what it is again. Because it was written up but I didn't know what it meant and I also didn't know what an account man was – it was their decision. I thought the place was such fun and would be a lovely place to go so I said all right.' He can't remember anyone explaining what planning was. 'David Cowan just said it was very interesting. John Siddall interviewed me and gave me a maths test. And then Stanley Pollitt interviewed me and he mumbled and dropped ash – I sat there nodding and smiling. Not a word did I understand.'

There was a sharp disagreement. John Siddall, reflecting on this, says, 'The best service I gave BMP was standing out against Stanley Pollitt to hire James Best. James wasn't Stanley's kind of planner. He was Martin's. Stanley's idea was the Jesuit approach to planning. You take an Oxford graduate and you turn him into a clone of John Madell and Jane Newman. Or both. For life. This was the only time in four years I was in a meeting with Stanley Pollitt. We sat down and went through the candidates. Stanley wasn't sure that James was right for the agency because he wasn't in that model. And I thought he was the best person I had ever seen. He was like the "suits" I had seen in J. Walter Thompson but with a brain! It's the honest truth. I remember asking him what his father did. Not a question I normally ask. And he said "He doesn't do anything. He's a gentleman." But he was so sharp. And I felt that BMP should hire the best brains that we could find, whatever discipline they came from.'

It wasn't long after James Best joined that he found himself in the firing line, debriefing John Webster about an ad for Colt 45. 'The animatic had a cowboy with a broken down old mule. It was all a bit slow and boring, and I came back after the groups and said it wasn't going to work and John went bonkers and wrote a house note about this planner who had said this nonsense. Stanley said, "Don't worry, you're a planner. Your word is the one that counts. John will have to do something else." And being John he did it quickly and he did it better, maybe thanks to something I had said. He had to accept my interpretation.' This is a delightful and very specific example of how Stanley would champion the judgement of junior planners against anyone, however powerful in the agency

We can draw several conclusions from these first planners at BMP. The first is the focus on scientific and analytical skills though this was never as pure, or as elitist, as you might imagine from talking to David Cowan. These hires combined analytical thinking with creativity. This wasn't a department of analysts but of graduates who were passionate about advertising – this was one of the reasons they were drawn to work for the agency in the first place. Not all of the hires were from Oxford or Cambridge. Certainly several of the graduates came from there, but the best candidates were not chosen on purely elitist grounds. Their work was dominated by pretesting research but this was not all they did by any means. Their ability to judge advertising was also shaped very consciously as part of their craft. They are very far from being the kind of planners who spend their time 'tweaking ads,' to use the slur famously cast on them by Stephen King. Then there is the level of support they received from management. These planners, even at a junior level, were able to make important judgement calls about whether campaigns went ahead in their existing form. We will look at the role of John Webster a little later as a creative director who was willing to be directed by planners – without whom this system could not have worked.

So we turn now to the fledgling JWT planning department. The first planners in the department. And who Stephen King recruited to grow it.

The first planners at J. Walter Thompson

> *'The rationale was that if you took the media division and the marketing function and put them together under this new thing called "planning" then it would be more cost-efficient for the agency and not only give the agency a competitive edge and produce better strategic planning, but it would save money as well.'*
>
> David Baker

We'll start with those who joined the J. Walter Thompson planning department when it opened at the end of 1968 and those who followed after, recruited to the new function. What characterises our first three is their background as media planners. Not media research analysts as they were at Pritchard Wood, but those responsible for laying down media schedules. There was also another strand of recruit who came from the marketing department.

John Bruce joined J. Walter Thompson's media department three years before to work on Rowntree, a particularly demanding client. He had been recruited from Masius, which was one of the strongest media agencies in London at the time. John hadn't got a place at university and had started in the Masius mailroom and worked his way through media buying into media planning. He was particularly interested in developing computer models to weight media campaigns better. Though he hastens to add that he was responsible for choosing the inputs – he wasn't a programmer himself. This would have been when computers filled entire rooms and were fed with punch cards.

What attracted John to JWT was not its media reputation but being a 'thinking' agency. 'That's what I loved about it and relished from a personal point of view. I had come through Masius where we had started looking at computers in terms of helping us to understand advertising. At JWT I continued thinking *how* does advertising work? Which meant that, when I got into account planning, I was really in my element because we were really talking about how advertising works and how we could use it most efficiently.'

He remembers the memo announcing the new department – he still has it at home. Stephen's pithy summary explained that the new department was going to be the new marketing department for J. Walter Thompson. Its job was to market the advertising which the agency did – surely the earliest and one of the best summaries of account planning. And because he was already working for the then media group head Tony Stead who also moved to planning, John was keen to join the new venture, moving across to be a planner in Tony's group. As far as John was concerned nobody knew where planning was going to go at that time, but it was the way forward. As a media planner he was already contributing to the bottom line when the marketing department was starting to look like an expensive overhead. As he saw it, media was about negotiation with media owners and it was more appropriate that he move into a department which was focused on targeting: 'It was seen very much as applying those skills of targeting – for instance: determining exactly who you were showing your advertising to; who you were hoping it was going to appeal to.' Within a few years he would be writing Bowater Scott's marketing plan as part of the service in the new planning department, because there was no one within Bowater with the skills to do that.

John Bruce describes what it was like working in the fledgling planning department: 'I was dealing a lot more with creative people. The media department had very little to do with the creative department in any agency in those days. We had only just got beyond the point where we had a copy department and an art department – those two had been separate up until beginning of the 1960s. At Masius there was a copy chief and he was in charge of "the writing". He saw more of clients than he had been used to at Masius, but that was partly because Rowntree had dedicated media specialists working for them in York. 'Planning was a centralising force, integrating marketing thinking right across the agency before it got presented to clients.'

There was a lot of research to analyse – mostly quantitative but via Judie Lannon's creative research unit, there were qualitative findings to analyse. But no more work with computers.

John also mentions pitches and the way in which planning made itself essential because of the need to gather data fast and work in isolation from clients and often account management. There was no way of knowing whether one had hardly any, or most of, the available information. 'But you're just trying to pull together whatever you've got and put together a convincing argument that you're going to put at that pitch. And of course that's always exciting fun for young, competitive people.'

David Baker was next. He joined J. Walter Thompson's media unit as a graduate with a pure mathematics degree. He got into advertising largely by accident – if you weren't going to progress as a career mathematician then you need to do something different. 'I looked at something called the *Directory of Opportunities for Graduates* which is a big thick book. At the letter A, I looked at Accountancy and I looked at Actuary and then I looked at Advertising, and it said, 'It doesn't matter what you've done, there might be a place for you in advertising" – and I didn't get to B.' He says he was the first maths graduate the media department had taken on and they were quite surprised he wanted to join. They never tested his arithmetic skills which weren't very good. Like John Bruce,

David concluded that media people were brilliant at negotiating but not so good at manipulating figures and he was expert at it. 'But I soon realised that despite the fact that I could work out the best schedule of, say, newspapers, there was a lady called Nan Duran who would say – I've got a much better one than that because *The Guardian* has given me 50 per cent off. She could do that bit. I couldn't. I decided it would be more attractive for me to go into something that was a little bit more strategic. Hence planning.' Stephen King set up planning not only to improve the quality of campaign planning but also to save money. By moving media planning across with marketing it concentrated the strategic function within the agency where advertising spend would pay for it. The weakness was that media buying was relegated to execution and detached from the planning process.' But it did create a profitable branded consumer focused function.

What glued this disparate group together was Stephen King, 'less by management style and more by intellectual rigour. So he invented the T-Plan, the Planning Cycle, Planning Guide and all of the tools that drove a common way for the agency to communicate and for it to work.'

By the early seventies it was all centred around the Planning Cycle, so you were expected to use intellectual rigour to analyse. Where are we? Why we are there? And within that, there were certain other tools like the T-Plan defining target audiences and the philosophy of response – which was used a lot by Jeremy Bullmore and by Stephen and, at the time, was a big selling point for the agency 'because every other agency would be talking about messages and we would be talking about responses. At the time that thinking was innovative and gave the agency quite a distinctive edge.'

David also mentions Judie Lannon's creative research unit, and how this was used to check the strategy: 'We could take rough advertising and test it with people and get feedback.' But it was about analytical discipline. There was never the creative spark in planning that came out of agencies like BMP and later on at agencies such as BBH. The creative bit was done in terms of setting the brand strategy, working out the role for advertising and briefing people on that role for advertising. The briefing was strategic rather than catalytic so the emphasis was on the brand in total and communication in total rather than giving them a little creative gem that they could then work on.

Doug Richardson also came from the separate media research department. He had been working with Tom Corlett who led econometric modelling – he mentions winning a Thomson Newspapers Gold Medal for a paper they wrote together about the role of media in people's lives. He moved across into planning in 1970 a couple of years after the department started. He remembers asking to join. 'I think the marketing department had a reputation for being the intellectual elite and I suppose these people who were planners thought they were the inheritors of that. How far they actually understood what the job entailed or any of that, I'm not sure.' But his role in planning was very different from that of a media researcher and much more interesting. 'It was about creating advertising as opposed to saying this is where it should be put.'

Doug also mentions the use of the T-Plan. 'It was a valuable tool. I think that what was actually going on, people – and the planners in particular – were beginning to understand the power of brands, taking it upon themselves to become the champion of the brand. Actually this was a new idea and had to be sold.' He even describes planners as the 'thought police' for the agency, since every agency has a founding philosophy. The J. Walter Thompson philosophy began to evolve around brand, and the elements of the brand. 'The T-Plan was a discipline for organising your thinking, but at some point you needed to understand what were the elements of this brand, what was its power, its potential power – that took a while to evolve. So I think there was an awful lot of T-Plan filling in, where people didn't have a bloody clue about what they were doing!'

Doug mentions the famous double act of Stephen King and Jeremy Bullmore, proselytising brands and encouraging marketers to think about the stimulus response model – the process by which advertising might actually influence people. His perception was that Stephen King was functioning as a theorist rather than a head of department. 'Steven was interested in trying to find the big social picture. His "What Is a Brand?" booklet talked about evolution and all that. That was his area of interest. I'm not sure how really comfortable he was with actually kind of being part of a team, to evolve the solution. That sounds critical and I don't mean it to be. But he was brilliant at writing documents, and I don't know if he then thought, my role has ended and I'll hand it over.'

According to Christine Gray – another junior hired into the planning department – Doug Richardson's own contribution was the introduction of qualitative aspects of media. 'He anticipated Marshall McLuhan: "the medium is the message" which doesn't seem to have struck anyone before Doug.' Doug became a group head shortly after he arrived in the department. By 1976 he had taken over day-to-day running of the JWT department from Stephen King, the first head of planning.

Roderick White is somewhat wistful about his time in the marketing department. He originally joined J. Walter Thompson in 1962 with a degree in ancient history and philosophy. When the marketing department closed in 1968 he didn't move into the planning department but into the newly formed marketing consultancy unit. One suspects he would rather have become a planner but wasn't chosen. An alternative reading is that his consultancy skills were substantial enough that J. Walter Thompson could bill his hours out to clients successfully, which was what the remainder of the marketing department had to do. Roderick stayed within the consultancy unit for the next 10 years and then moved across to Lansdowne Marketing, another agency in the J. Walter Thompson group, as planning director so he got to planning eventually.

Roderick describes the planning department as doing the day-to-day thinking compared with the marketing department where they were working on consultancy projects like the creation of the brand Mr Kipling Cakes. And he contrasts the way they used the qualitative research produced by Judy Lannon's unit, with BMP where the planners did the groups themselves. 'Planning remained quite a strategic operation rather than a nuts and bolts execution operation.'

There is a consistent picture emerging here of the importance of analysis, the use of Stephen King's tools, the use of qualitative research carried out by the advertising research unit, and the continual thinking about the role of advertising. What all of these individuals clearly shared though, was analytical prowess: they all had strong numeracy skills. The use of the T-Plan and the Planning Cycle were more than form filling; rather a stimulus to ensure that thinking was deep and shared. There was also a strand of media thinking. Planning had by no means left media behind, but was contributing industry-leading thinking. And there was always Stephen King (and Bullmore) in the background to challenge you if you hadn't thought deeply enough. But although the required skills were similar to those of the BMP planners, the application was quite different: JWT planners' focus was on the longer-term effects of advertising, and less on the creativity of the work. The development or evolution of a brand was, in itself, seen as creative work.

The second wave of planning hires at J. Walter Thompson

> *'The job involved doing three things. There was hanging around the creatives trying to talk them into how you think it looked, what an answer would look like, and what you were trying to achieve. There was the talking with clients and finding out more about what they really thought the issue was, and trying to get that in a way that the reps couldn't as clearly. They had to be polite all the time, whereas I could ask more directly. And lastly there was a bit of time to write short, smart documents really. As a sort of, you know, here's the proof, see how heavy it is? Or light it is? Right!'* Jack Krelle

John Siddall joined in 1970. It was his second shot at advertising – an English graduate he started as an account supervisor trainee at Dorlands and it hadn't gone well. Stephen interviewed him for a junior planning role and John perceived that it would be much more intellectual than what he was doing before, so he took the job. His initial perceptions of the planning department were that it was full of much cleverer people than himself. 'I thought I really shouldn't be here. People like group head Tony Stead – brilliant talker and brilliant mind. There was another man there, Stuart Thomas, who also had a brilliant mind.' John was the youngest in the department when he joined and he was still the youngest when he left three years later so his perception was that the planners were relatively mature. John was in awe of the account supervisors: 'the smoothest people I had ever met. I was ex-grammar school and they wore pinstripe suits and were the 7th Earl of whatever.' He was also in awe of the creative department. He remembers their cleverness but also their accessibility. Creatives would invite you out for a drink in the pub. That never happened anywhere else he worked subsequently.

Lee Godden says she needed persuading that she knew enough to be worth interviewing. But her modesty conceals a shrewd ability to read people and develop brands. She joined in 1971 after working for five years in America and she needed to get a job, having followed a man back from New York: 'He became my husband,' she says. Unpacking what she had been doing all of that time, it turns out that after graduating she worked in the wardrobe department of Sadler's Wells, then moved to an agency called London Press Exchange[45] where she assembled and tested TV commercial ideas in a 24-hour cycle. She was sent to New York to start up the business there and after a couple of years moved to Benton Bowles to head up the 'day-after recall' research unit; from where she started a small consultancy 'which was basically planning by another name, taking raw information and with a lot of work, turning it into knowledge and then trying to make wisdom out of it.' In short, Lee had accrued five years' varied experience starting and running research and planning businesses. After she returned to London, Stephen King called her to ask her to come in for an interview. When he phoned her she mistook him for someone in HR. 'And here he was, this really clever, really nice man and I wanted to work for him because I liked him so much. And then he said, "I have no idea what makes a good planner but it seems to me you might do. Do you want to come and work for me?" I don't know what he saw in me. I couldn't think. I mean I'm certainly not as rigorous and smart as others. I think if I've

45 London Press Exchange was a UK agency which eventually was acquired and renamed by Leo Burnett.

got any skill, I'm quite good at listening to the heartbeat of brands, and I wouldn't have known that at the time because I wouldn't have thought of it that way. I don't know, he probably thought I was jolly and energetic.' Lee recalled some of the more bizarre questions she had been asked when trying to get a job as a graduate trainee at J. Walter Thompson including 'What team games do you enjoy playing and why?' Stephen King promised that if she joined there would be no more impertinent questions about team games. In fact the personnel department would never hold any records on her. 'And they never did, until by the end, I was in charge of HR and they really hadn't got any records about me.'

Peter Dart, from when he was brand manager on Persil, remembers Lee Godden as 'the mother hen.' 'There were quite a lot of little chicks running around.' He talks about the sheer depth of planning expertise: 'The planning team was always consistent – Stephen King, Jeremy Bullmore, you know . . . it was the golden era. The real richness about how brands functioned and worked and behaved. I learnt more as a human being from JWT, you know, in my career than I probably learnt from all those Unilever courses that I went on.'

Of all the former JWT planners interviewed, Lee has been the most instinctive. She prided herself as a person spotter – it was partly down to her that Christine Gray got offered a job in planning. Much later, she moved into the HR department to spot and develop people. A reminder that planning is more than analytical capability, but the ability to read others and to take them with you.

Christine Gray is next. She started work at BMRB whose work was mostly quantitative research, but she worked in a small qualitative research unit running depth interviews, often to do with advertising. She was too junior to meet the planners face-to-face but often spoke to them on the phone. Jean Grundy and Lee Godden recommended her. Stephen King interviewed her. She can't remember anything about what he told her about planning. At the time she was more interested in the possibilities of working in the West End in the world's largest advertising agency. When she arrived she was put in Catherine Butler's group. And as she put it, she was taught to think.

Catherine Butler is mentioned by several of the planners as the most formidable intellect they ever encountered. She was the niece of the politician Rab Butler and is described as a 'bluestocking' – a woman academic. Catherine was one of the first planning group heads. Here is Christine's account:

'She essentially taught me to think. Don't get me wrong, I had been to Oxford and everything. But nobody had taught me to think in a disciplined way in the way that Catherine did. And she made me sit down and write and rewrite. These were the days when you wrote documents rather than produce charts, and she would make me write, and rewrite, and reorder, and categorise in a way I had never been taught to before. It was fantastic. It was a real education.'

Catherine had to be kept away from clients, according to John Siddall, because she could be withering: 'She would always tell them exactly what she thought.' Catherine's other main trait was her spartan taste. 'Her idea of a good lunch was a sandwich at the National Gallery. Which wasn't mine!' says Christine.

Lee Godden describes Catherine as a little bird of a woman. 'She used to bring her lunch in a string bag and hang it out of the window on the stairs and you would not in a million years ever guess that she worked in advertising. Going to talk to her about work was like going to a tutorial and you always thought her eye or her tongue would fall on something you'd forgotten. She was very clever, but very nice. She injected a bit of rigour into things.' Catherine Butler died many years ago. The current Archbishop of Canterbury Justin Welby, a cousin of Catherine's, told us that Rab Butler described himself as the last man in the family with brains. Seemingly, the women in the family had inherited all the intelligence!

Ev Jenkins arrived in 1974, the first planner to be hired from a client background. She had studied at art college in Manchester and as she put it 'blagged her way into a job with Unilever'. The way she describes it, it seems almost as if they realised their mistake and didn't want to admit it, so persisted with her. She says, of the five years she spent at Unilever, a full two years was spent on training courses. She answered an ad in *Campaign* magazine for planners at J. Walter Thompson, and was interviewed first by Doug Richardson (who fell asleep while interviewing her: 'God, was I that boring?') then Stephen King. She thinks what attracted them to her was her Unilever experience. She joined on condition she didn't have to work on Unilever because she was fed up with marketing toothpaste. 'Stephen was brilliant because his brief to me was – "Ev, I have these two clients that are driving me nuts, one is Andrex and one is Oxo. I want you to take them off me, I'll work with you for three months but then I'll measure your success on whether or not they are ringing you direct and leaving me out of the loop." What a great opportunity! So I worked on Oxo and after three months Stephen disappeared because the client was calling me. Then Unilever bought Oxo and they said – in for a penny – so I got Elida Gibbs as it was called then. Then I got Persil. And I was Miss Unilever again.'

Jack Krelle is the first creative who found his way across into the planning department. He had a degree in psychology but got interested in advertising through a tutor, Mary Tuck, who had written the 'Ricicles are twicicles as nicicles' line, and so took the copy test at J. Walter Thompson. He was another whose reasons for going into advertising were being allowed to keep his beard and haircut when other graduates had to shave theirs off. He describes working in the creative department as not drawing on his psychology at all. 'In fact if you mentioned avenue advancement, or social class, or motivations you'd get a look off the others.'

After two years Jeremy Bullmore called him into his office and suggested that he would make a better planner than a creative. Bullmore's argument is an intriguing one. 'We would much prefer it if you were a planner. Because you understand what we are doing, and you could understand for more people and accounts than you can write on.' It was a reverse argument about the planner representing the experience and agenda of the creative department. And if he changed his mind he could always return to his job as a copywriter. He moved across to the planning department to work for Doug Richardson in 1974. In fact the new role suited him. 'It made no difference to the number of lunches or the people I hung out with, or my interests. It did mean that I could do stuff, I could have different sorts of conversation more easily with people and my degree sort of came in handy at that time, because quite a lot of stuff I knew about – and it meant that I could also dress up simple observations if necessary.' What Krelle brings to planning is something different – he loved the T-Plan which some of the others were inclined to dismiss, particularly the part about the sensory map of the brand – which was eventually dropped but which as a creative he felt was the most important part of the advertising brief. 'The sensual is crucial to a great number of things that people do, a great number of their habits and behaviours. Many things that one buys and likes are actually driven by sensual pleasure, you buy a new car because of the experience you get from driving it. You don't drink Guinness for any other reason other than it tastes delicious. And those things: the velvet, the beauty in the eye, the pouring of the pint of Guinness are sensual to start with, and I think that the problem was that everyone was embarrassed by sensuality.'

Terry Prue was the last of the JWT recruits we interviewed.

He had been working for Southern TV as an analyst evaluating how film and TV commercials performed in test markets. He moved to J. Walter Thompson to work in the media department as a researcher and says the reason he moved was because he had hired Phil Gullen who was so clever he thought he ought to do something else. He asked Doug Richardson 'can you tell me what account planners do?' 'And he said, in his normal unhelpful way, "No I can't, they all do different things, but we'll interview you." Christine Gray interviewed me and we just had a general chat, which I seem to remember was mostly about why I liked Paul Simon and liked words in songs and she said "Oh, you're the right type. Come and join us in planning."' Once again an indication that there is no standard type of planner but that through discussion of something entirely unrelated the interviewer could tell if they have the potential for planning.

He worked initially with Christine. The training wasn't formal. 'There were training courses in the sense that there was a philosophy laid down by Stephen King, so that there were times where you were given documents. There was a lot of doing what you did by talking to other people, but there was a core of certain philosophies: like always go back to the Buying Cycle, always go back to people and how they react to the product.'

Terry's description of planning bears out what the others were saying. 'It was very much to try and realise what was happening with our brand and to bring it down to people's needs and understandings. To try and evaluate whether it was successful, and to recognise what you were doing and whether you were getting a return. I think, because in JWT the original idea of planning came from the marketing department, the marketing side was pretty hefty and therefore the mathematical side also.'

There was some qualitative research but very few of the

planners did groups themselves. 'Some planners would do it themselves although they were the minority and it was slightly frowned upon. There was a sense that planners were not impartial and they would buy in qualitative research rather than do it themselves.'

Terry's focus on analysis was so strong his main work was on defining advertising effect. 'It was absolutely luxurious. You had all these resources, none of them were charged to the account in any way and so you were expected to use them. You did have to pay some charges if Judie Lannon did groups, but beyond that, the analysis of TGI, the use of media research was all there. Which is why I think we were very effective in the very early years in winning effectiveness awards – because we actually did it, we had it all there, we could work it out, and there was a sense that econometrics was in its early days and you were actually encouraged to experiment and do it, to try and prove that advertising worked, and try and actually make that breakthrough.'

He had relatively little input to the creative development process. 'Once the planner had worked out the strategy for the advertising, and had written the creative brief, whether it was good creative work was solely the responsibility of the creative department and the management of the creative department; it was said at the time that the only involvement that the planner could have at the time, was to say whether it was on strategy. And I think that many of us felt that it was very often that you got on-strategy but dull work.'

The relationships between the planners and the creatives were not as close from his perspective. 'There was one particular creative team that I got on very well with, and almost as a joke we would leave the building separately and meet at the pub. So the creative guys weren't seen to be hobnobbing with a planner, and actually we would spend whole afternoons together and get involved in writing the early stages of the work. But this was all clandestine.' Which means that the relationship between planning and creative was there, but that it was an informal one and it would seem that the relationships between creative teams and individual planners were quite varied.

So we can see that the planning department broadens out to include a whole range of skills. Almost as if there is a repertoire of planners to be drawn on to work on different advertising accounts. No planner was expected to deploy all of the skills and planners were encouraged to work to their strengths. There is also a sense that the planners worked with other planners – there was a strong collegiate sense.

But we need also to acknowledge a key factor in the success of account planning which was outside of these departments. And that was the role of the creative director as guardian of creative standards and protector of the creative teams.

The godfathers of planning – the influence of John Webster and Jeremy Bullmore

'The other unique thing about BMP in those days was John Webster, who is as much a father of planning as Stanley.' John Madell

'Jeremy Bullmore and Stephen King had worked on the T-Plan. They had invented the Planning Cycle together. The T-Plan had been around before account planning. You wouldn't have said that about John Salmon and David Clifford, for example, or John Webster and Stanley Pollitt, or John Webster and David Cowan. They were not twins the way Jeremy and Stephen were twins.' John Siddall

John Webster and Jeremy Bullmore were leading their creative departments at the time the planning departments were set up. Both were closely connected with the development of planning. It is not surprising that the creative leaderships were directly involved and adapted planning to their ways of working. Planning doesn't exist in a vacuum. If the creative department can't make use of it, its days are numbered.

First John Webster – who has earned a place in the annals of British advertising as one of the best ever creators of television commercials. In a poll run by Channel 4 of the top 100 commercials, John had personally written 11 and another six were written by teams that reported to him. The obvious question to ask is how a creative so gifted could have tolerated the innovation of pretesting groups, where nobodies who had never seen a rough advertising concept in their lives, could destroy days of work in a matter of a few minutes. How could John Webster stand it? Most creatives couldn't.

Peter Jones, who as a junior partner at BMP was the same level of seniority to John Webster, talks about delivering John bad news from pretesting research. 'Even when he became creative director John Webster actually liked finding out what real people thought of his work.' There is a story that when BMP was in its heyday, John became so distrustful of how others at BMP judged his work that he took to coming to the agency at six in the morning so he could run his ideas past the cleaning ladies, because at least they would give him a straight answer. We have already recounted the story of James Best turning down a campaign for Colt 45, which John Webster was not at all happy about. But several of the planners cited Webster's ability to calm down, put the idea away in a drawer for future, and use it later on another account, and in the meantime come up with a brand new idea within the next couple of days. Though our interviewees also note that not all creatives were as sanguine or as capable of bouncing back.

Dave Trott describes Webster's ability to turn research failure into a creative triumph in football terms. 'The BMP managers thought all creatives could work in the same way as John Webster. We couldn't. That's like assuming every football player is going to be a genius on the pitch like Lionel Messi. You could have stuck John in a block of concrete underneath Mount Everest and he would still have won awards. It was phenomenal. He was Lionel Messi and the rest of us had to fit around him.'

John Madell recounted how planners and creatives both played significant roles in the birth of planning. 'John [Webster] was as much the father of planning as Stanley.' Without the resilience of creatives such as John Webster (and Dave Trott), planning couldn't have survived. Most of the rough ads taken out by planners to pretest, failed. Madell's experience in other agencies was that very few creatives could survive that failure rate and think of something better. John Webster had a genuine psychological and mechanical interest in how advertising worked. So much so that the idea at the testing stage was almost incidental. 'When you came back he wanted to know: Did it work? And if so why did it work? And how could it work better? Creative people conventionally see the idea as everything because it's all they've got, whereas John was so prolific that he could bounce back. He could be less committed to the idea – so planning worked extremely well. We took stuff out. If it didn't work he genuinely wanted to know why and that enabled planning to remain as one of the three power points.' Few other agencies had creative departments who could survive the kind of failure rate of two out of three. The strength of this way of working was the speed of turnaround. Because planners did the research they could turn around ideas within 10 days when global agencies like McCanns would take six weeks to do a round of research.

Trott wasn't that resilient: 'I knew the guys in our creative department were really good. If we could do this here, we could go to CDP and bury them where they didn't have planning. It was like running with lead boots. At CDP all they had to do was to write a great ad and then it ran. What we had to do was write a great ad, get out of the trenches, run through the machine guns, try to get to the German lines, and conquer them. Writing a great ad for us was the beginning of the process – for them it was the end of the process. The only thing that kept you there was John – it was like learning from Picasso. I could have had an easier life learning from not such a good painter. Every day I would do an ad and it would get turned down. And John would do one and I would think, Why didn't I get through? But John did it, so I knew it could be done.'

Co-creation, the idea that consumers work in partnership with the agency or marketing team to generate ideas or new product concepts, is a fairly modern view. But one way of casting the BMP model of planning is to see it as essentially a piece of co-creativity between the creative team and real people, mediated by account planners. John would use even the way people commented on the drawings to develop his opinions on how an ad should be filmed. After all he had drawn the key frames with shooting angles himself. So the pretesting wasn't just used as a way to develop the strategy but even the executional elements of the advertising with the creatives taking note of relatively minor comments.

James Best goes further: 'Planning succeeded because of John. You came back from groups having tried out the creatives' ideas. Most creatives would panic and blame the respondents because they didn't have anything else. You killed the baby and they didn't have another baby. John got upset but would listen and had the confidence that he could do another one and he had listen to what you had to say. He was genuinely interested in what ordinary people thought about advertising.'

The other strength that John Webster had in abundance was patience. Just because an idea didn't work in research didn't mean it was finished. It would be filed away to be used for another project and often that is exactly what happened since John would, as a consequence of the research, know what made a particular idea fail or fly.

Jeremy Bullmore was a very different figure from John Webster. He and Stephen King had both been at Harrow, a year apart. They were even at Oxford at the same time. Jeremy Bullmore joined J. Walter Thompson as a graduate. It was Jeremy Bullmore who got Stephen King an interview at J. Walter Thompson in 1957. They became a great double act, Bullmore rivalling Stephen King in wit and intellect. They were described as twins by more than one of those interviewed. And Bullmore is described as much as a planner as a creative. During the 1970s as the duo leading the agency, they worked naturally together to win pitches – deploying over and over advertising that people responded to and which created long-term branding. Jeremy Bullmore's role was critical, just as John Webster's was for the new BMP planning department. J. Walter Thompson's reputation for outstanding service depended no longer on the account representative's charm and persuasion skills, but on a theory about how advertising worked that was endorsed by the creative department at the highest level. We have cited Bullmore's contribution to the T-Plan and the Planning Cycle. When Stephen King made a film based on his booklet *What is a Brand?*, he insisted on Bullmore as co-presenter.

Jeremy Bullmore wasn't the only creative leader in J. Walter Thompson at that time, but he was the one with whom Stephen King is most closely associated. Bullmore rejects the 'twins' label as myth. 'Stephen and I tended to work in parallel and only come together when we had to do something jointly like a joint presentation. It was quite creepy how often we found ourselves asking the same question unprompted. The way the Planning Cycle came together was a perfect example of our collaboration – an accident of simultaneous thought, rather than him and me sitting down and inventing it.' The reason tools like the T-Plan and the Planning Cycle were so valuable was the creatives at J. Walter Thompson didn't see them as an obstruction to be surmounted (as pretesting at BMP appeared. It made it much easier 'to persuade clients quite dramatically that unexpected work was appropriate.' It's a roundabout way of saying it helps to sell adventurous, creative ideas to clients but significantly Bullmore can't bring himself to use the word sell. That's how far his thinking has moved from the persuasion model. And he continues by saying that 'cerebral companies like Unilever knew that behind what we were doing, even if it looked frivolous, there was substantial thought, based on a workable model.' It's better advertising, working better for creatives, and making it easier for clients to accept.

When asked about his role in supporting the development of account planning, Bullmore is a little wistful. He observes that he knew he had a planning brain as well as the ability to write, but he wishes in retrospect he had spent more time writing.

Planning changed the way the agency functioned but these changes were gradual. Bullmore describes it as 'something that became what you did, like breathing. There was no sudden uplift in quality. The evidence of our thinking had a more overt effect on new business. The work before planning hadn't been bad. The big mistake is to assume that no planning was happening before planning. You can look at the introduction of planning as undramatic, as a codification of what we did best anyway, so that more people could do it and do it more often.'

The cast assembled

Before we move onto the specific skills it is worth reviewing the planners we have met so far and to attempt some kind of classification. At least what they brought to the job at the outset. It should be clear that planners have a diverse range of skills and that a simple template is not easy.

Even if you take the Pritchard Wood first experiment as mostly improvised, you had a core of analysts – those who studied it to degree level such as David Cowan and Peter Jones – and Tony Mortemore who got into the department because he was perceived to be grounded in such skills. But that's not all they were good at – they also needed to cultivate *judgement* about what constituted good advertising. It is clear that the way Stanley operated was that he expected there to be continual debate about what made advertising effective, and how you could use research to make it better.

We suspect, through David Cowan's influence, the fledgling BMP got the best graduate trainees it could from Oxford or Cambridge. There was a desire for planners to be an intellectual elite and this is the shortcut for doing that. But this wasn't the only place where they recruited. Lancaster University produced two recruits at postgraduate level – Jane Newman and Leslie Butterfield – who were there for their business skills. They recruited Oxford historians like Chris Cowpe and James Best, so it was more than a stream of science graduates. And even the scientists they did hire were much more than scientists: the 'mercurial' chemist John Madell, as Peter Jones describes him, and Jim Williams for whom drama and Jungian psychology were more compelling than a physics PhD. Paul Feldwick comes in sideways from account management. Jan Zajac came from the research agency NOP.

Moving on to J. Walter Thompson we have the initial three media planners coming into the planning department when it was founded – David Baker, John Bruce and Doug Richardson. Tony Stead would be another. All of whom have good analytical skills but soon show their creative side. Catherine Butler came from the marketing department. The next group of hires: Lee Godden, John Siddall, Christine Gray, Ev Jenkins and Terry Prue come from a variety of places. The head of department is not looking for a particular type of training or set of technical skills. Lee's background running small communications-related businesses; John's and Christine's in research; Ev's in Unilever management training; and Terry's working as an analyst for a media owner. Roderick White trains as an ancient historian and moves into the marketing department. It is very diverse.

CDP poached planners from elsewhere (Tony Mortemore, John Siddall and Jack Krelle) because they didn't train – they hired senior people. They also hired an advertising researcher, David Clifford, to become the first planning head. Cathy Simmonds, like Ev, came from the client-side. John Wood came from a research background.

It is also interesting that no one feels pressured to do or be everything. The range of things they have to do is such that each focuses on what they are good at. The planning function works at the level of the agency providing planners to work on different kinds of business. There is no job description that each and every planner fulfils. Which is why it is all the more remarkable that the planning role is so consistent, given the diversity of planners and the number of different things they do.

We should stress that these individuals are not the only

planners who worked in the agencies at this time; nor are we assuming that they are necessarily the best – however the level of cross-referencing by other planners indicates that all of them played a significant role in the development of account planning in the agencies we are looking at.

Once they were in a role, all of these individuals were trained on the job and mentored as they did it. They were dropped into the deep end. They survived by thinking and consulting with colleagues. Planning was a social not a solitary function.

Now that we have met the entire cast we will let them do the talking – covering a familiar range of topics for account planners. We have opted to do this thematically, not incorporating them within a campaign development process – because these planners were not working on an assembly line as so many planners are in agencies today. The requirement for analysis, the judging of the role of advertising, the way planners worked with clients – all of these things the agencies had in common. It was the style, rather than the objectives, that differed from agency to agency.

Chapter 4

The professionalisation of planning

And now we turn to the planning skills, which as time passed became established but also systematised.

Doing due diligence

> *'It was about upfront analysis of the situation with quantitative research. Which was probably more influential in setting the objectives for the advertising.'*
> David Cowan

> *'It was, stop, think, wait for your brain to catch up with your mouth, don't say anything until you've thought it through, and it was common sense half the time. If you were reasonably numerate you could look at quantitative data and make some broad conclusions, you could read qualitative data, you look at the market stats and then you think, what would I do if I was in Tesco's now? You know, it's not rocket science.'* Ev Jenkins

The first skill has never changed and is essential. It is applying numeracy and analysis to understand how the market works. Whether from J. Walter Thompson or Boase Massimi Pollitt, the planners, like the researchers in the other agencies who didn't have planning departments, were still expected to do the due diligence to make sense of the marketplace. In the 1960s the volume of market data available was considerable.

When Leslie Butterfield found himself working for David Cowan, who had neither recruited nor interviewed him, it's interesting to hear him recount what David started him doing. 'David Cowan was a very powerful and brilliant tutor and one exercise he made me do was to give me the TCA (Television Consumer Audit) – a mound of data. He explained what a gains/loss analysis was, and then he said "Here is the data from the second half of 1974 and here is the data for the second half of 1975. I would like you to work through and come back to me tomorrow and show me how it works: who was new to the brand, who loved the brand, who was new to the market and who left the market." And I did a manual gains/loss analysis of these two periods. I worked deep into the night, doing this by hand. And the purpose wasn't to punish me. The purpose was to say that an understanding of the data is not about reading reports and reading statistics that are nicely prepared for you. It's about really understanding that an individual bought that brand in this period or didn't buy that brand in that period. Why did they stop? Why did more people stop buying the brand than start? He wanted me to really understand the intricacy of the data and the detail and meaning of the data, rather than just reading a report.

'This was classic David Cowan – get deep into the data until you reach the limits of what the data is capable of telling you. It was not the case that quantitative research was in any way second division. It was on a par and it was equal and you were expected to understand and be able to design surveys, understand confidence intervals, understand sampling. Some of that I could draw from my degree, the statistics experience but some of it I learnt along the way.'

John Madell tells a story about a late night at BMP: 'We were pitching for the government energy-saving campaign.

We had all the charts. I added what the average heat loss in a house was and I showed David [Cowan] what I had done. I told him, "Look, it's absolutely rigorous." But then he disappears into his office for four hours. He sits there at 3am. No charts could go to slide until everything was right. And at 3am he came out and apparently I was wrong at the second decimal place. David had to get everything right. The name of his company "Forensics" says it all, doesn't it?'

At J. Walter Thompson, Roderick White spoke about the need for an understanding of numbers too, one of many who emphasised the need for *numeracy* rather than mathematics or statistics. 'I was quite good at maths which helps. But only up to O level. I didn't ever have any formal sort of training, but what I did do was read one or two books on statistics, and I did understand what standard deviation was and things like that. I'm still not any good at manipulating them, but I do actually understand what's going on. And as for reading survey reports and large quantities of numbers, I find that's quite easy actually and it comes naturally.'

Christine talked about the amount of time she spent buying and analysing research. 'It was 75 per cent using and 25 per cent doing – I spent a lot of time designing omnibus surveys. The smaller unsophisticated clients used their agency to do research for them and the planners would get the clients to commission it.'

The planners didn't just do the analysis; they put together the media plans as well. Peter Jones perceived that BMP planners were unique in that they planned the media schedule as well. But JWT planners were also expected to do it too. Here's John Siddall talking about the way media planning was done at J. Walter Thompson: 'So many had come into the department from media planning that the media strategy was the responsibility of the account planner. How money was allocated, was it burst or drip? How many TVRs?[46] That whole media analysis side rested with the planners.' But he comments on how this emasculated the media department at JWT, reduced to negotiating media deals. Lee Godden also mentions having to assemble media schedules on Persil Automatic, to which David Baker, with whom she shared an office, would have to make extensive amends: 'David knew a lot about media so he'd fall about laughing, but he was immensely helpful.'

Of the people we spoke to, Lee was the only one who claimed she was not good at the numbers, but her argument was that the Unilever client had more than enough people who could do that kind of work. 'I stayed on Lever for 25 years and I just suited them. They knew I was lazy, but they had all the marketing skills and the analytical skills, but they believed that I knew what that brand was about. It saved my bacon really.'

Here's David Baker explaining how this analytical skill supplemented the creative department and the account supervisors: 'There was an opportunity to have some clever people there who were not necessarily very good at account handling, and couldn't write ads. Planning was an excuse to have another leg to this stool, of people who are clever, good analytical thinkers, inventive but from a different point of view. Along with them came other clever people like Tom Corlett with his media research unit because that's what it was to begin with. They were clever at analysing numbers and things like that and, because that was quite a different way for an agency to operate, it was very successful.'

Because planners knew how to use data well and how not to be deceived by faulty logic or inaccurate analysis, there was

46 Television Viewer Ratings are the percentage of the total TV audience which is viewing at any given time. They are a unit of measurement but also a currency since the media planner needs to calculate the proportion of the total audience reachable with multiple exposures.

often the naïve expectation that by telling the truth, the planners had done their best. *Realpolitik* is not so simple.

Jane Newman – former senior planner at BMP – years later, having moved to the USA when account planning was unheard of, got a job working as a lowly assistant account executive at DDB Chicago, decided to establish how Miracle Whip advertising was working. She tells of how she quietly analysed the campaign performance figures and discovered that the advertising was having zero effect. 'Miracle Whip Margarine was a classic horrible piece of creative work. It's what they called the "doughnut commercial", so there was a song, two vignettes in the product shot and then a final lifestyle vignette. I analysed all the data available and I proved categorically that when the advertising ran it had no effect on sales.

'I was so naïve – I came from BMP where everything was about getting it right and as effective as possible, so I called a group meeting with the group manager, the account supervisor, the creative team and I presented all this data to them and I said we should explore a different strategy for this. I had all the charts and everything. At the end there was a deathly silence. It was awful and nobody ever mentioned it again.'

Terry Prue tells a similar story from J. Walter Thompson in London. 'My first account as junior planner was Brooke Bond Tea, and I remember that it wasn't seen as being terribly helpful when I came to the conclusion that the improvement in the decisions-to-buy was actually correlated with money-off vouchers in Sainsbury's. I managed to prove that the offer price meant that more buyers came in and more people said they were going to buy in the future. That went down really badly. So as an assistant planner I went to Brooke Bond and said that all this stuff that you are doing is rubbish, it's all being driven by short-term promotions. I virtually got fired off the account. That was my first experience of account planning.

'Luckily the next account I worked on was the TSB Trust business and that was creating a demand curve to show when advertising was appearing, how the demand for their business went up. And that was my first experience of doing that kind of work.'

J. Walter Thompson had Tom Corlett and later Jeremy Elliot, to provide support in econometrics. BMP hired Louise Cook in the mid 1980s. But the impression conveyed through the conversations with these planners is that they were competent enough to do a lot of the analytics themselves, and indeed felt that it was an important element of doing the job fully and properly. And the ethos for these departments was doing it properly. John Bruce comments, 'We were far more interested in finding a good solution than a quick solution. That was Stephen King – not the pragmatism.'

That's the analytical side. Next we move on to the advertising itself and how it was supposed to work.

The role for advertising

'One of the things that Stanley was so much against, was the assumption behind so many of those advertising techniques that they were about recruitment. So many campaigns were all about getting new users and persuasion, whereas the role of advertising was usually about reinforcing and we weren't persuading anybody of anything.'

David Cowan

'The real medium isn't TV or a newspaper – it's 55 million minds.'

Dave Trott

We have already introduced the core idea that drove the invention of account planning – the switch from input to output, and consumer response. Allied to that was the related question: what is the role of advertising? This needed to be agreed before creative ideas were developed, as a standard against which the ideas could be evaluated.

Account planners were dismissive of broadcast-led theories of advertising – that's why they took customer response so seriously. AIDA – Attention, Interest, Desire, Action – was treated contemptuously because it legitimised a process approach to the development of advertising. Where the metrics you used in development and execution told you how much attention you had got (versus competitors), how involved your audience was, whether they liked the product, and whether as a result of the advertising they had done something. Like buy the product. Because the planners were deriving their perceptions of advertising from what customers actually did with it, their views of advertising and how it worked were very different and were often diametrically different to the inherited persuasion model.

They didn't see advertising as very good at customer acquisition – what it did much better was to reinforce the beliefs that customers held. Here's David Cowan talking about how they used quantitative models – for example the one developed by Parfitt and Collins – to forecast what market share a new product would have if it succeeded. 'Within 18 months you had recruited virtually all the buyers. Advertising is about reinforcement. So we talked to heavy-users or light-users but never non-users. If you wanted new customers, advertising was not the best way to acquire them.' Quantitative research was carried out before any advertising was made to calculate the scale of likely demand.

James Best explains that the way John Webster liked to use creative ideas was to create personal connections so that the brand became familiar and loved. 'We were not trying to be challenging. We were good at bringing something no one had heard of, and was struggling up from number four in the market, by making it interesting and lovable and appropriate. And people feeling good about it and feeling *that* is for me. We weren't good at doing the "In your face, let's revolutionise it." The whole development process was about smiles and laughs and people singing along because it seemed to work. Rather than be shocking.' This is a different idea because it suggests that BMP planners thought it *was* possible to acquire new customers by making advertising that they like – so their warmth towards the advertising drives trial and sales.

Leslie Butterfield refers to Alan Hedges' seminal booklet *Testing to Destruction*. 'There was a passage in that book that we thought absolutely captured the model of how advertising actually works. It's about two-thirds of the way through and he talks about a woman becoming aware of a new cleaning product for her kitchen: he talks about the little nudges that occur in that woman's day, or in her life that make her think, "Oh, maybe I should try that?" The thing we always felt was that advertising was something that could always win people over through affection, through charm, through nudging, through cuddling, just giving them a different slant on a subject. It wasn't something that had to be rammed or banged or hammered. So intellectually that meant models like attention and interest, desire and action, and all those kind of stepwise models of how advertising works, didn't really cut the mustard in BMP. We don't believe that's how advertising works; it may be harder to articulate. We think it's probably more to do with that, put your arm around the consumer, entertain them, involve them, engage them, persuade them but do it gently, do it with charm, do it with panache, not a bang over the head.'

At J. Walter Thompson, in Stephen King they had a master theorist in-house. Christine Gray references one Stephen King model – the Buying Cycle. 'There was the kind of contingency theory: the ladder that Stephen developed, which worked at different points for different people, depending on their existing relationship with the brand and on their history of the brand. So you started with selling off-the-page where it was immediate, and then ended with the long-term effects building on brand personality, incrementally building up to the even longer-term brand effect where you never sold anything but everyone admired you enormously!' So people took different things out of the advertising depending on how often they bought the product, and how long they had been using it and watching the advertising. Her concern is that so much effort was placed on the longer-term effects that advertising could get made where there was no demonstrable immediate effect.

David Baker talks about how the focus at J. Walter Thompson on strong strategic thinking made for brand-building but not always creative advertising. 'Advertising would always be in the right direction because of planning. There wouldn't be big mistakes and it had a very powerful effect on the clients and on the brands and overall strategic direction.'

Jim Williams describes the way you identify how advertising works with customers as being more intuitive than anything else, because he had watched so many people processing advertising and listened to them talking about it. It was like a kind of radar reception that picked up on feelings and thoughts that they could barely articulate.

Tony Mortemore takes us through the emphasis on understanding how the advertising worked that was also key at CDP. 'It was about doing the early stages of setting the strategy in a way that made sense: like refreshment, or sustainability, you've got something quite simple. We had a client brief from Johnny Walker and we managed to go through it and articulate exactly what the campaign needed to achieve. The work I felt worth doing was always *before* the advertising.'

It was John Wood of CDP in the early 1960s who articulated the idea of the pre-emptive generic campaign that became such a definitive way for creating advertising at that agency. John Siddall explains: 'John had the idea that if you are first to market you should adopt the pre-emptive position of the generic. You find out what is the key satisfaction in a market and you indelibly link your brand with it. So he would say "What is cigar smoking about?" and he would rely on research as well as his own observation to tell him what it is about. So it is people sitting down, leaning back, with their feet up after the troubles of the day, drinking, relaxing. And then people get full satisfaction and they're happy and that was Hamlet. And that was typical Woody.'

At J. Walter Thompson, Jeremy Bullmore comments, 'We were doing the same. We called them motivators and discriminators. If the brand leader left the motivations territory unoccupied we could go in there and take it over.'

Another famous campaign from the CDP stable was the 'Heineken refreshes the parts that other beers cannot reach' campaign. 'That was a typical Woody strategy,' says John Siddall. Start with what lager drinking is about. Who is saying that? And if that was already being covered then the job of the planner was to find something else. And to make that central. The point of the refreshment idea is that it didn't belong to beer at all. It belonged to gin and tonic. So it was imported from another drinks category and applied to lager which, as a relatively recent market entrant, was perceived to be not a proper beer. This is a brand strategy rather than how advertising works per se. But the CDP position was that if the creatives worked with the goal of creating a simple association – the more impactful the creative treatment – the more effective the work. Note that messaging came secondary to creating a brand impression and an emotional response.

CDP's famous opposition to researching advertising ideas (which is starkly different from Boase Massimi Pollitt or J. Walter Thompson) was because they believed the work would be so different from the rest of the category that drinkers shown the work wouldn't know what to make of it, and would distrust it because it looked unlike any other advertising in the category. CDP would argue that such advertising was untestable. Research was still essential in the CDP model mainly in order to find out what benefit needed to be owned by the client brand. Once they had chosen that connection, the advertising which created it was free to be category-busting.

If the experience of using the product was negative then there were strict limitations to what advertising could achieve. And the role of advertising had to shift.

Here's Ev Jenkins talking about bank advertising after the crash: 'You can't get money out of your bank and you haven't been able to pay your rent, there's no amount of advertising that's going to change someone's attitude to a bank. Don't do product advertising. Just get people into the banks somehow.'

We turn now to choosing the best creative ideas. How did planners help to do that?

Choosing creative ideas

> *'Working at JWT challenged my earlier view from BMP that you have to get a good advertising idea and the brand goes with it. Jeremy, the creative director, said – you can't sell a sizzle without a steak. BMP thought it was all about the sizzle, it doesn't matter about the steak.'*
> Jan Zajac

The first point to make is that it was never down to the planners alone to select the appropriate creative idea. It was a collective decision. However brilliant or forceful the creative director, the decision to present an advertising concept to the client was never theirs alone. Account supervisors played a significant role as well.

Agencies also take a range of approaches to how many ideas were developed at all. CDP presented one idea only. BMP might have tested some variants but used the research process to fine-tune one creative idea at a time. J. Walter Thompson presented several variants which were developments of the current brand campaign.[47] The judgement call was not left to the planner, nor was the planner allowed to delegate the decision-making to respondent opinion, though this is a widely held external view about how BMP operated. It's interesting that Jim Williams could come back and tell the creatives that

47 Note that none of them put a scattering of ideas in front of the client hoping she would buy one of them. Adam Lury offers an alternative which is showing the early ideas to the client and then refining them down to a single route.

the positive response wasn't nearly positive enough. The body language of the research respondents suggested boredom: actual or imminent.

The watchwords at BMP were *relevant* and *distinctive*. That was the criteria by which they judged work. Relevant was determined by the pretesting research. There had to be a connection with real customers. But unless the work was distinctive it wouldn't get noticed. No ordinary person would care about it. Jane Newman: 'Relevant and distinctive equals more effective was BMP's mantra.' At that time most other advertising agencies would be using quantitative research to develop the message, the creative ideas and the aftermath, so had limited feedback on what people thought of the advertising – the relevance factor.

Leslie Butterfield talks about the judgement calls required in order to interpret research results 'Creative development was the scariest bit for a planner. You had to develop a holding story, as you were thinking about the debrief. The other thing you learned was how do to deal with creative people, manage expectations, translate what people have told me – not just into reportage – but into interpretation and helpful commentary that will move the thinking forward – rather than just saying that didn't work, or that colour is better than this colour. It had to be interpretative and constructive and helpful.'

Peter Jones uses a rugby analogy of the team game where the team fail to score, rather than any individual or specifically the creative team dropping the ball. 'It was part of the BMP ethos that only one idea was ever put to the client at a time. But if that bit the dust for any reason it might be because it wasn't right and needed tinkering with. More often than that, it was substantially wrong because the intuitive leap made by the creative didn't actually play through to consumers. And then that would add to the learning bank of knowledge. So the creatives would feel that it wasn't their fault that it hadn't worked. It was a collective failure of brief and proposed execution and that helped build the sense of trust. It's a team game and it's essential that you all agree the stages in the process as you went through.

'I used to say I spoke with the voice of a thousand housewives so it was they who didn't quite understand what you really clever creative boys were trying to do. So we needed to approach it from a different angle. It was very much a matter of personal relationships.'

We have already referenced the Sugar Puffs Honey Monster as a successful character which didn't work in research till a single element – his height – was changed. Similarly the first incarnation of the character from John Smith's beer started as a variant of the newspaper cartoon character, Andy Capp. This reinforced all the worst stereotypes of beer drinkers as slobs who never got off the couch. But as soon as the character became a trickster who took his dog out for a walk and made a detour to the pub – a character who represented the worst of all beer drinkers transmogrified into the best of all beer drinkers – somebody you wanted to emulate.

Dave Trott talks about the basic error so often made in advertising, of imagining that people find advertising interesting. 'It isn't until we realise how trivial advertising is to them that we can start doing it well. Advertising is less interesting to people than washing your milk bottles and putting them out on the doorstep. When you start realising it's nothing you can make it big.'

The agonising calculations planners have to make, is whether the creatives have it in them to fix the problem or come up with a new creative idea. After Jim Williams moved on from BMP, he talks about how much more difficult it was to work with creatives to get them to come up with new ideas. 'They had given it their best shot, so beating them up and saying this isn't good enough didn't help. They would say: that's all there is, and you would mainly tinker with it. I felt brutal. It was about understanding the nature of the creative folk. It wasn't just about producing a strategy then the ad follows automatically. It doesn't.'

John Bruce talks about how research was used as a supporting opinion to help the client to make a decision, particularly when being presented with several creative ideas. 'It wasn't a difficult sell. It's a lot easier when you've got two or three ideas that you're pitching to the client and you say "I'm not really sure which is the best of these". But if you've only got one idea it was still pitched very much on the basis of "Let's check it out, let's find out if it's doing what we say it's doing". We had a lot of experience and we had the contacts with the researchers. Some of that research was done internally through Judie's lot – because Judie Lannon had two or three researchers and they would be doing routine discussions on a regular basis.'

Tony Simmonds Gooding, CDP's Heineken client, used to say 'great advertising needs brave clients'. Cathy Simmonds: 'It did, it needed brave clients because we didn't pretest. What you were showing them was very basic drawings. The visual expression we showed people were extraordinarily limited. They had to use their imaginations. There hadn't been much of this kind of advertising around. They had to do quite a lot of work themselves.' A reminder that approval of creative ideas is collective. The process model of developing communications actually inhibits creativity, because all along the conveyor belt individuals are given the right of veto. What all three agencies show is that planning enabled decision-making to be informed and more collective.

Demonstrating effectiveness

'Effectiveness mustn't be confused with accountability. Accountability interferes with effectiveness. The need for accountability is nothing to do with rationality or effectiveness or results. It is probably from a psychodynamic point of view a defence against anxiety, because it creates the illusion that you are in control of things. When the reality is that you're not in control of anything. It doesn't mean you can't make a sensible decision. It is not a science. It is not a simple cause and effect. A lot of those basic assumptions are in the service of something completely different.' Paul Feldwick

One of the planner's responsibilities after the advertising campaign has run, is to show how it has performed. This is different to the analysis, now common in many media companies, demonstrating how effectively the advertising has been in reaching a mass audience a given number of times. Stephen King explains the task of evaluation in the following elegant way: 'If you run an advertising campaign you expect people to notice it – that's not evaluation. What you want to know is whether it performed better than other campaigns with a similar weight of spend.' The agencies where account planning began, took the evaluation of advertising seriously because it helped them to learn about how the advertising worked. Did it fulfil the role that was expected of it? This was more than simple accountability. Or ROI for that matter.

Jim Williams, who went on to set up the Brand Asset

Valuator system for Y&R Worldwide, talks about how he used to do a qualitative assessment of the impact of advertising. 'You're looking for signs of interaction between the ad and the consumer. It's not just brand tracking, no. Brand tracking I thought was an enormous waste of money most of the time, because you don't ask the right questions. When you do qualitative research you can see what works and what doesn't, but with a brand tracker you just have a line that goes across the paper and it isn't at all clear what it means.'

One of the triumphs of account planning has been the setting up of the IPA Effectiveness Awards – a biennial scheme that will only award campaigns where the effect of the advertising has been isolated, so that the attribution cannot be made to any other aspect of the marketing mix. In recent years the IPA Effectiveness scheme has come to resemble a contest not unlike Formula 1 motor racing, where only the richest teams can compete. You need extensive resources and deep pockets to afford the services of an econometrician to isolate the advertising effect.

The IPA Effectiveness Awards were set up in 1980. The chairman of the working party was Simon Broadbent of Leo Burnett who very nearly might have employed Tony Mortemore. Broadbent and Stephen King represented the agencies among the judging panel. And Stephen King's definitions of the criteria for advertising effectiveness are extensively quoted in the 1980 book of published papers[48]. There were five categories: new products from consumer goods and services; established products from consumer goods and services; direct response, consumer goods and services; industrial; and financial and other non-consumer goods and services. The first Grand Prix winner was Davidson Pearce for the launch campaign for Krona margarine. From the other categories two more first prizes

48 *Advertising Works 1981 IPA Effectiveness Awards*, Ed. Simon Broadbent, IPA (1980).

were handed out – one to Masius for Dettol and one to Damian O'Malley of BMP for Tjaereborg. Leslie Butterfield talked wryly about not taking the new awards seriously and allowing Damian to submit the case and claim the glory. 'It was his idea. I said to him, you go ahead, I'm not sure I've got time for that right now. He wrote it up and it won, won a prize. And I thought, bugger, I should have done that. So his name is in the book: Damian O'Malley, Tjaereborg case study. And good luck to him as he wanted to do it. Maybe that was the kind of thing that started to change people's attitude. A new breed of people were coming along saying actually this is quite important, it sort of goes back to what I was saying about David Cowan and the Account Planning Group (APG). There was a quite isolationist, sort of insular culture at BMP, which was, we know, something special. We work in a special way and we don't need to broadcast this to the world, it's working for us, let's just keep doing it. So don't get involved with the Account Planning Group and maybe a little less interest in the IPA Awards when they were first announced. BMP were fantastic after that. It brought in the whole econometrics system. BMP's track record is probably still as yet unbeaten in that area.' This win helped to get BMP to take a greater interest in sharing its successes with the rest of the industry. But David Cowan commented that there was a measure of irritation at the time with how other agencies started to introduce their own planning departments. 'Looking back we were very precious and stand-offish, we thought we had a USP and didn't want to talk to our competitors. Stanley was very against the Account Planning Group for that reason. We were very miffed that agencies that hadn't made the structural and organisational changes that we thought necessary to move from the old research department model, just started saying that they had planning too.'[49]

49 Email correspondence with David Cowan, Nov 2014.

JWT were runners-up in every single award winning category. In 1982 John Smiths took the Grand Prix for BMP. It wasn't until 1986 in the fourth round of awards that JWT captured the Grand Prix.

We mention this because it should be evident by now that BMP was every bit as rigorous as J. Walter Thompson in determining the role of advertising and its effectiveness in the marketplace. And David Clifford was quick to say that CDP also submitted and won Effectiveness Awards.

What rankles the BMP planners even now, was a paper given by Stephen King in 1989 at the tenth anniversary of the founding of the Account Planning Group, the trade body for account planners, where he offers a typology of account planning as a scale running from 'Grand Strategists' at one end to 'Ad Tweakers' at the other. And he criticises those ad agencies who have imitated BMP's style of planning and converted qualitative researchers overnight into account planners. There is too much ad tweaking, he sniffed. Even though Paul Feldwick, who if you recall had scraped into BMP's planning department without maths A level, was by this time the convenor of judges for IPA Effectiveness, having followed Simon Broadbent and Charles Channon into this heavyweight and high-profile role. Stephen King may have been feeling defensive. Terry Prue reports that at an awayday of JWT planners, BMP was the department's first choice in where they would like to work if they weren't working at J. Walter Thompson. And the reason given was the status they enjoyed with the creative department. BMP planners had power rather than influence and they were protected.

Leslie Butterfield, stung by a reference to JWT 'grand strategy' marketing, retorts, 'Did I consider us to be ad tweakers rather than grand strategists? Well, no, I didn't think we were that. Ever.'

But BMP planners have had to endure the tag of being ad

tweakers ever since – glorified qualitative researchers who scurry back and forth from research groups relaying whatever respondents told them about the advertising concepts. It wasn't like that at all. James Best claims that BMP didn't need to assemble IPA Effectiveness case studies – they already had these because they had presented them to clients following the campaign. Evaluation was a normal part of the job. 'It was never just about writing the brief and doing the creative development but measuring and monitoring the results. The planner had to stick in there and to carry the can. So one of the reasons to get the ad right was because it was your job to understand it. If it wasn't working, it wasn't the creatives' or the account handlers' fault. A failure would impact the whole agency. Then the finger would point back to the planner. Evaluation and measurement was part of the brief.'

David Baker talks about how seriously J. Walter Thompson took evaluation – seriously enough to set up a separate unit to make sure that it happened. 'J. Walter Thompson was stricter than most other agencies on evaluating the effects of advertising. So there was a complete unit that was set up. We would call them in – Tom Corlett, and John Davis who was very good as well. So that function grew and became merged with a unit from Henley as well, so we had a whole market modelling unit.'

Terry Prue talks about how evaluation was so basic to his work that it was only latterly that he got involved in creative briefing. His skill set pushed him towards evaluation. 'I was always fairly self-sufficient because that was the side I'd come from. I used Tom, but as an adviser. I think I was involved in possibly the second or third IPA Effectiveness Awards because I certainly had been involved in four winning papers, and I've judged four times since then. The spirit of the Effectiveness Awards was very close to the spirit of JWT and what it was doing – and JWT felt, as BMP did, it was very important to win them.'

Ev Jenkins is more sceptical about evaluation. 'A lot of clients think that you can absolutely prove and you can isolate the contribution of advertising – which I don't think is always true. In fact, rarely true, unless you are pushing for direct response "Great, I'll buy that one now." So you end up spending a fortune with somebody who talks in a language I do not understand, and can prove that he can isolate the effect of advertising and I'm sitting there thinking – I believe all those numbers but I don't believe you . . .' Often clients were more interested in having an advertising property like the Andrex Puppy or the Oxo Family, than setting clear communication goals. 'Everything works. if you had a £17 million budget in those days, it was going to work!'

Christine comments: 'It was a terrible shock to JWT in the first IPA awards that BMP did extremely well and we realised they could do numbers as well as qualitative; they had this dual capacity. They had econometric modellers, as we did with Tom, but somehow they had been pushed away and planning in those places was about consumer behaviour. BMP had somehow cottoned on the thought that it was about selling things. In some ways the concept of the brand and the brand personality did a great disservice to manufacturers, some of whom went under because we were so busy selling them the long-term effects of advertising that they didn't have any short-term effects.'

Jeremy Bullmore presses home the attack on ROI. 'The characteristic of the great work, which I don't think anybody ever really talks about, is that every pound you spend behind it, works much harder than a pound against ordinary work. So the big thing is this concept that people have forgotten all about, called "value for money". With great work, you get better value for your money.'

We leave the last word here to Paul Feldwick – arguably the most distinguished of the planners interviewed when it comes to proving effectiveness of advertising. He talks about the limitations of effectiveness

'Trying to take an ad campaign apart and say it's 30 per cent to do with this and 20 per cent to do with that is like taking a cake apart and saying it's 10 per cent to do with the eggs, 5 per cent to do with the butter, and 60 per cent to do with the sugar. And the bit on the top didn't have to be there at all. It's kind of a nonsense. When it works, it all works together.'

Brand effects

> *'I conceived it was about building brands. Putting numbers on brands is notoriously difficult and I always preferred to do it qualitatively. And qualitatively doesn't necessarily mean qualitative research, it's seeing how various measures go up and down. And we were looking for correlations with market effectiveness. And share movements.'*
>
> Jim Williams

Brand building is one of the great triumphs of account planning. The idea that the intangible value of the company, over and above the actual assets, represented the ultimate wealth of the company, was not thought up in an advertising agency. That was suggested by Lord Leverhulme at the start of the twentieth century. Leo Burnett also focused on the way advertising could establish brand properties and keep on working with campaigns such as those featuring the Marlboro Man.

But following Andrew Ehrenberg and Stephen King's work, agencies were keen to claim that advertising did more than generate sales. It built up these intangible values to such a level, that the brand would continue to influence purchase long after the advertising had stopped running and the memory of the advertising had faded. Many parts of the marketing mix contribute towards brand building, not least purchasing and using the brand. Being in places where the brand identity is prominently displayed is another. However, advertising is one of the quickest and cheapest ways to build this intangible value with a mass audience – and advertising agencies took full advantage. We can see that Boase Massimi Pollitt and CDP went about this differently from J. Walter Thompson. But all of them pushed the emphasis away from the physical exposure of advertising to what people did with it. Or as Rod Meadows of Benton & Bowles put it: 'How people consume advertising'. And what was left, which was much more than recall but conversation, emotion, belief in the superior efficacy of the product, or that it justified a premium price. CDP's pre-emptive generic idea enabled brands which were being comprehensively outspent lying in third or fourth place in the market to become market leaders – because the advertising made them look and behave like category leaders. Clients without the resources to spend their way into market leadership used radical advertising to leapfrog their way into dominance.

Stephen King developed the idea of the emotional proposition, where the purchaser's attachment to the product was such that if it was out of stock, they would go to another supermarket to purchase rather than buy a substitute. These effects were measured quantitatively and the cost of creating these effects was also measured. Andrex and Mr Kipling being the great case studies that vindicated the concept of premium pricing for products that would otherwise have been a commodity. This isn't startling to us now because in large part Stephen King's ideas won. They became normal.

Even with Stephen King in the building, the sharing of these radical ideas was problematic. What exactly was a brand? Christine Gray talks about how she struggled as a junior planner when she started at J. Walter Thompson with this brand patois being referenced day in day out. 'You're talking to someone who didn't know what she was doing to such a degree that I remember howling my eyes out in the loo because I didn't understand what a brand was and everyone else did. Because people kept on talking about brands and I didn't know what brands were.'

Geoff Howard-Spink, one of the first account handlers hired at BMP before he moved on to CDP and ultimately to start his own agency with Frank Lowe, talks about how Stanley Pollitt used to reference the campaign that CDP ran for Harveys Bristol Cream as an example of how an agency could perfectly understand and articulate a brand. 'He felt it captured the values of the brand in a way that was just completely correct and wholly admirable. And he wanted to know, or struggled with the idea, that "how did they do that, why can't we do that?"'

The planners we interviewed played back a view of the world where brands were not central and clients didn't expect advertising to have long-term effects. Some felt that brand building would backfire as an idea. Like marketing, this was something that clients themselves would take responsibility for. At BMP branding talk wasn't separate from advertising. David Cowan warned that if the two were separated that marketing would take brands from agencies and nothing would be left for the agencies to do except execute. The other challengers here were management consultancies.

Here's Jan Zajac: 'At Added Value my boss's view was that we were there to take business away from advertising, not creative work but all the thinking. My colleagues there were all Unilever marketing people, not planners. The thing about the brand personality. All of that thinking, branding, naming and so on, originally came out of Unilever thinking. That's what drove Added Value and it's not just about advertising, it's the role of marketing, too.'

His then boss at Added Value, Peter Dart backs him up: 'At the heart of what we sold clients was that we had invented a formula – several points that all, kind of, come together. When you're running a consultancy the first thing you realise by the time you've employed about five or six people, is that you've got to have a system – because if what happens is everybody comes with their own mini-view of what a brand is, and what makes a brand tick and everything else – you're going to get chaos very quickly.' He explained how they invented the 'brand bullseye', a process to supplant the expertise embodied in the advertising agency team. After developing dozens of them for his former employer Unilever, the client brand team decided that this way of working should be proprietary to Unilever. 'Eventually Unilever said, "We've worked out we've bought 56 of these brand bullseyes over the last four of five years, we'd like our own proprietary thing," and it went on to be – so we added a bit down the bottom and called it the Brand Key.'

Likewise Leslie Butterfield, who was global Chief Strategy Officer of Interbrand, makes a distinction between advertising and brand building. 'Probably because at Interbrand it suited us to do so, but obviously back then it felt like the two were merged, you know brand and advertising did kind of become the same thing: love my advertising, love my brand. You know even the language I just used about it, implies that the brand, the way the brand communicates, is the brand. It's how I feel. The brand was almost seen as a function of how it communicated. So I think there was much less distinction then between brand and advertising and brand communication, than there is today.'

David Baker is still holding a candle for brands being dependent on an idea – usually expressed through advertising. 'I still believe fundamentally that brands actually have to have meaning, they have to have fame. There's got to be an idea at the heart of it. I believed that the idea had to be more tangible than just a philosophy, it actually had to have some sort of communications that it was famous for, that wasn't transient as well. I still believe that, even though you use all these different forms of digital and I still think that something has got to be there that is the magnet that everything else is attracted to from a communications point of view.'

Doug Richardson is a pioneer who applied brand thinking to corporate communications when, years later, he joined Tim Bell in his PR consultancy Bell Pottinger. 'It seemed to me that, all this insight and knowledge about the consumer brands could be applied to corporate brands, and institutions, charities and all that kind of stuff. So Tim created a consultancy, to advise people on big strategy. I could play a part in that by introducing what was, in that world, completely new thinking: to persuade the PR people that you should apply the same rules of advertising – to think about what your core message is. And to use communications across a broad range of activities including advertising to persuade, not just simply inform.'

He gives the example of rebranding the BBC. 'The BBC was seriously under threat of losing its monopoly of public service broadcasting, and we advised them on how to get the charter renewed on their own terms. A key part of that was that they had absolutely screwed up their branding, and they had allowed their organisation to determine what the brand was. You had this situation that only one of the outlets was actually using the BBC brand when BBC2 was just called 'two' and you had Radios 1, 2, 3, 4, and 5 – none of which mentioned the BBC and with them wanting to break that down even more. So not surprisingly the BBC wasn't getting credit for what it actually did. We built the strategy around becoming one BBC – recognising the future value of the BBC and what it brought and why everybody had to be in it, and why they needed to start building awareness of their value and use their own airwaves to have commercials – so we did that.'

Jim Williams was architect of the Brand Asset Valuator, a global research tool he build with a budget of $2 million when he moved to Young & Rubicam and needed something to enable the agency network to stand out. The ingenious idea behind the Brand Asset Valuator was a common way to understand brands that made it possible to compare brands from very different markets and categories. There are now several similar analytical tools available to measure brand power, but the Brand Asset Valuator was one of the very first. Listening to Jim Williams talking about it, we got the sense that his original vision was for so much more than a scale and a common currency for evaluating brands. He did a lot of work with Margaret Mark, who has since written *The Hero and the Outlaw: Building Extraordinary Brands Through the Power of Archetypes*. What Jim was looking to do was to build not so much a valuation system based on share price, but one founded on Jungian archetypes. As his wife explained, 'Jim would come and look in the kitchen cupboard and from the brands he found there he would tell me which archetypes were most influential on the things I bought. Archetypes which were in me.'

This is perhaps the most radical of the brand ideas and one which is in danger of getting lost as brand thinking separates itself from advertising and attaches itself to share price and the management of assets which are all under the marketer's control. That brands, in the final analysis, belong to customers and are an expression of their values more than those of the brand owner.

Lee Godden, the intuitive who guided the Persil brand for nearly 20 years, puts it like this: 'It was absolutely true that Persil mums got a whiter wash, it was nothing to do with the washing powder, it was entirely to do with that they were Persil mums, they were more careful, they sorted their washing better, they never washed colours with whites, they were better washers. It's a fact! The most we can say is that we probably reinforced their behaviour.'

'The brand is the consumer and the consumer is the brand,' Jane Newman says. So categorically that we asked her to explain what she meant. 'The aspects of the product which you decide to brand are aspects which appeal to the target audience, so you can't have a brand without a target audience. It's the desires and aspirations of customers wrapped around the product.' So in this way of looking at brands there is nothing that belongs to the marketer at all. It's a way of articulating and orchestrating customer perceptions.

Judie Lannon warns, 'With the amount of different communication vehicles the whole brand story that advertising is so good at, has been lost. In the digital world the whole brand idea is in real danger of getting lost.'

Peter Dart again: 'Brands exists to make life simple, and how many times have brands made your life more complicated? You go in, again, you see the shelves on washing – with liquids, powders and the concentrates – and we've forgotten the brands are there to become a relationship, something you trust, something that simplifies your life, not complicates it.'

The reason that planners talked about brands was to get the attention of the marketing people even if eventually the responsibility of brand building moved towards clients. So we turn now to see how else planners worked with client marketers and the value that they brought.

Working with clients

> *'It was a totally collaborative team effort, so you would have the planners, the creatives . . . the account director would run the meeting, you as the brand manager would have your junior brand manager, the junior would have an assistant. For some huge big meeting you would have the marketing manager in the room too.'*
>
> Peter Dart

The account planning idea was consumer-led not client-led. Stanley Pollitt's Pritchard Wood experiment, taken over to Boase Massimi Pollitt, was carried out in the interests of the agency to ensure that the agency's work was not hostage to research techniques he didn't believe in. And after the failed Smash commercial, qualitative pretesting became a hallmark of the BMP style of planning. It came about to prevent clients losing confidence in the agency and the power of its work. Stephen King founded the J. Walter Thompson planning department in part as a preventative exercise, as he saw budgets and power leaking away from the agency's marketing department. The planning department embedded marketing thinking inside the account team to make it possible to sell advertising campaigns to the marketers that would build their brands.

So it is interesting to hear how much contact the first planners had with clients. There is some overhang from the marketing department days. Planners carried out marketing activities for free that the client company was unable to do themselves or lacked confidence in. John Bruce, in his early twenties, even wrote the Bowater Scott marketing plan (including Andrex toilet paper). Planners routinely conducted product research and either worked in parallel with the client research department or performed the research buying function for their clients. They also worked in new product development, whether conducting desk research to find gaps in the market for entirely new products or line extensions, or getting involved in brainstorming new products. This has been part of the service from the beginning. And BMP, J. Walter Thompson and CDP all did this kind of work. The actual research might be conducted by third-party research companies so the planners acted as research buyers, but all of the agencies had researchers who could carry out fieldwork themselves.[50] Each of the agencies was simultaneously a research agency and a buyer of research from third parties on behalf of the client. This would give the agency more contact points with the client and kept them close to market intelligence, strengthening their position when it came to the development of advertising.

The planners from J. Walter Thompson don't give specific examples of persuading clients, because their work with marketers was much more like being a permanently connected brand consultancy. Peter Dart, as a Unilever brand manager working with JWT in the 1970s, talks about the strategic leadership the agency took: 'You spent Thursday in J. Walter Thompson – one day a week was the agency day. And you'd arrive at nine o'clock every Thursday and you would go through a sequence. In those days of course we had good market research of our own. I was up to Port Sunlight every week working on brand development, innovation, looking at

50 Boase Massimi Pollitt employed three qualitative researchers at one stage. This was confirmed by Roddy Glen who was recruited to BMP to improve the quality of the research being carried out.

the future, what do consumers want, what's round the corner and so on. It was a time of change. But in terms of the deep understanding of how brands functioned I would say that, at that time, JWT were teaching brand managers.'

Likewise John Bartle, then the research manager at Bournville, recalls Thursdays when the confectionery and foods marketing department of Cadbury closed for the day, made the weekly train journey down from Birmingham and then from Euston, and fanned out in different directions to the ad agencies for the day. He would go to BMP. 'You never had a small meeting. So those were days where the big agencies had loads of people. And they used to match person for person, but then there were always more agency people. You'd have people in meetings that you wouldn't see from one year to the other. This is a packaging expert, this is a consumer panel expert, this is our research advertising staff . . . And then you might have a drink before lunch, depending on which agency. Then we'd get back to Euston at four o'clock, and then back to Birmingham. And it would be very productive. That's the difference between then and the way it is now.'

In effect the marketing communications tasks were devolved across the agency and the client marketing department. Sometimes, as happened on Rowntree, the client team would even include media specialists, but the evaluation of marketing activity, the understanding of the brand – these would sit across the agency and client organisation. Planners like Terry Prue would take the lead on evaluating the success of advertising. But where you had planners, such as Ev Jenkins and Lee Godden, often the client would consult or defer to them on the question of whether an ad was on-brand or not. Marketers who were new to the team, would be directed to get an induction at the agency with the planners who would tell them how the brand worked – because they had a deep understanding of how consumers viewed the brand.

Doug Richardson comments that the focus at J. Walter Thompson was much more on client handholding than working with creatives. 'A lot of it was about writing reports and doing analysis and that kind of stuff, rather than building those relationships with the creative teams, sharing your insights and trying to help them, help the process.'

But when advertising was controversial it was the bravery of clients that gets mentioned. Ev Jenkins describes how key the role of James Stewart, the Brooke Bond client, was when the Oxo Family was launched for the second time in the 1980s – holding the line against the hostility that true-to-life advertising stirred up. 'I have to take my hat off to them because James and the then chairman, were getting a sack full of nasty mail every week and he just threw it aside, and we had everybody telling us "Take it off-air, it's not doing anything for sales" – this is in the first four weeks. You really do need a committed client to do that kind of stuff. James had seen Persil and they were very empathetic in that respect. He wanted to break the family mould on television advertising, because if you looked at advertising about Proctor & Gamble brands, you had mums smelling armpits and going, "Oh, April freshness". It was that happy families advertising. When you looked at what was on television at the time and it was *Boys from the Black Stuff* and *Butterflies* – it wasn't fantasy, it was semi-documentary and dark comedy. So people had all these worries, their kids not being able to get jobs perhaps, or the cost of universities, it all kind of brings you down a bit. So it's important if you want someone to open up to you, to actually do it in a way that makes them relax and talk about this little thing in your life called advertising your brand, or creating your brand or whatever it is. I don't think you can just do this with analysis, to be honest with you.' It's a beautiful example of the agency being able to exercise its intuition to go into the fragile space for making a customer connection, and with the client able to back that hunch by sticking to the strategy once that had been articulated, and not panicking when the postbag got nasty.

Turning to Boase Massimi Pollitt, the purpose of the qualitative pretesting was not just to provide evidence that the creative ideas were popular or 'worked' with real customers, it was an opportunity for clients to sit in the same room with them and hear them talk. James Best explains: 'Research allowed the agency to sell John Webster's surprising, otherwise unsellable, work to clients who found it frightening. The risk was being diminished. Clients were allowed to join us in the groups and sit in the back of the room and ask their own questions at the end. Some clients would come with us and attend a lot of groups. We always insisted that they attend more than a single group and it had a remarkable effect on them because they weren't use to talking to their customers. So to see people in their home lives or in the pub talking about stuff gave them reassurance.'

David Cowan and John Madell make exactly the same point. 'By doing qualitative research quickly and at virtually no cost, it meant that clients could accept at script stage, ideas that they wouldn't have been brave enough to accept under other circumstances. So that was terribly important.'

Occasionally it might go awry. There's a story of the BMP planner and the client failing to turn up to groups for two days in succession. When the frantic researcher phoned to report them missing, a search was started only to discover that both planner and marketer had gone on a two-day drinking binge and hadn't managed to reach any of the groups sober!

For CDP this was where planning performed its most important role. The planner was expected to articulate an advertising strategy which the client could commit to so strongly that they would then buy the single advertising idea which would been developed as the solution. The way in which John Wood got his job at CDP in the early 1960s is a good illustration of this. He was a researcher working at RSL, debriefing Gallaher executives with some CDP directors present. They were testing the idea of basing Benson & Hedges advertising on the gold packaging. Having explained that the groups didn't like the ideas – with only a single group coming out in favour – he, as part of his recommendations, told Gallaher to proceed because the negative response couldn't be trusted but the minority in favour could. The working men of Tyneside liked to smoke a more aspirational cigarette at the weekend when they weren't at work. The majority wrote off the idea of a gold packet as pretentious nonsense. He was employed at CDP on the strength of this highly irregular interpretation of research findings. This story became part of the mythology at CDP. Several of the planners mentioned it. The point of the story is not that research doesn't work, but that it informs judgement and in this case the concept was used, in spite of what most of those interviewed said.

This did mean a ferocious focus on product research. It's simply not true that CDP advertising was not research-based. But clients needed to know what they expected the advertising to do. The other reason CDP used research in this way, is that the real decision-makers were at the top of the organisation. Advertising as creative as this was high-risk and those owning or running the business had the power and confidence to make such decisions. Research had to be used clearly and intelligently, and presented to those who weren't themselves research specialists or professional marketers but business people. And a John Wood or a David Clifford would be working alongside Frank Lowe or John Ritchie (father of Guy Ritchie the film director) to make the case for the campaign. This was hugely irritating for middle-ranking marketing managers because the decision was taken out of their hands to the highest level. But it usually delivered CDP from the perils of having to sell a commercial all the way up the client organisation – with the almost inevitable result that the ad would be challenged and changed so many times that ultimately it would either be rejected by somebody or changed out of all recognition.

CDP used the high-pressure sale like no other agency. From the point where the client had accepted the advertising strategy and signed it off in the creative brief, it became almost impossible to turn down the advertising the agency subsequently came up with, however outlandish it was. And although CDP never fired clients as often as they bragged that they had, turning down creative work to a brief you had signed off was a sure-fire way to stir the agency's ire. John Bruce tells the story: 'Ford said "we want another idea" and CDP said "no sorry, that's it – either take it or leave it and, if you don't take it, we won't handle your business any more". Ford thought they were calling their bluff. But Ford really did get fired.'

Adam Lury, who had worked as a planner at BMP, felt he needed a far less confrontational way of selling in creative work when he came to start his own agency at Howell Henry Chaldecott Lury (HHCL). 'We built the client into the process, early on. We made sure the client was inside the process. We would present a series of ideas to the client at a very early stage. We would present them with five or six very rough ideas but we need a check as to what is right and clicking, and how far you want to push things, rather than go to the usual confrontation meeting.'

We turn now to creative briefs and creative briefing, now a staple of the planning process and ask how planners summarised their thinking on paper.

Briefs and creative briefing

> *'We didn't have a creative brief. For a very long time it was all about the briefing. It wasn't formalised.'*
>
> James Best

It may seem odd that a review of the main responsibilities of the planner should conclude with briefing rather than start with it. Particularly as for today's planners the creative brief is now central to the job; the document which above all others planners are expected to write themselves. However it was not always thus. If you conceive of the development of advertising as an industrial process, the defining of the specification is indeed fundamental. But if you are trying to develop the best advertising possible or even the kind of advertising that no one has ever seen, then a written specification may not be possible.

J. Walter Thompson had the T-Plan from 1964, long before the planning department was thought of. The T-Plan would define the way in which advertising had to build long term brand effects through rational emotional and sensory communication. Because a creative team was permanently assigned to work on a particular piece of business they would already be familiar with the T-Plan. This way of working continued for years. Charles Channon was brought in to manage quality control of the T-Plan and that team was part of creative services and not part of planning at all. Eventually the T-Plan was radically simplified into a creative brief. In other words, the creative brief was a relatively late development at J. Walter Thompson. Some of our planners never wrote them.

Christine Gray talked about how little protection planners got from creatives who didn't want to cooperate. 'One of the planners told me that the creative locked the door so he had to post the brief under the door because the creative wouldn't let him in!'

This is where what Dave Trott calls creative planning, comes into its own – refining the creative task to push the envelope to get great creative. So the creatives may not have much to do at all. Krelle again, this time talking about Elastoplast: 'The core observation was if you can see the holes, the germs can see the holes, and the creative team said, "That's really neat, Jack. If we win the business, we will use that as a line if that's alright."' Where there were relationships of trust, the creatives were perfectly happy to take lines from the brief and use them in the advertising itself.

Dave Trott, working at BMP in the early 1970s, tells this story: 'Jim Williams was doing a pitch on fire prevention. The account man Dave Batterby came down to brief me and said, "Jim and I have had a thought," and you could tell he was excited because he was so fidgety. "How will you know if fire prevention is working? How would they measure it?" I said "Fewer fires?" "Yes and fewer call-outs, so the brief changes to "Get call-outs down." If we tell people how to put out their own fire, they won't have to call out the brigade. Our brief to you is to make you so scared about what it's like to put out a fire that you never want to have one." I won two silvers at the D&AD for that and it was nothing to do with me. That's the planner and the account man working together.'

There was no formalisation of the brief at Boase Massimi Pollitt until some 10 years after it was founded. James Best comments: 'Since we put a formal brief in place I have seen hundreds of creative briefing formats come and go and every new planning director and creative director has to have another one. But if you don't have the framework and the discipline, people will use them until they don't need to.'

David Cowan says rather wistfully, 'I never felt that we got the briefs right. We tried to work out what would motivate the customer. We wrote what would keep people's feet on the ground when looking at creative work. The creatives wanted a hook that would stimulate the idea and we weren't doing that.' This is the danger of the creative brief when it becomes a contract for commissioning a piece of work and evaluating its quality – the brief became about accuracy and not about inspiration.

Leslie Butterfield talks about how the brief format was deliberately left unstructured 'You were expected to write the brief as appropriate for that brand or that product. There were certain bits of language that were around which were a kind of touchstone: the idea of proposition – the offer you made to customers – the idea of target audience, the idea of insights, although I don't think we ever used the word insight as such. But, really the thrust of writing a creative brief that did fall largely to the planner was not prescribed in the form of a template, and I do remember that the reason for that was it was seen as restrictive. Templates encouraged box filling. It encouraged inanity in terms of: well, I've got to put something in there, so "C1, C2," here, rather than giving it thought. It was suggested that it was better to think about the problem in its own right: think about who you wanted to reach, what you wanted to say, what the message was, what the core benefit was, or whatever the language was (and there wasn't even necessarily an agreed language that you had to use). It was more informal than that. I know it's surprising for such a rigorous culture. That whole process was scary because, maybe even as I'm describing it, an awful lot of responsibility went onto your plate. At quite a tender age, 23 or 24, you were making decisions about budgets, ratings, expenditure patterns, creative treatments and production budgets and you knew the associated risks with that, making big decisions at a relatively young age.'

When he moved to AMV to start the planning department there, Leslie used the creative brief as his tool to reduce what he saw as the wastage in the repeated cycles of creative pretesting until the creative idea was right. 'I did feel that that was the one change I wanted to make, I wanted to do more of the work upfront, get the brief more right early and then hopefully be more efficient at the creative development. I also figured that working with someone like David Abbott at AMV, I couldn't just use his kind of work as fodder in the way that the creative work sometimes got used at BMP.'

CDP had a love-hate relationship with briefs – the legend was that the creative wouldn't even let you into their office to hand them a creative brief. But there are similar stories at JWT. The brief was an ideas starter for CDP but it wasn't there to provide inspiration so much as the diving board from which the creative team would jump to somewhere entirely new. So the legendary Heineken campaign had a proposition which the account director, David Gray, came up with – which said simply 'Refreshment'. When the work was discussed inside of the agency, all the brief could be used for was to check that the creative idea connected with the advertising strategy.

John Bruce talks about briefing the media team being just as important as briefing the creatives. And how the brief was used as a tempering device to head off bright ideas that weren't appropriate. However the brief shouldn't exclude all bright ideas that were not on-brief – it was a balancing exercise. 'I would brief the media department as much as I would brief the creative department. If you started with the creative brief, then you started with something fairly concrete and so, if they produced something that was totally off-brief, then you might think "Oh I wonder whether I can rewrite this brief", which sometimes you could and you did because that was the best way of making the whole thing fit together. But other times you would say "this isn't on-brief".'

Likewise Judie Lannon running the Creative Research department at J. Walter Thompson agrees that the documenting of the thinking might take place after the conversation with the creatives rather than before.

Years later, Jon Steel, moving to Goodby Silverstein to start one of the earliest planning departments in the USA, asked Jeff Goodby why he wanted planning. 'He said, "I need somebody in the agency and some group of people in the agency who are charged with saying no when it's necessary to say no." And I think that was the moment I realised that it would probably be fine for me to go there.'

Jack Krelle warns of the commoditisation that took place when planning was turned into a process and the brief a request for work 'A lot of people rather neglected what King actually said and have tried to over simplify it. If you over simplify it, you do diminish its value. Therefore clients don't want to pay as much, they don't understand that it's as difficult as it is. So I think JWT, and all the others, dug a hole for themselves by making planning and that sort of stuff, presentation drones, research managing drones, rather than serious thinking. And serious thinking backed with a properly structured point of view. So there was a creative brief system called the T-Plan, it was one page, it did have headings, it did say desired response when there was a perfectly clear and good structure.'

Now we turn to another area where planning made early and speedy gains: the new business pitch.

Pitching for new business

'In new business clients loved planning. Because here was an agency that had gone out and taken the creative ideas to the consumer. Almost always, every client is frustrated when they come to you, because the previous agency had dug in their heels or they felt the work wasn't effective, so we clearly demonstrated flexibility and a willingness to do work that was effective.'

Jane Newman

Pitching to win a new client was not allowed at J. Walter Thompson through the 1950s because the owner Stanley Resor forbade it. Speculative work for a client who hadn't paid yet, was done at the expense of clients who were paying. So if a client wanted to come to J. Walter Thompson they should apply in writing and the agency would consider their application. In 1961 J. Walter Thompson London broke a rule. And pitched for Ford. And lost.[51] Not a good omen. But through the 1960s the top agency in the country gradually got used to the idea of competing with other ad agencies for business. They spent more time talking about J. Walter Thompson and its resources than the client's business though with some justification, since the resources available to the client were indeed dazzling and dazzled many clients through the doors.

Being reminded that pitches are not inevitable is a useful reminder that the world was not always as it is now. And that

51 *Fifty in 40* previously cited.

the genteel world of the pitch to select a suitable agency partner, where the outcome was a foregone conclusion, has now been replaced by not only searches for new creative ideas but an auction to bid prices down. J. Walter Thompson won the Tesco account for 24 hours until Jack Cohen affably introduced the topic of a discount on the full 15% commission only to be told that that was non-negotiable. He found a new agency the following day.[52]

John Bruce describes how as a junior planner at J. Walter Thompson he enjoyed going after new business. 'In the early days the account planner became a key member of all the pitch teams whenever we were going after new business. We would do all the investigative work and start pulling it together – it's unlike working on regular business. You're working almost in isolation. You have no idea of what the percentage of relevant facts is – so you don't know whether you've got 10 per cent relevant facts or 80 per cent, but you're just trying to pull together whatever you've got and put together a convincing argument.'

Sometimes you could be too clever. David Clifford explains how in a pitch for Ski Yogurt at CDP they measured all the ingredients for all the yogurts in the category. And they concluded that Ski had twice as much fruit as any of the competition. They built their campaign on that and took it to the prospective client. 'And the MD turned to the Marketing Director and said, "Is this true?" He said, "I don't know I've never thought about it." And I said, well, it's true because we weighed it. And the MD said, "Why the bloody hell are we putting all this fruit into the thing for?" That's the most expensive part. So they stayed with Masius and fired the marketing director!'

Boase Massimi Pollitt on the other hand as a start-up

52 *Fifty in 40* previously cited.

needed to pitch constantly to survive and grow. Account planning is never shown to such an advantage as when the speed and intuition of planners is put to work at short notice to develop new ideas for a client. And the intensity of the work led to breakthroughs which were life changing. Here's Roddy Glen talking about working on a pitch in the middle of the night with David Cowan: 'We lined up all the products in the category. We didn't know what we were doing, we didn't know about semiotics and all of that, And we got a breakthrough in the tea market in the middle of the night. It taught me to interrogate the client as much as the customers. Get all the packets and line them up and ask them until they confess. Why are they the way they are? Why do you have teapots with tea on the front of the pack? The reason the packs were the way they were is because 'er indoors has to reach out and adopt and own and pay money, put it into the trolley, take it home, put it in the kitchen and put it in her caddy – to look like something she wanted to own. The big preoccupation with the tea advertising as opposed to the packaging, was reassuring people that it was real leaves in the bags and not dust from the factory floor. The pack was assigned with the job of bringing user values at the touch point. But I didn't know that before the middle of the night. Then it all happened in half an hour. I came in my pants!'

When planning was taken to other agencies, often the best way to demonstrate its viability was to only use it on pitches and then on the business once it was running. Jane Newman and Jon Steel, both alumni of BMP, followed this policy when Jane introduced planning to the USA at Chiat/Day in New York, and a few years later Jon became planning director of Goodby Silverstein in San Francisco.

Jon Steel talks about how he introduced planning: 'I would only introduce planning to the agency through new business, and we would not go to existing clients and say – you've been doing it wrong. We took the view that if things were fine on existing business, they wouldn't introduce me, and that we would simply pitch new business. Let's say we won two or three pieces of business, I would then hire another planner to come in and work with me on them; that would give me a bit of space to pitch more new business and so on, and we'd roll it out that way. After about probably a year and a half, there were other accounts in the agency that were seeing new business we'd won, campaigns we were winning creative and effectiveness awards for, and saying, "hold on a minute, can we have some of this too?" a simple and very effective strategy – not least because at the peak the success rate in pitches was above 90 per cent, so existing clients got to hear about and see the new work the agency was doing.'

Jane talks about how in New York at Chiat/Day they were able to make the case for planning by researching concepts when they pitched for business. Introducing planning on existing business was a much more difficult sell. 'Planning comes into its own on new business because you've got a blank slate and a client who's very receptive and teams who have fresh ideas. So every new business pitch had planning on it and in every instance, the client liked it. So right from the beginning we researched advertising. We'd take out a storyboard and do the research ourselves. We could have used researchers. But it was better from us because we weren't saying, "Is this idea right or wrong?", we were saying, "What is it in this idea that is going to work in the marketplace? How does this work and how is it going to be effective?" So we could articulate that to the client team. It's like detective work. You don't have a set list of questions. You explore what's going on and it's the serendipity of asking a question that you didn't think was going to have an interesting answer, but it does, and then you can explore it from there.'

Jay Chiat eventually went on record to say, 'Account planning was the greatest new business tool ever created.'

Notice how this is exploring how the advertising is working and never asking whether it is right or wrong. Respondents aren't being asked to judge, but to shape and to think out loud. And clients were being given a deeper understanding into how their customers' thought – something their incumbent agencies may not have been giving them.

We turn next to research the final tool in the planners' armoury and how planners bought it, used it, and did it themselves.

Using research

'The whole idea about planning is that it's evidence-based, it's not just another opinion. It had meat behind it. It wasn't personal.' Paul Feldwick

'The blinding light was qualitative research which told you why. But all the clients wanted to do was to research whether the advertising would work. What we were researching was why people might or might not buy their products, so we could get underneath. This may seem very obvious now but it wasn't being done very much at the time and it was certainly an insight to me.' Cathy Simmonds

It should be obvious by now how integral research is to the account planning role. If you can't back your intuitions up you are just another opinion. Those in the early experiment at Pritchard Wood market planning department were called researchers, not planners. And it isn't clear whether the Boase Massimi Pollitt planning department were called planners from the day the agency opened, or researchers. Stephen King, rearranging the pieces to form a new department, was determined to call it something different. Those in it were not to be researchers – they were not to conduct research themselves but to be called something different. And the account planning name attached itself not only to the department but to those working in it. Judie Lannon and Tom Corlett continued to be called researchers.

It became obvious from very early on that this new type of researcher operated quite differently from other researchers in ad agencies. John Bartle was a research manager at Bournville who dealt with researchers from four agencies including Pritchard Wood. 'Researchers were absolutely back-room. Just like a lot of us at the client-side were. Good and very nice. We used to have meetings with Young & Rubicam and talk about research. You never thought that those researchers ever saw the creative work. So people like Peter Jones were a completely different breed. They were sort of itching to get out. And from the moment they were liberated at BMP the whole thing became much more flexible, much more informal, much more chatty. They were absolutely miles apart in terms of formality. One way of describing it was quantitative-ness versus qualitative-ness. It was formal, numerical, statistical versus chatty and colloquial.'

It should be clear that these new planners were still expected to be fluent in the commissioning and analysis of research. Most of which was still quantitative. This was a golden age for research as it became possible to link media consumption with the purchase and consumption of goods in the home, allowing detailed analysis of trial and switching. And that research companies – many of them closely linked with advertising agencies – were starting to provide syndicated services. Clients, led by agencies, were putting together brand-tracking and campaign-tracking studies which measured brand performance as well as advertising. Government sponsored research was also being used with the thought leaders such as Tom Corlett, moving between government departments, research agencies and advertising agencies. The biggest advertising agencies were commissioning their own studies. In the early 1960s, J. Walter Thompson devised a system to grade every poster site in the country by the volume of those walking past and their demographic profile. There was a day-part study to determine whether it was worth booking TV slots earlier in the evening when the rates were much cheaper. One discovery was that TVs were left on at certain times of the day and that a third of the living rooms were empty with the television left on. So media tracking relied on set-top boxes, diaries and surveys. No single source of information was taken as gospel.[53]

When there were objections to particular quantitative research methods it was because of the use of benchmarks which could be spurious – based on different market sectors or other parts of the world and on respondents who neither bought or consumed the products concerned. But the deeper concern about benchmarks was the way in which they became the bar to beat. What planners wanted to do instead was to create the best advertising they could, not simply to exceed a lowest common denominator. Quantitative research proved too limited to do this work. And it was because of this that qualitative research was appropriated from motivational researchers and their occult theorising, and redeployed to allow ordinary people to explain how they used products and what they thought of advertising. Copywriters were using this kind of research and doing it themselves before the invention of account planning.

But the borrowing of the creative workshop concept from Chicago by John Treasure in 1965, and the setting up of the creative research department by Judie Lannon in 1968 made qualitative research accessible and simplified its use. The projective techniques such as asking people to personalise the brand were discovered to be extraordinarily effective. People who had never been researched before in their lives could say

---

53 *Sampling the Universe: The Growth, Development and Influence of Market Research in Britain since 1945*, Colin McDonald and Stephen King, NYC Publications (1996).

with utter confidence, 'My daughter is a bit like Palmolive', as if Palmolive were a real person.

Applied to roughly drawn key frames with an audio commentary, ordinary people were able to explain what a TV commercial concept was about and to discuss the role of the brand in a way that quantitative research simply couldn't do.

The planners at Boase Massimi Pollitt used simple techniques over and over, until they got an understanding of the advertising idea, the specific elements of the execution – because you could have a good idea which was poorly executed – and a creative of the calibre of John Webster was capable of using the feedback to decide his shooting angles and lighting. As a blunt instrument, research could be used too literally, when it could kill off good advertising ideas. Dave Trott as a junior copywriter hired by Webster at BMP complains that the planning department should have been called the testing department. 'It was like walking around with lead boots on the whole time. Everything got blown out.' There was even a report of a BMP creative team who got hired by Frank Lowe at CDP on the strength of a reel of their work – all of which had been rejected in group discussions.[54]

Not even the one-to-one ratio of an account planner to an account man was enough to meet the demand for research at BMP. Roddy Glen, one of the researchers who was hired from Schlackmans to improve research standards at BMP, talks about the grounding he got in researching advertising before he left and started his own research agency. 'A lot of the way I worked was poured into me, not from Schlackmans, but by BMP. It was a great way to solve communication problems. And by now I spoke the right language for the agencies.' The fascinating thing is that both J. Walter Thompson and Boase

54 Geoff Howard-Spink is the source of this story about Derek Apse and Mike Stevenson hired by CDP.

Massimi Pollitt were in effect large qualitative research agencies but never bothered to work out how much income research was bringing into the agency. Paul Feldwick comments that it wasn't until the recession of 1990, when his department was threatened with a 15 per cent cull, that he saved it by pointing out how much research revenue his department was generating and offset that against the salaries, which had never been done before.

Consistently we found that nobody knew or cared how much research cost, or how much it had cost the agency to find the right solution. At BMP Leslie Butterfield talks about the lack of interest in the agency's financial fortunes, particularly running a successful research business at the same time. 'It was a weird thing. I never came across the concept of profitability, I don't think, in the whole time I was at BMP. Nobody ever said, Leslie could you dial back your work on X because you're doing so many days' work and it's a very small client. And nobody ever said the opposite: which is you really need to lock that client down, because they are incredibly important to the agency, blah, blah, blah. You decided what you did on the basis of enthusiasm, interest and need.'

Similarly almost all of the research resources available to clients of J. Walter Thompson were not charged , as they were part of the service. Though this changed as the commission system faltered and died.

The volume of research being commissioned kick-started a whole new research sector. Paul Feldwick talked about the 'industrialising of market research' when Wendy Gordon and Colleen Ryan founded the Research Business. This was a quotation of a public slur from a paper given by Mary Goodyear at the national MRS research conference, aghast at the qualitative research consultancies springing up under her nose, diluting the purity of the academic methods her company MBL used. Not every ad agency was ready for planning – but their research departments and the agency clients wanted groups. And qualitative research agencies sprang up like wild flowers. Wendy Gordon told us, 'I didn't set up to have a competition with the other agencies. But Mary, and Peter Cooper of CRAM, got aggressive with us. I thought I'll show them. So we fucked them on the numbers!' The Research Business after a relatively short time became the largest qualitative agency in the UK, built largely on advertising research. And so a new category was born.

Qualitative research was not supposed to be holding up a mirror to the consumer but interpreting what they said. Jan Zajac comments that at BMP the training was as much in developing their creative judgement, as being able to run a group discussion properly. 'To begin with, you go along with your senior planner and watch them do it and after that you go and do your own. You were given guidance on how to get insight and I think that was a huge job you learnt as a planner, and the other one was artistic judgement about advertising'

The idea of planners doing their own groups was not at all approved of at J. Walter Thompson. It was perceived to undermine objectivity. Judie Lannon: 'Stephen was quite firm on the subject. Largely because, God forbid, he should ever do a focus group. He would be terrified. He would never have done it. He also thought, "Are clients going to buy this?" if the groups are done by planners? Remember he had come from the marketing department. It's a bit like asking the marketing director to do their own groups in a client company. It's sort of naff! You want to be a bit more professional than that.'

So it was a few years before Ev Jenkins who had proven herself as an able planner at J. Walter Thompson, opted to run her own groups. She did so partly because she found it very useful as a way of keeping conversations going with the creative team, who would also view the groups. But also because it was much cheaper than employing an external researcher and having to bill that through the client. She reckoned she could run four groups for the cost of every group charged out.

Planners started to use groups in ways not envisaged when it was simply a way of asking simple questions about product use or advertising. John Siddall ran a group where they showed 50 TV commercials for Fry's Turkish Delight going right back to the 1950s, in order to get the language of the Turkish Delight brand and how the brand had changed during its history. But this was research with customers, not a piece of backroom semiotic analysis. Qualitative research allowed you to experiment much more quickly than surveys which took weeks to turn around.

And Jim Williams, years later working at Young & Rubicam, put together qualitative and quantitative research to develop the Brand Asset Valuator. 'Well, from the qualitative research I would explore the archetypes. So, for example, you have the "Maiden" or "Innocence" as one of the archetypes – you have got brands like Dove, Johnson's Baby, Danone, Olivio and Crayola. What you were doing was plotting which brands were closest to the brand values.'

Cynics might regard this as a green light for planners to make money by charging clients for conclusions they had already come to. But the whole point of the research apparatus was to get a deep understanding of the customer. If anything, they were naïve about that. Martin Boase tells the story of the pitch where the planner who had researched the creative work the preceding night, told the client he had never seen creative work research so poorly but that, based on what he learnt, he was confident that they now knew how to execute the campaign. Strangely enough BMP didn't win that pitch. But the point of the story is that the planner thought that the integrity of saying the ads had researched badly would be a tipping point. Of course it wasn't.

But this did not mean that planners were always so literal.

Judie Lannon comments on the difference between research conducted inside an advertising agency and that conducted by a third party.

'The pure researchers I knew wouldn't have been happy in an ad agency. Mary Goodyear and Wendy Gordon from an ideological point of view were much more committed to the findings. But when you're in an agency, it's true of the planners and true of me, you don't follow the rules in the way a real qual researcher follows them. And you have to be good friends with the creative people. I was on very good terms with them. I loved them. I married one and the other was my best friend: Digby, my husband, and the other Jeremy Bullmore. You had to have that kind of a temperament.'

We have still to explore CDP's famous antipathy about putting any of their work into research. Tony Mortemore cites one of the creatives, Tony Brignull, who was responsible for the Mr Spock Heineken poster, commented once, 'If we present something it's our best effort. We don't test it on animals.' But that didn't prevent CDP being pressured by clients to research their advertising. The failure of the CDP campaign for Heineken in research is now the stuff of legend. But they went on and ran the ads anyway. Tony Moretemore recalls, 'It wasn't the research agency's finest hour. "Woah, this isn't beer advertising", which, of course, it wasn't.'

John Siddall points out that despite all the bluster CDP's clients did actually force them to research their work. 'When it was a very big client like Gallaher who insisted on doing the research CDP would reluctantly agree. They would say "We don't believe in it, we won't take any notice of it, but if you want to do it and pay for it then go ahead."' He goes on to say 'But what I learned from Colletts and John Wood was not to take what people say literally, but to use my judgement based on my years of living, to say what I believed and didn't believe.

So I never ever believed in straight reportage but always in analysis and interpretation, and in judgement.'

Christine Gray at J. Walter Thompson is just as sceptical of negative results from her experience of the Maureen Lipman BT campaign. 'I have never been a great believer in advertising research in the sense of looking at storyboards or rough cuts – I truly don't think it can tell you very much. I think it can only tell you that you're possibly saying something relevant, it can't tell you if you are saying it well or saying it in a way that's going to be effective.'

The provocative point is that it doesn't mean the research shouldn't or can't be done, but that the results need to be used judiciously to decide how to take the creative ideas forward. Creative pretesting by sudden death has given research and qualitative research a bad name. But that is when the planner hides behind the research rather than using it to understand what the creative idea is capable of.

Adam Lury, who worked as a planner at BMP in the 1980s, offers some of the most trenchant criticism of the way in which, in later years, their research could simply become a macho exercise in how many groups could be done and how thick a report could be written off the back of it. A lot of it was just qualitative research, the level of thinking was not about thinking differently. When at his start-up at HHCL he was researching Molson lager, and research respondents praised the scripts as great lager advertising, he told his startled creative partners and the client that they shouldn't be run. 'It will go in one ear and out the other. We don't have 10 million pounds to spend and if we did I still wouldn't want to do it.' Molson, as a new entrant to the lager category, needed to find a way to break the rules of lager advertising, not serve time as a kind of junior comedian leaving the headline acts firmly in place. So they created advertising which sharply divided the audience to create an impact which couldn't be appropriated by the brand leaders.

So to summarise – the first planners had huge capacity and capability with research but were never defined by it. There continued to be advertising researchers in agencies who rebadged themselves as planners, and researchers who deployed ever more creative techniques to understand customer motivation. But the planning function, whether they did their own groups or not, was supposed to rise above research and make creative leaps with it.

Left brain, right brain, and the higher powers

'Stephen King talks about creative imagination subjected to critical control. And that left brain–right brain thing that planners have to have. And I've generally found that the critical control part of it is sold to clients. That's the external benefit. The internal benefit is the creative imagination part, in the work that they can do in stimulating ideas and informing ideas. They've got to do both at the same time if they're going to do it properly.'

Jon Steel

'I was always positioned as a planner because my skills from the theatre were artistic, and my experience in a scientific laboratory was relevant, so I like to say that nuclear physics and the theatre would have made an ideal combination. And it seemed to work. But it's quite important that planners who made it had abilities both in the analytical scientific side and the creative side of things – creative sensitivity. And that was me.'

Jim Williams

In this section we close in on the core abilities of the planner and what characterises the stars whose effectiveness came from their interpersonal skills.

It should be clear from the people who have been interviewed that not only are they a very diverse collection of individuals but they represent a whole range of capabilities – whatever agency they worked at. Even at BMP when there was a serious attempt to recruit a graduate elite; those who passed the recruitment process were an intriguing blend of analytical thinking and creativity as well. All of the planners seem to be intellectuals. Jan Zajac comments, 'You're supposed to have a brain that other people haven't got. I think planners should be able to do thinking things that the others can't do. Otherwise I don't really see a role.' But Adam Lury, another BMP trainee who went on to be a founder of HHCL – one of the barnstorming agencies of the 1990s – is critical of the focus on cleverness at BMP. His concern is that the focus on intellect among planners is as unhelpful as the designation creative is upon the creative department, as if nobody else in the agency is capable of creativity and if they do, they have to call it something else. He suggests that intellectualising gets in the way of getting the job done and can distract.

The skill sets of individual planners differ. The way each was trained seems to have been to help them to become better at their strengths and not to shoehorn them into a particular way of working. The task was clear – how they carried out that planning task was not prescribed. And very different ways of working emerge. So much so, that one of the responsibilities of the departmental manager was to match planners to particular accounts. And the planner who ends up working on a particular piece of business regards it as a piece of luck that they ended up working on the business they were given.

Actually the left brain, right brain nomenclature is not a term than any of the planners use – Roger Sperry's experiments were carried out during the 1960s and he won his Nobel award in 1981. So the terminology came much later. The analytical side has great prominence for them but they boil it down from physics and higher maths into 'brute numeracy.' Their focus on analysis was about rigour and solid groundwork. It's how the data is interpreted and presented which makes all the difference. This is where planners shone because they were capable of taking the data and making intuitive leaps with it.

Jan Zajac talks about what he did at JWT after he had had stints in several agencies including BMP and CDP: 'At JWT, I got quite a lot of respect instantly, just through spotting insights that a lot of the others hadn't. For example, Thames Television – the creative director was in one of the teams working on it. He didn't know why we were advertising. And I told them it was because they want to boost the share price in case they go public. It didn't say that in the brief but that's the reason why, and I could bring an extra dimension of thinking to help people along. I did a similar thing with the British Airports Authority (now BAA), when they were being privatised, which we won. I think I wrote about a 10-page paper on what the role of advertising was and they took it and we got the business.'

On the other hand, Lee Godden, who doesn't think of herself as analytical at all, recounts a conversation with the intimidating J. Walter Thompson planning group head Catherine Butler. 'I said to her one day, "Catherine, I feel awful because I'm very undisciplined and I'm very sloppy and I do everything off the back of the envelope" and she said [changes accent to RP] "I am very good at analysis but I am not so good at synthesis. You, on the other hand, are fairly good at synthesis and not very good at analysis," [laughs].' Synthesis is an interesting skill because it is not only about combining multiple sources of hard data and balancing discrepancies between them, it also involved soft skills – being able to integrate qualitative data and to judge when it matches and when it does not.

At several points in the interview, Lee mentions Christine Gray, whom she perceives to be one of the best planners she ever worked with, because of her ability to synthesise. 'Christine even got a job in the creative department by acing the J. Walter Thompson copy test. Six months later she came back and said it's so boring because all the interesting work has been done by the time you get to write the copy. Because that bit of the thinking is what really determines the way that the advertising should be, if you're any good.' In other words thinking up creative ideas wasn't creative enough in Christine's book. She wanted to shape the strategy.

A quality which was commended more than once was what was called the 'terrier mentality', a more dynamic variation on synthesis. 'She sort of took all that information and had a lot of intellectual energy and she transformed it.' Which wasn't just about understanding or rigour, but the ability to persist and the intellectual energy to follow the trail through to its conclusion, which was to create a strategy out of formerly disparate elements. Here's a quotation about another planner on condition that they weren't to be identified: 'An amazing mind and a totally terrier mentality, someone who'll keep going and going until they get there.'

Another skill however, which only a few were perceived to have and when they did so it was highly prized, was the ability to take other people with you. It is ironic that planning was founded on the insight that customer response is more important than what advertisers want to say to them. And how so many planners work on an opposite transmission model – not being focused on the responses they require from colleagues.

The first of these could be called the listening style of planning. Doug Richardson, who took over as head of department from Stephen King at J. Walter Thompson, was known as the 'Zen Planner'. Partly this was because he had a reputation for falling asleep in all sorts of situations but mainly because he was so quiet at meetings sitting in the corner with his eyes closed. When we asked him why he did this, Doug's response was that so much of the time he simply had not yet formed a point of view, so did not wish to commit himself. The rituals of smoking, when this was allowed in meetings, allowed a semblance of activity without saying anything. And he decried the banning of smoking because it required him to contribute to meetings before he was ready. Jon Steel makes a similar point, that he could go through an entire meeting without saying anything while carefully weighing up the ideas in the discussion and the alliances forming and changing around the table. From which he was able to go and steer the group towards a strategy knowing what needed to be done.

Geoff Howard-Spink, who was an account handler at BMP and then CDP before heading up planning at his own agency Lowe Howard-Spink, commends listening: 'It is what I always thought the job was about. I was much happier if I was trying to tease something out of somebody, the client or the creative people. I just wanted to understand what they were on about, really. It's so difficult these days – or even then, not even just these days – when you know so many people don't know how to listen, they're forever stepping on other people's words, they'll say something and then they'll switch off trying to think of "what am I going to say next?" and don't hear all of that.'

The next variant in these higher skills was the 'spare pair of hands' approach. Conspicuous in that it was never about displaying cleverness or trying to batter down with counter-arguments, but about being useful. David Baker, before taking over as head of planning at J. Walter Thompson, did a stint in account handling because as he said, 'If you're an account director with good strategic planning, you know how to get the best out of planners. So that's a win-win situation.' John Bruce says much the same: 'I eventually left account planning partly because I thought I could do more and better account planning as an account director than I could as a planner.'

Jon Steel again: 'The most important skill of a planner is being useful. And I've worked with some planners who have brains the size of a planet, and who are so far my superior in intellect, it's sort of shrivelling in its effect. But they're not useful. And intellectually they can never make the connections they need to make with creative people who they need to persuade, or clients they need to persuade that they're right.'

Lee Godden: 'It depends what sort of planner you are, there are the incredibly analytical ones who put the brief under the door, probably don't have much in the way of social skills [laughs] but they do really clever, valuable work. And several planners are described by their peers in such terms – brilliant but you need to keep them away from clients, because they can't and won't be tactful.'

Leslie Butterfield talks about the people management skills: 'Managing expectations, debriefing, explaining complex things to creative people who didn't necessarily think the same way you did. Both aspects of the classic lateral and logical differences of thinking.'

The final group were those who were so empathetic that they came across as positively disingenuous in their apparent disinterest in talking you round.

Terry Prue describes being in awe of Ev Jenkins: 'She managed all levels of the agency extraordinarily well. I think it's very difficult to be good at everything. You have responsibility, but you don't have real power. You are forever being an adviser to people, and I think that Ev was particularly successful at being able to push through her views. She got her way well. Whether she got on with them well or not, I'm not entirely sure.'

Here's Ev talking about her clients: 'I had a lot of sympathy with the clients because, to be honest with you, advertising was only a part of what they did. They had a lot on their plates, there were far fewer of them then than there are now. So coming to the agency was a bit of a day out, it was a chance for them to relax a bit. So we'd have coffee or breakfast or lunch or something. Because they were relaxing, you set yourself up for clients to tell you what's worrying them, to become part confidante, part planner. When you're on that level, as opposed to whatever, it's much easier to discuss issues in communications that are worrying them, because you've already got a much more relaxed relationship. And so I didn't find it that difficult. It's a bit like doing a group discussion but with your own people. If you can talk to people and communicate with them, then it's not that difficult to understand where they're coming from – what are their personal worries. Because everybody brings everything to the table, what you've left at home in the morning you bring to the table when you have a breakfast meeting, so it's affecting what you do and say, so it's a question of understanding.'

And here's a typical piece of self-deprecation from Lee: 'I was really lucky, I worked with smashing creative people. I worked with Larry Carter's group and I worked with Geoff Weedon's group and it was just heaven. There was a set format. I was very bad at it because I procrastinate terribly and I would have talked to the creative people a lot before there was ever a brief on the table. But there was something called the T-Plan. Do you know about the T-Plan? Well that was really the brief. I didn't much care for the planning tools. I didn't much care for them (not that I thought Stephen's thinking was bad) but it didn't seem to me a very good way to talk to creative people, to get out a piece of paper . . . Yes, slide it under their door and run for it! I was so lucky. I worked with such smashing creative people. They were just fine.' Of course they were. A prized skill was the ability to empathise, rather than identify the big idea and then try to persuade everybody else of its rightness. What it reinforces is both the relative isolation of the planning role and the lack of authority – a planner can't tell anybody else what to do – and how effective strategy involves the entire group and persuading everyone to be of one mind. Also important as ideas develop, as the whole group needs to move on together. If planners make themselves central to the strategy then once again they have to do another round of persuasion.

Jane Newman, one of the first planners in America starting planning at Chiat/Day, talks about having to simultaneously build up a team and a case for planning. 'Definitely, you're a catalyst for focusing on the end result and getting people to understand their piece of that, their role in that, and work together. Planners are very good at defining the end result so it becomes like a flag planted on a hill that you're going to go for. It's that, more than anything else. Everybody wants to know where they're going, and if you get everybody passionate about where they're going then they'll start to work together and move forward.'

It seems that of those we spoke to, it was the women who, in particular, had the ability to persuade and used it to the full. Lee again: 'You've got to be comfortable with not being in the front line and not getting the medals, which is why I think girls are quite good at it. I don't mean boys are necessarily bad, but it comes very easily to girls because an awful lot of it is just patting things and sliding them around.'

Notice how far planning has outrun its founders. More than one planner at J. Walter Thompson mentioned that, despite his brilliance, Stephen King preferred theoretical solutions to the haggling of the front-line planner's daily life in the trenches. And it was Stanley's protégées, rather than Stanley himself, who found how to take others with them and had the patience to take them there.

But we'll conclude this section with Paul Feldwick who talks about the facilitating role he has grown into as a senior planner then consultant: 'I'm not sure what it is and I'm not sure I would call it planning. But the best planners have always done this. And that is why this image of the isolated planner in the ivory tower is the misleading one. Because where planners have made a contribution is precisely in that interaction –

working as a member of the team. This is why writing creative briefs is really not where it's at. It's not important, it's the quality of the dialogue that you help to produce.'

Now we move to look at how the function is organised and managed. What does it take to run a planning department? Starting with finding and training planners.

Finding and training planners

'I don't think I ever had a single idea of what a planner was, it was about the individual always, rather than the model.' Doug Richardson

'The informal training came through using it, doing it, involvement, reading . . . that kind of thing.'
Leslie Butterfield

The beginnings of planning are illuminating because it was part pragmatism and part aspiration. They used the people they thought could do the job, even if they weren't quite sure what the job was. It's interesting that when they came to hire planners BMP, although a start-up, felt they needed to train planners themselves and went out to find the brightest graduates they could, who could combine strong analytical skills with a love of advertising and a strong creative streak. J. Walter Thompson on the other hand as the largest UK advertising agency sourced their planners first from the media and marketing departments, but then recruited planners from wherever they could. They weren't recruiting graduate trainees – actually their planners were already very experienced and were recruited because they were already familiar with the issues. The two agencies also recruited people from advertising agencies doing a variety of jobs including planning. After the setting up of the planning departments, there wasn't any more recruiting externally from media departments. Though internal transfers from media continued for some years at J. Walter

Thompson. They hired from research agencies too, despite David Cowan's misgivings about the ability of qualitative researchers to transition into planners. But recruits came from a variety of sources including from client-side.

What were the recruiters looking for? Doug Richardson as the first head of department after Stephen King, took exactly the same view that there was no template – but it was down to the individual. He saw the department as a stable he had to keep stocked. Planners had to be persuasive and persistent so he tried to find 'gritty people' as he called them. One of the characteristics of the J. Walter Thompson planning department was the number of women in it. Advertising agencies always employed a lot of women. but not in executive positions. It was comparatively rare to find women working as account supervisors at a senior level and even less likely to find them working as copywriters or art directors. J. Walter Thompson had a relatively large number of women planners.

Was this something Doug was aware of and was recruiting for? 'It's going to sound totally corny, but I mean I genuinely went for the people that I thought had the most to offer. I never ever thought that I needed to recruit fifty-fifty. It was always as it happened, the people that, at the right time, had the most to offer. It just happened, that they were jolly good, talented, clever, engaging, insightful, all those kind of things . . . Again the nature of the job was different from other styles of planning, which were very heavily dependent on qualitative research, and people actually getting out and doing the groups and all that kind of stuff. We deliberately separated those two things. So I didn't recruit qualitative researchers. I recruited people who I thought would be able to problem-solve and having done that take their case and carry it forward and be the engine for the business. They were guardians of the brand. They were taking a long-term perspective.'

Interviews were interesting partly because often the

candidates didn't know what planning was and had to be told and persuaded. And this meant that the interviewer had to judge the candidate on different criteria.

Leslie Butterfield remembers asking Stanley Pollitt whether this new planning function was a bit career limiting: 'I asked him if this planning thing is so special and unique to BMP, what happens if I want to move on at some point. Where do I go if nobody else is doing it? His answer was "There isn't anywhere else to go really. It's us or nobody."' Despite this discouraging reply Leslie took the job anyway.

Even in those days getting employed was by being interested and interesting. Terry Prue got his job offer by talking about guitar playing and Simon and Garfunkel.

When Paul Feldwick was head of planning at BMP he regularly interviewed potential planners. 'Whether it was the graduate level or the level above, the criteria was the same. It was primarily a case of "Did that feel like a really interesting conversation? Were we stimulating each other to be curious and to come up with something we hadn't thought of before?" It didn't feel like an interview. I never got much out of tell me what you've done, tell me how clever you are. It was more a case of find something they're interested in that I am interested in, and then let's talk about it. And if at the end of an hour you went, "That went quickly!" It was looking for like-minded people. That was about it really. The times I made mistakes was when I overruled that. By thinking they have too much experience and I have to pay them too much money, or they won't fit in, and stuff like that.' He looks back ruefully on some of the successful planners who slipped through his hands.

'One was Mary Stowe and the other was David O'Hanlon. My misjudgement in both cases was that I didn't pay enough attention to *them* and too much attention to their experience because David came from the accounts department and we were all a bit snotty about that at the time: "What do you know about planning? Get back to your ledger!"'

Leslie Butterfield had to build a department from scratch after he joined Abbott Mead Vickers – when Chris Powell came in to his office with a copy of MEAL (Media Expenditure Analysis) to persuade him to stay at BMP, since there was no listing yet for AMV, it was too small. Here is Leslie's criterion for finding a good planner. 'It hasn't changed at all: in a word, "detective". Somebody who has got a curiosity, enthusiasm, thirst for knowledge, almost a childlike inquisitiveness, pursuit, you know, those sort of characteristics. Some of the basics are great, the quantitative skills, the qualitative skills. But above all I'm looking for people who love brands and advertising. And in those days we were really fascinated by the kind of relationship that you can build with consumers through advertising and communication and brands. How advertising works, what triggers does it pull? That kind of deep human interest, inquisitive nature, scientific in the sense of a natural science model hypothesis testing. I like people who think in that way. So I'm looking for solid deductive thinkers. One of the great flaws in the planning world, I think, is the concept that ideas alone are enough, and there was – maybe you remember a breed of planner who were just kind of wacky thinkers, ideas people, and I've never seen that as being particularly admirable. Basically bright people of any discipline can have ideas. The skill for me lies in the ability to sift and sort and prioritise, and express ideas, and evaluate ideas, and put them in order, and then present them in a compelling way. Just having an idea is not enough. I want somebody who has got more focus than that.'

Turning to the issue of training, most of the planners we spoke to had simply learned on the job – they were mentored by senior planners for whom they worked and who checked the work they did. This raised issues for junior planners who were employed by agencies that wanted to buy in planning on the cheap. Who were they supposed to learn from? It's even problematic when a single planner is hired to 'do' planning for the agency. The planning function depends on dialogue and debate. And that's the best way for planners to learn.

Ev Jenkins had to learn fast by taking over Unilever accounts from Stephen King until the client started to call her instead. But she was careful to choose and use mentors. 'I learned from Jeremy [Bullmore] too. He and Stephen were very close. Their whole education was parallel, and Stephen was pretty creative and Jeremy was pretty thoughtful, so the two of them worked brilliantly well together. Doug as well, in a different kind of way. He was more practical in some respects. Then there was Catherine Butler. She was pretty scary. But when I got to know her, actually, picking her brains was really helpful. If you're not sure about something, if you don't know, unlike my blagging at Unilever, I thought it might be best to go and ask and admit I didn't know – but everybody's doors were always open so I could go to Catherine. She was always pretty good on quant. I'd go to Stephen if I had a dilemma, and to Doug, if I had a dilemma where I was stuck between two good choices.'

Clearly Ev was a self-starter who went to get the advice and support she needed. But the training was never particularly formalised. It was Ev who broke ranks and began running her own research groups – something that was disapproved of at J. Walter Thompson. She talks about how she got the confidence to do it: 'I'd watch Judie doing a group and think – okay, projective techniques that she was using and so forth. There were such a lot of people at JWT who were good at things, and wise and thoughtful, if you kept your eyes and ears open, you learnt so much and you were able to do more stuff.'

Christine Gray is more succinct: 'Sitting by Nellie' or being interrogated by Catherine Butler to teach her to think. There was also the requirement to write and rewrite documents so as to be able to communicate clearly and straightforwardly. 'It wasn't formal processes but sitting by Nellie learning to do it by doing and being supervised and monitored. It was much later that the toolkit came and people were actually taught how to do it in a formal environment. It was an apprenticeship which is probably the best way to learn: I do and I understand. There was an enormous pride in having disciplines that other agencies didn't have, recognised and using approaches that were more sophisticated.'

Jon Steel colourfully describes learning the job as being like a chimp watching to see how the others went about getting food from a termites' nest. 'I watched other people doing it and not only watched the way that they did their data analysis or their qualitative research, but the way they operated in meetings, the way they developed presentations, the way they delivered presentations, the way they followed up. And in being mentored by two or three different senior people, I was able to take the best of each of them.

'When I ran a department in San Francisco, that's how I tried to set it up, so that I mentored the first two or three people I hired, I then brought in another senior person and those two or three youngsters worked with both of us and then there was another senior person. I basically had a rule whereby each new trainee planner would work with three different planning directors. And I'd pick those planning directors carefully according to the skills that the individual needed. Some individuals were naturally brilliant researchers, or naturally fantastic in their creative abilities, but less good at some of the other stuff. And that sort of mentoring I think is imperative in a department, and you've got to do it on a consistent basis, you've got to train people in all the core skills, you've got to have a community whereby people share experiences – and it's got to be open enough that people can share their work and bounce things off others, and be quite confident about doing that and not feel threatened by it.'

Later on in their careers many of those we interviewed went on to train planners around the world. But it's interesting how they say much more about the talent of those they trained than specifically what they taught them. Detached from the day-to-day – the environment in which most of them were trained – the training courses they ran seemed to be about inculcating a culture of planning. And more than once these trainers commented that their agencies didn't know how to harness the talents of these young planners. This is something we will return to in the section about culture. What is perhaps also worth mentioning is how much they enjoyed doing this kind of work. Several described it as being a highlight of their careers. It would appear that part of being a planner is mentoring others and those who had the opportunity to do so found it deeply rewarding.

We turn next to running a planning department.

Managing the planning function

> *'Good planning has always been very well-rounded in terms of business skills – but it requires a commitment from an agency to having enough planners that planners can actually be involved in the business. In a lot of agencies today, they don't have enough planners and therefore they can only be involved on a very superficial level.'*
>
> Jon Steel

Managing the planning function was, at one level, simply one of matching the right planner to the account where they would do best. But increasingly the head of department would develop other concerns. In J. Walter Thompson it was more than recruiting enough planners and making sure you had matched the right planner to the right account. The question was how to capture, store and disseminate the wealth of experience that planners gained working on particular accounts.

A planning head needs to match the skills and strengths of each planner to what might be needed on a particular account in a particular situation. As we have seen there was a whole array of talents and temperaments which needed to be aligned with accounts which could be very different from one another.

Doug Richardson talks of planners as being a kind of thought police. 'The personalities of the people I brought into the department were a key element. It was quite fun watching someone come, you know, having been in a small goldfish bowl, throwing them in, knowing that they were tenacious and good at getting their own way and being persuasive and all that, as well, talking of missionary zeal.'

Leslie Butterfield talks about the way in which a planner built up a huge body of knowledge about the client. 'The whole model of using a planner on that business over a period of years was really very good, as you built this huge kind of database of personal knowledge about that client.'

John Madell talked about the depth of knowledge built up by a Jim Williams or a David Cowan. 'Today there's less . . . with the demise of the commission system because you can't afford to put that many people on a piece of business. And there may be something about recruitment criteria where you aren't getting scientists. Take Jim Williams, he was working on Smash at the time. He did some fantastic analysis and he knew more than some people at Cadbury about what their consumers were doing. David [Cowan] is one of the few people who knew the formula for what was the AGB gains/loss analysis which is probably why they don't let the data out in raw form any more. You would have to travel a long way today to find a planner who knows the formula for gains/loss analysis.'

But the sheer volume of information gained was too irresistible for people not to try to build up a data repository. One of the first was Doug Richardson. 'A key part of the planning role was how do you shape the future? And it seemed to me that at JWT in particular, we were in a unique position, because we had so many brands, consumer brands, that the body of case law that you could build up was such that you could begin to recognise and know what was possible, what wasn't possible, what was a priority and what wasn't a priority; to think more deeply about what the advertising was there to do and to get that sort of out and agreed – because quite often there were different expectations, of the client and the agency. So if the agency is plodding along thinking, "Oh well, we are all about justifying a premium price," and the client is thinking, that "I want my sales to go up this year," there is some kind of tension. So what I would do is spend time, not explicitly, but spend time with the planners just talking through with them, issues, problems, whatever it might be, or listening to their analysis and what they were thinking, and trying to input into that in some way.

'I brought in somebody from a business school who I hoped would actually help me do that, but I never managed it, so I suppose you know it existed in the minds of planners based in their own experience, and what had been said. There was a very good system that JWT had in place for really quite a long period of time – it was called a review board, one of the most hated things in the world, but what you had was, every year, the team presenting their planning for the year ahead. And I think that you could have examined the analysis and say: what about this, what about that? But I failed. I never got people to talk about their experience, and to distil that. You needed some sort of typology and all that, but after a while, most planners would tell you that they begin to recognise patterns and they begin to know what other people have done in similar sorts of situations, and what the effects were.'

David Baker was also a system builder with his total branding system, based less on advertising than on integrated communications. 'I pulled together the 12 best planners from J. Walter Thompson across the world, and together we wrote a whole new way of planning communications looking at the brand in total. All touchpoints and much more than that. We wrote software for doing it, an expert system for doing it, which was extremely well thought out, so thorough, it went right the way through every form of communications. It was based on taking the Planning Cycle that Stephen had done, and giving it a lot more depth and breadth in terms of communications and bringing the emphasis away from just advertising. It was called Thompson Total Branding. For a period of about five, six, seven years, this was used across the world as the way in which we were going to move ahead. And we had Total Branding awards. The agency took it very seriously and the first award ceremony took place on top of the Twin Towers in New York and the winners were given $25,000 which was a lot of money then. And it was done very seriously with a massive investment by the agency. The trouble was it was just too daunting; it would have worked for McKinsey's. It wouldn't have worked for JWT or for any agency in fact. You would need to have exceptional people with enough time.

'I over-engineered all of this, I accept that. Just a few tools that people could use as support to do a better job could have been more effective.' This contrasts with what Stephen King did with his Account Planner's Toolkit. To design a system so simple that anyone can use it.

We have already seen Jim Williams at Young & Rubicam build the Brand Asset Valuator – a database containing the performance of hundreds of global brands.

Ev, who went on to run the planning function at McCann for over a decade, is scathing about the size and scale of the head of planning's job. 'I think the role of head of account planning is totally redundant. I don't think any agency needs one, because what tends to happen is the number of planners just grows. I was part nanny, part therapist. I mean I had so many roles there. I still had my own accounts that I planned on – that was what kept me sane – but doing everything else is a bit stupid. I think that the best way to run planning in an agency is to have five or six really senior planners who know what they're doing and get them to employ their own juniors, and have the senior train the junior and so it goes on.'

John Bartle tells a charming story about when he left Cadbury Bournville in 1974 to set up a planning department at TBWA. Boase Massimi Pollitt threw him a leaving party which Stanley didn't attend. 'After six weeks, he rang me up and said,

"Come and have lunch with me!" And he sat there in the smoking room and he just said, "Right, how are you getting on? I bet you're finding these things difficult, aren't you?" And then he talked me through it. He said, "Just think about this, and just think about that." Way beyond anything to do with an agency. It was not quite parent–child but a teacher–pupil thing, it was brilliant. A very special man.' That mentoring role deployed so effectively on graduate trainees was apparently also hugely helpful in helping a new planning director find his feet.

A major role for planning heads is the creating of a culture within the departments and to support a culture friendly to planners in the rest of the agency. So it is to culture we now turn.

Creating culture or keeping departments inspired

'In America, we talk about a "waffle" of planners as a collective term . . . because you can guarantee if there's more than five planners, they'll stand on a street corner for at least half an hour deciding where to go, and then breaking off and talking about something else because they waffle. And that was Stanley. He never talked about anything trivial, he always talked about serious things, going round and round about something.'

Jane Newman

'What will happen in the places that survive long-term is much more breaking down of the silos which have grown between those departments. That was where a lot of the blockages and obstacles came in. And where you could transcend those barriers through personal relationships, that was when it worked because the barriers weren't good.' Paul Feldwick

It should be clear from all of the above that both Boase Massimi Pollitt and J. Walter Thompson created a sustainable planning culture. The function was exported and imitated widely. But creating the culture was more difficult. In the next 10 years, agency after agency set up planning departments. The fledgling planning departments would have had the same issues as Stanley Pollitt first reported. Researchers unwilling to be involved in the day-to-day making of advertising, or unwilling to make creative leaps before there was time or opportunity to gather all the evidence. Account handlers who felt that their strategic abilities had been overlooked, as planners took the responsibility for identifying the role for the advertising. Creatives who felt that "now there was a spanner [for which read planner] in the works", making advertising had become even more difficult. Planners needing a measure of protection that they didn't always get. Planning directors needed to ensure that the agency and ultimately clients valued the contributions of the new department. These growing pains were evident at J. Walter Thompson and BMP even with strong founders and strong sponsors in Jeremy Bullmore and John Webster. We start with the culture within the department itself.

Planning culture is both internal to the planning department and in the fragile ecosystems represented by agencies. Doug Richardson talked about having to protect his planners from anti-intellectualism. 'A key part of what I was there to do was to give the individual planners space and protect them. To help them grow.' Creatives who thought all you needed was a great idea saw planners as just getting in the way. So it took continual work to make sure that planners were a key part in any team.

The Thompson planners didn't feel protected from the ire of the creative department if the creatives didn't find briefing helpful or if the work did badly in research. Christine Gray tells a harrowing story of being punched by a creative director in the cab on the way to a research debrief for the Maureen Lipman BT campaign, because she wouldn't change the research findings to say the campaign had performed better than it had in research. 'On the way over he was saying you've got to rubbish this research and I said to him I can't rubbish the research. I was there. The clients were there. We all saw what happened. And he actually leaned across the art director and hit me. The minicab driver screeched to a halt and said to him shut up or get out. With the art director in the middle holding us apart. Fortunately because the commercials were made BT had to go ahead with them, And it's a wonderful example of research being destructive and unhelpful because it was an amazing campaign.' There's another account of the same creative director breaking up a meeting by marching down to the J. Walter Thompson basement and returning with a pick-axe handle. Agency cultures are fragile – and while much of the debate was adversarial, BMP and CDP are spoken of as peculiar democracies which worked for a long period of time, because whoever was able to make an effective case could win. At BMP this enabled juniors to challenge and override senior people.

Stephen King's way to keep the planners focused was through the laying down of tools such at the T-Plan and the Planning Cycle, which he didn't need to police personally, but the planning group heads could make sure were carried out. There was a commonality of understanding which meant that the same language was being used in the account groups with clients.

Because these processes were in place, the managing of people was with an altogether lighter touch. First from Lee Godden: 'Stephen was very accessible, he was in his office, the door was mostly open, or he'd come in. He used to come and see David and me a lot, but I think it was because David made him laugh. And I think we had a very jolly time. Because everybody else had their offices done so they had their backs to each other and David and I just had one great big long desk, all piled up with stuff.'

And this slightly less complimentary story from Christine Gray about being 'managed': 'They sent Tony Stead who was head of planning on a course for how to motivate your employees and for weeks afterwards you had to hide. He would go off for lunch and have far too much to drink and then cruise around the department trying to motivate his employees, and once he came into your office you could not get rid of him!'

Paul Feldwick warns against what he calls 'scapegoating' where planners take on pressures which aren't properly theirs but represent a problem for the entire agency. 'I know a lot of planners who have allowed themselves to be made deeply unhappy by taking on that sense of scapegoating as you say. And scapegoating goes on all the time in organisations. It's not very productive. These are questions about planning – there have been endless debates for 40 years about what should planners do, which planners endlessly introspect and agonise and beat themselves up about. I think almost all of this is a projection of questions that should be faced by the agency as a whole. Is it my problem or our collective problem? Do we really want to produce effective advertising? Or do we just want to win creative awards?'

One of the questions which our interviewees constantly came back to was whether planning was viable after the collapse of the commission system. When the gross margin fell from 15% of all media booked to separate percentages for creative origination and media planning; and then when the fee was unlinked from percentages all together, so that a major advertising account was only more profitable than a small account because more work needed to be done – then the role of the planner became commoditised and planners had to justify their work by the hour. Tricky, when thorough analysis of a market takes months, and when a brilliant idea can strike within seconds. To survive planners now work on so many accounts that they never learn any one market in sufficient depth to be able to plan on a piece of business effectively the way our interviewees were able to do.

Here we want to explore what it is that makes agency cultures supportive of planning – because not all are. We have already covered how people left J. Walter Thompson and Boase

Massimi Pollitt to start off the planning function in a new agency, only to discover how different and unreceptive the culture was.

Culture outside of the planning department depends in no small part on creative leadership which is why we have already cited Jeremy Bullmore and John Webster as being, at the very least, godparents of planning, but here we explore the wider factors in each agency, starting with J. Walter Thompson.

Thompsons was already known as the advertising university. Although Jeremy Bullmore comments that that reputation had been earned in the US, they were delighted that that nickname became associated with the London office. Once King and Bullmore were in management, often pitching as a double act, they came to embody the culture of the agency as intellectual and witty – whether acidic or self-deprecating – and this set the tone for the whole agency: how it was regarded by clients and by the rest of the advertising industry.

Thompsons had a strong account group structure which meant that there was continuity for creatives and planners. The whole agency team would meet weekly including the creative heads who were permanently assigned to an account. In fact part of the planner's role was to have the conversations and only to use the documentation of the T-Plan once the whole account group had agreed the direction they should go in before presenting to the client. This didn't mean that the account groups sat together but they did work together constantly.

As of 1961 the copywriters and art directors started working in the same offices. It wasn't just CDP who, in the same year, followed DDB New York and brought them together. This contrasted with J. Walter Thompson New York where the lady copywriters sat in cubicles waiting to be briefed, and the wearing of hats at the typewriter was mandatory in the J. Walter Thompson dress code! But through the 1960s the growth of television meant that art directors and writers worked together rather than being in different rooms or on different floors. There are mixed reports of how planners interacted with creatives. The safest thing is to say that it varied. Terry Prue tells of going for a beer with a creative team but they insisted on leaving through separate doors before reconvening round the corner in the pub. Jim Williams on the other hand, reports playing cricket with the creatives at Young & Rubicam. 'We socialised with them, which was what helped us to spark off each other in a relaxed kind of atmosphere.'

Before Boase Massimi Pollitt was founded there had been some experimenting at Pritchard Wood. The copywriter and art director sat with their producer and the account man. It turns out that a very young Frank Lowe – an account manager – found himself sharing an office with John Webster and Brian Mindell and their producer. Martin Boase sniffs that he always felt that Lowe spent all his time with John and Brian, enjoying the creative experience by infectious association. 'He should have spent more time looking after his clients rather than messing about with creatives. But he developed a great deal after leaving us.' A massive understatement as Lowe went on to become one of the great account men of his generation, able to coax brilliant work out of CDP creatives and sell it to nervous clients. Or as Geoff Howard-Spink put it more colourfully, 'playing Stalin to Colin Millward's Lenin', reforming the creative chaos at CDP and implementing systems that made the agency function rather better than it had before.

Lowe was not a democratiser. But Martin Boase was. In conversation Boase was keen to point out the significance of the first Goodge Street address where the fledgling BMP set up in an open-plan office – one of the first of its kind. The reason for the move to Bishop's Bridge Road a few years later was, in part, because it was possible to put the whole agency on a single floor. He recounts with satisfaction Peter Marsh's disdainful put-down of BMP as 'that democracy in Paddington.' 'I took that as an absolute compliment. I personally was very obsessed with the feeling of an equal voice for everybody and being un-hierarchical. I was neither a craftsman nor a major intellectual contributor, but I felt I had an important role in its promulgation.' Jeremy Bullmore warned us not to take Boase's diffidence at face value. 'Every successful agency has someone who epitomises it, and Martin epitomised BMP more than John Webster. He wasn't just putting brainy people together. He always pretended that he wasn't as brainy as these other people. He knew very much what he was up to. You could tell that by the way he picked people like Chris Powell and James Best. They were all interesting, clever people. None of them were stereotypical frontmen.'

These most successful agencies weren't successful because of planning. The deep secret is that there was a culture which valued thinking, which made space for creativity – and didn't expect creativity to emanate from just one department. These cultures didn't crumble after a few months. Nor did they last forever. Planning didn't create them. But planning flourished in the environment which they created and enabled the work that came out to be better as a result. One of the factors behind the success of account planning is that it is a certain way of thinking and working that successful agencies do anyway inside the planning department and out. The successful completion of a creative brief by a planner doesn't make great work intrinsically more likely – what is essential is the thinking, the creative leaps and persuasion.

'Descent from Olympus': starting up account planning elsewhere

> *'I suppose the key question is what influence you have on the output of your company. That output may be a commercial, it might be a complex econometric model – but the key thing is you have got to try and get inside the most important function of the company because then people look to you for help.'* Peter Jones

One of the most interesting aspects of the interviews was finding out what happened when they in turn went to other agencies to found the planning function. Many of them underestimated how difficult this was going to be – discovering too late that part of the success of the planning function at BMP and J. Walter Thompson had been the culture which protected planners from the consequences of bringing unwelcome news, and recognising that planning did make a contribution to helping clients to have the confidence to run more challenging advertising and to demonstrate its effectiveness. Planners did not have to prove themselves on a daily basis.

Jim Williams, before he went on to happier experiences at Young & Rubicam London, went through a difficult period as planning head at the BMP sister agency SJIP, which was, in contrast to BMP, dominated by account management. Creative standards were much lower, and he struggled – lacking the status he had enjoyed as a planner at BMP. He discovered that the creatives did not have the resilience to bounce back if the work did badly in research. Instead of challenging them to do better work, all too often he succeeded only in demotivating them. There was nothing left in the cupboard. He elected to switch to account handling where he found that he was able to make his accounts work better, and to be profitable. It is one direction planners have taken as they became more senior in an agency because they can do the planning work on an account without necessarily needing the job title. David Baker at J. Walter Thompson made a similar transition – so much so that at least one of the other interviewees who had worked with him when he was an account handler had not realised that Baker was already a highly experienced planner.

John Bruce recounts the difficult time he had leaving J. Walter Thompson and becoming an account director in a small agency, which became the CM partnership and was eventually acquired by Lintas. During this time he ran his accounts and did the planning on them at the same time. 'When I was working with those clients, I don't think I mentioned account planning. I just did it. I think it's something you just do rather than you are, and that's how it was and it worked. When it came to, let's say, backup skills, I knew lots of people in the market research field, so I had those contacts so I could go to this or that research agency. I could write a questionnaire easily enough and get that sorted. Then you would have to analyse the results and present them.' He was rueful about how much harder the work was than when he was at JWT, but justifies it by saying, 'When you're 35, you suddenly think you can rule the world.' Outside of the JWT environment where planning had all sorts of support systems, then planning and research was much more hand to mouth. His perception was that some agencies started their own planning departments but many just ignored it.

Leslie Butterfield is sure he improved the BMP planning model by improving the quality of preparation and brief writing at

Abbott Mead Vickers and then in his own agency, Butterfield Day Devito Hockney. He regards planning as a success because of the way it has become the norm at so many agencies and the skills are now embedded in marketing consultancies like Interbrand, where he was working when we interviewed him.

Ev Jenkins went on to run the planning department at McCann Erickson for a number of years. The instincts she had developed for the Oxo Family she now used on the Nescafé Gold Blend couple. A mix of brand values and being able to tap into the values driving the most current TV dramas – the idea of the soap opera where particular themes engaged the audience and they waited for the next episode. According to Jan Zajac, she even wrote at least one Gold Blend commercial herself. She was diffident about the need to lead and manage a department. At McCann she hired senior planners to do the job and to work in a self-contained way. 'The planners I hired knew it was going to be a nightmare job, they would be well paid so, yes, it was difficult. I ended up hiring people I already knew.' She talks about the discipline that planning gave her for working on large accounts. 'Planning put a structure on my thought processes and it made me more goal orientated. When I was working at McCanns we had so many accounts – being able to compartmentalise something, put it aside and get on to something else. It does actually impose a good discipline, I think.'

John Madell ran his own agency and then started a market research company. He sees research as borrowing a lot of the cleverness of planning. And planning has become weaker since it has lost a lot of the understanding about how research works and how to make the most of it. The difficulty with research is the descriptiveness of it. What senior clients want is problem-solving – and often their own research departments aren't oriented to solve business problems.

After BMP, John Siddall started his own research agency, Reflexions, with Chrissie Burns, one of the BMP qualitative researchers. He says he learned a lot more about planning from working directly with client businesses like Proctor & Gamble (P&G). 'When Reflexions was in business P&G was an important client of ours. We learned a whole other set of planning disciplines that would not be called account planning from what P&G did and it was how they operated. Elsewhere what the agencies were looking for was creative development research that would help them sell the advertising. The same as BMP, though BMP clothed it rather better.'

Paul Feldwick found himself sent around the world by DDB with the brief to persuade various agency owners whose agencies had been acquired by the network: 'I gave up trying to persuade them to take planning. It turned into a pointless debate about how can we persuade the client to pay for it. The clients don't know what it is, we don't know what it is. And I think that is where planning shoots itself in the foot. There are too many agencies in the States where people hang around saying I am the planner and people say we don't know what you do. The planner is desperate to impress. I am not even particularly interested in the idea of planning being a separate department. If you really understand what you are trying to do you will probably get there eventually, but the whole business is changing so much anyway, all I would try to talk about is this is how you go about creating effective advertising?'

Doug Richardson found he had his work cut out. Sent to New York to start planning at Ogilvy & Mather, he was pitted against a culture that believed Americans weren't interested in brands, they wanted to be sold to. 'Nobody in their right mind would have taken the job. I recognised at the beginning that I couldn't transform this overnight. What I did – and I knew I was only going to be there for 18 months, that was a deal I had made – I picked a handful of people out of the 85 in the department, who I knew I could turn into a virus that, after I had gone, would bring the whole thing down.'

Doug's strategy was to start with language: to claim that, in fact, brands started with audience response – and to say this wasn't a British idea: this principle was already known within US advertising. But it had been forgotten. He constantly talked up audience response and long-term brand effects to challenge the orthodoxy of selling. The breakthrough came like this. 'There was a wonderful Italian girl, called Nadia Regoni and she was second generation Italian from Chicago and she was the most buttoned-down yuppy that you could ever meet, and for the first two or three months I would challenge her: what do you think? But I would get a stock response. One day I was sitting in my wonderful corner office on Fifth Avenue with my feet on the desk and she wandered in, closed the door and said, "I have to tell you something: I'm not like that at all, in fact, I'm completely barking mad". At which point she did the splits. And the real Nadia felt confident enough to actually then start saying what she believed in, and what she felt and all that kind of stuff. She could begin to turn others. That was a key moment.'[55]

Jane Newman was summoned to an interview with Jay Chiat at such short notice that she swapped clothes with a colleague for the interview. 'Before he had even bought me a drink, he said, "When can you start? We need an account planner."' Jay had just returned from a trip to the UK where he visited CDP, and was convinced by David Clifford that account planning was the point of difference that allowed CDP's clients to buy

55 Nadia Regoni, now a freelance researcher, has confirmed the story with most of the details intact including the splits.

their extraordinary work. She tells the story of how she walked into a meeting room on her first day. 'It was the launch of the Apple Macintosh. This small room was plastered with print ads and headlines. There must have been a hundred of them and the floor another five hundred which they'd already rejected. And Jay went through that room, he took three ads out. One was "Why 1984 won't be like 1984". Another was "Why we'll never call our product an AKZ1010" or something. And another one was "Think of it as a Maserati for the mind". And I couldn't believe it. I was so appalled, all this wasted creative effort and time and we'd ended up with three ads. I could see immediately that what planning could do was help the creative team home in on an area and in fact within those three ads were the strategic thought, which was "friendly". In fact I think Steve Jobs talks about that in his book, how that became the strategy for Apple.'

Jane built up the planning department at Chiat/Day by hiring, as she saw it, planners smarter than herself. She ensured that all pitches had planning input and that all business the agency won had planning involved. And that just as at BMP, the creative ideas were researched. 'It was relentless, I constantly had to pitch planning within the agency. There were account people who just hated it because they thought it was cutting off half their brain. Some of them adapted and went with it, others resisted and eventually left the agency.' After a few years she moved to a start-up consultancy, Merkley Newman Harty, where the hours were more manageable.

Jon Steel grew his department at Goodby Silverstein in San Francisco 'firstly by hiring really smart kids straight out of school, or from their first jobs doing other things, and training them in the same way that BMP had done. And the other tactic was, if we won a big account, I would bring in a more senior, experienced planner. Although those more senior experienced people generally I hired from areas other than planning. I hired an account director and converted her to a planning job. I hired a very, very good qualitative researcher and converted her to planning. But of my early planning trainees, I hired a killer whale trainer from SeaWorld and a lawyer and somebody who'd been doing a job with a dance studio in Los Angeles, I think. They were all from very different backgrounds, but they were just sort of smart and interesting people. And I hired them for their human qualities and their potential as part of an ideas community, I suppose, before I hired them for specific planning characteristics.'

Jon Steel again, about adapting the way of working to American pragmatism: 'There were some aspects of BMP planning that I wanted to embrace, and there were other things that I wanted to experiment with because, not only was the agency culture different, but the surrounding culture, the American culture, the American business culture, was very different. BMP had this philosophy of "late but great", that it was okay if it was late if it *was* great. But American clients wouldn't stand for that at all.' And he goes on to describe how a client requires the agency to put the idea on TV the following Tuesday – which then happens. 'If I'd still been at BMP people would have been arguing about how they needed at least three months to think about it.'

Peter Jones took a different trajectory to all the others. He is far more business-minded than most planners. All the way through his career he ran businesses or worked in horse racing in parallel with his career in advertising agencies, which took him to being chairman of the Tote and a stint in New York on the global board of DDB – and including writing what he claims was the first ever book deploying the planner's mindset – reissued annually using hand-compiled data showing how to train a winning race horse![56] Within a few years of starting at BMP he was working on buyout and mergers, and what he principally remembers about the thousands of hours spent running discussion groups is how useful interviewing skills can be when transferred to the boardroom. 'I have found it is quite helpful to let people have their say. And then draw a conclusion from it rather than tell them what you want them to think. The traits of qualitative researcher are very useful at the board table.' He looks at planning and brand consulting as an owner and manager of businesses rather than from the inside.

What this cavalcade shows is that planning outside of the agencies that started it wasn't necessarily the same, but that the planners adapted what they did. They had to learn to work differently. And they more or less reinvented themselves when they had done so. There was never a simple, single template that they worked to. In different agencies, and in different parts of the world, planning would take on new and different forms.

56 *The Trainers Record*, Peter Jones, reissued annually from 1973.

The professionalisation of planning

'Planning became defined by the planners. It was what they were like, as opposed to a rigid way.'

John Bartle

In this chapter we have reviewed the things that the first planners did from day-to-day and also how their heads of department found, trained and motivated them. Even though planning, as we have seen, was different in the agencies where it began, there are still strong commonalities, which we've highlighted. It was inevitable that as account planning became established, and as other agencies set up planning departments, that what planners did and were supposed to do became standardised. However, what emerges here is very different from what followed with the demise of the commission system with what might be called 'professionalisation – the fitting of planning within a production process. It should be clear from much of what has been said, that the most effective planners resisted silo thinking and ensured that ideas and customer perspective were communicated right across the team.

It should also be clear from the skills we have outlined that account planners were evidence-based – and that required quantitative skills. They also needed to have good creative instincts and to be clear about how the advertising was expected to work. They needed to be able to demonstrate that the advertising was effective, but this did not stretch to accountability at any price. Measurement came at a cost.

Brand building was considered to be one of the main benefits of advertising, but branding became so prized that eventually it transcended advertising and a whole new raft of brand and management consultancies succeeded the first planners in providing branding advice. Surprisingly writing creative briefs was not central to the process – this came later. What was important was briefing the creatives so they were clear about the task that was being asked of them. New business was one of the areas where planning was able to win its spurs, and this was one of the ways in which agencies were able to persuade clients to sample planning when incumbent clients were not so sure. Research was part of the planners' powerbase, but they didn't follow it slavishly. Actually they could overlook it – not to make compromises, but because the research fell short of what real customers were doing and thinking.

Planners combined intellect with creativity but the most effective of them had formidable interpersonal and social skills, able to persuade and take others with them. Intellect on its own could be a handicap, creating resentment and even opposition.

In recruiting planners the new managers were never prescriptive, but looking for interesting people who would not take things at face value. Building a department was more than building a stable of planners with various skills and temperaments; but planning heads also worried about how the agency was managing knowledge as an agency resource. Culture also became an important preoccupation – it wasn't enough for planners to be right or protected, the agency environment had to accept discussion and argument. And many planners leaving J. Walter Thompson and BMP found that life in other agencies was much harder than they had anticipated and the cultures were often hostile to the factors that had allowed planners to flourish.

With the demise of the commission system planners found themselves having to justify their hours. They were expected to work on many more accounts. If this notionally increased productivity the disadvantage was that there was no longer time for the thinking and discussion which had made account planning such a game changer in the first place. And it was hard if not impossible to bill this thinking back to clients. So less a case of professionalising than industrialising the planning process. Doing, rather than thinking or challenging.

Chapter 5

Where does account planning go from here?

Is planning for life?

One of the idle but usually unanswered questions that flits across the mind of a young planner is: where do planners go? Do you find planners doing the same job until they retire? What do they get into next? Advertising continues to be a young person's business. None of the interviewees we spoke to were still employed full-time as planners in advertising agencies. But all of them were interested in what the planning role involves now. You can find out what became of our planning pioneers in the Appendix, where you'll find questions we put to all of them, one of which was: 'Do you ever stop being a planner even when you no longer do the job?'

Here we wanted to address the idea implicit in much of what they said: that planning is a very particular role that you play in an agency and that eventually you move away from it. It's not about youth per se. The first planning department at J. Walter Thompson wasn't full of young people. And many of the planners in the agencies we spoke to had, by the time they were in their 30s, gone off to head up a planning function in other agencies if not in their own – so were responsible for resourcing and developing the agency function rather than doing the job day-to-day.

Their strict definition of planning would be a role that gives you day-to-day responsibility for working on particular accounts in an advertising agency. You would be responsible for the strategy, the development of strong advertising ideas and showing how they have performed in the marketplace, using tools or templates that would ensure the thinking got done, whether by the planner or others in the team. Part of the contribution of a Stephen King was to make sure the thinking got done. Without having personally to check off every T-Plan or creative brief. Planning is a departmental function because of the range of types of business and the variety of personalities and skills which planners bring to the table. No one individual could expect to provide it all. This function was something that many of our interviewees described growing away from. Not all – some did largely the same job throughout their careers. But when they moved away from that pure understanding of planning they went and did something else.

We make this distinction because there is the spectre of the freelance or roving planner who isn't involved in a piece of business day-to-day. Or who may even function as a consultant who ducks in and out as a kind of problem fixer or occasional expert. Such roles focus on the contribution of the individual, rather than the utility to the agency which is buying it in and deploying it. That is also the flaw where very senior planners involve themselves in accounts once or twice a year, but otherwise keep their distance. In this, their role is not much different to the role of a board account director or creative director who by virtue of their experience and seniority will make a similar contribution to a senior planner. As planners gain experience their utility diminishes as they become more expensive and their expertise converges with the expertise of senior managers from other functions. It is when young, bright people employ their intellect, their creativity and their powers of persuasion to a piece of business that magic happens – at a much lower price point than in conventional management structures. And in this lies the power of account planning for agencies.

Planning doesn't belong to the individuals who are paid to do it, but to the agencies who are investing in it. As long as the thinking is being done it doesn't matter who is delivering it – in some ways the younger and brighter the gatekeepers, the better they provoke better thinking from the colleagues in their account group.

The broader planning skills mean that planners can expect to move into diverse areas in marketing whether client-side, or in research, product development, or in other roles where business problem-solving is prized. But the question mark is whether this is still the planning function or the application of planning skills to other business problems.

Here's John Madell talking about why he moved on. 'When I was at Euro, I interviewed a chap who came from Bombay. He said if you can't write a creative brief by the age of 28 you never will. But if you can by the age of 28 there's nowhere else to go. And that is absolutely true. That is why planning is the Michael Jackson of disciplines, it has always stayed young. It has not gone anywhere. I got fed up with planning. I got bored with it.' He goes on: 'What David Cowan is doing with Forensics is completely different to what he was doing at BMP. I now use consumer insights to develop growth strategies for start-ups. There are common elements shared with what I did as a planner but they have been built on.'

It was clear though that although they had moved on, these former planners shared a great affection for the function. It was more than an interesting job – it had given them opportunities they had never considered and they were still reaping the benefits.

What happened to planning from 1980?

Throughout the 1970s and into the 1980s planning blossomed across the London advertising agencies. Not only were BMP and JWT, in particular, conducting lots of research and consumer testing of advertising, they were still heavily involved in media recommendations to the client and in some cases even still creating the clients' marketing plans. And then there were still substantial departments to support planning: Judie Lannon's research unit, BMRB, and Tom Corlett's econometrics at JWT. And at BMP qualitative researchers as well as econometric modelling when Louise Cook was recruited to strengthen evaluation.

By this time, CDP had set up a planning department. However, the intention was to use planning not to understand, but to sell the work to clients. CDP started to acquire clients from mainstream sectors like Birds Eye, and clients were starting to ask questions about whether the creative would work, and how could they be sure? In contrast with BMP who developed one creative idea and iterated it until it was right, and JWT who developed variant ideas as the latest chip off the long-running campaign block, CDP insisted on presenting one agency-recommended route that the client could either buy, or not. And planning was needed to support that single option.

As the clients got bigger the agency needed business analysis. If they could get the client to buy into the overall strategy before seeing the creative work, then the debate would be about whether the work was on strategy or not. For CDP, the job of the advertising was to get the consumer to like the brand, not to understand a selling message.

Creative development research wasn't seen to be either useful or necessary because of the type of advertising that the agency wanted to produce. CDP wanted to engage consumers in the ads, which is partly why the agency sold longer spots making proper storytelling possible. But they also wanted to create unexpected, iconic creative work and saw no benefit in putting their original and imaginative advertising ideas in front of a consumer for a rational response. That was just a waste of time and money.

They were trying to find a way to connect with the consumer through identifying with them, rather than telling them a rational message about why the product was better than a competitor. Clients still wanted to do research, so any research that planning did ended up being more focused on understanding why people would or wouldn't buy the product, rather than whether the advertising would work.

Meanwhile the professionalisation of planning continued. In 1980 the IPA Effectiveness Awards were created under the chairmanship of Simon Broadbent. In the first decade JWT, CDP and BMP were prominent among award winners – all agencies with some kind of planning expertise. The Awards encouraged evaluation to become part of the brief and to put the accountability for evaluation more squarely with the planner. Whether for good or bad, over time, this encouraged a belief that if the advertising didn't work, it was the fault of the planner. It is acknowledged in many of the interviews that the planners at BMP were smarter than the account men (though not so at JWT), and the dedication to effectiveness and evaluation promoted by the IPA Awards increased the sense that when it came to accountability, it was the planner, not the whole agency, who should carry the can. Yet in other ways, external awards pulled BMP out of its introspection and relative isolation from other agencies, and encouraged it to become more aware of what other agencies were doing and how they were doing it.

When the Account Planning Group (APG) was founded in 1978, BMP hadn't been keen to join. Initially they boycotted it, believing that they had a competitive advantage not to be shared with others in the agency community. The APG had a two-fold objective: to promote the discipline of account planning within the advertising industry and related fields, and to raise the standards amongst those carrying out the planning role. Charles Channon was the first APG Chair whose expertise at JWT was in tracking studies and large-scale attitudinal research surveys. He was also one of the creators of the IPA Effectiveness Awards, becoming Convenor of Judges in 1984 and 1986.

In 1979 Stanley Pollitt died. He was 49 years old. In professionalising and drawing apart the discipline of planning, cross-agency collaboration and that feeling of 'planner as part of an account team' was under threat. John Bartle got very concerned at one stage that the APG, or any group that turned planning into an enclave, would become self-serving. Bartle spoke at the second APG event ever in 1978 and at a subsequent event gave his 'Planning Myopia' speech, warning planners not to isolate themselves: 'don't get up yourselves, this is all about collaboration'. And as this book shows, in its earliest form in both BMP and JWT, collaboration was at the heart of what planning was really about.

Throughout the 1980s, in direct contradiction to the professionalisation of the planning discipline in the industry, clients were starting to lose trust in agencies, and were taking research and insight in-house, creating their own teams of researchers and insight managers. And as the money men bought up agencies and consolidated them into large holding groups, planning seemed to be one area where they could cut back. The 15% commission system was disappearing and it became unclear how planners could charge for their time. Meanwhile smaller independent agencies were starting up which had a planning ethos, not just a planning department, the launch of BBH in 1982 being of most note. These start-ups were named after their founders – with account planners replacing media directors on the headers.

With media departments being spun off into separate, often independent, companies and agencies under pressure from clients with additional insight and research resources themselves, agencies moved into a more and more executional world. The well-respected and renowned agencies of the 1960s and 1970s – the agencies who enjoyed relationships with the CEOs and chairmen of multinational corporations – became diminished, as pressure built on those company CEOs to deliver shareholder value, and management theory gained hold. Agencies lost a lot of that strategic ground as the management consultancies moved in. Markets had become more and more competitive since the 70s and that was putting businesses under pressure to cut costs: if they couldn't grow the market then they would have to become more efficient. Management consultancies were happy to advise on new product development, how to reduce costs in the supply chain, and who or what to acquire to broaden their market.

But one of the aspects of the job that planners had been doing within ad agencies was working out, using market data, how a client could either maintain a price level, or indeed justify a price increase. John Madell speaks enthusiastically of how he got interested in shareholder value and retail models that sell 80 per cent on promotion, and pricing strategies too. He points out 'agencies and clients just want to sell more product. The whole role of advertising stems out of identifying what the business objective is, but that has got lost along the line.' Increasingly, big businesses and their boards were not visiting ad agencies for advice, but using management consultancies who were independent of execution and, supposedly, objective in their advice. Business strategy started to drift away from the agencies.

As a counter-trend, independent branding agencies started to sprout up, like The Value Engineers and Added Value. Independent research agencies also grew in number. All of them seemed to be exploiting some of the gaps that had opened up in strategic consultancy. Peter Dart set up Added Value to do just that. 'We basically drummed it into clients, of which Unilever was one, that in order to even begin to brief for advertising, you had to understand – really understand, based on insight – what your brand DNA was.' Of course that needed research, from which these consultancies made a pretty penny.

Later on, clients started to realise that they needed their own proprietary model that expressed *their* brand DNA, and each one produced their own version internally, without the aid of the ad agencies. Even later, in the 1990s, the likes of Unilever and others created their own processes for creating and judging advertising and communications. Coca Cola has its CCI, Johnson & Johnson has its IMP, and Unilever has its ABC model. Peter Dart again: 'The ABC process, Advanced Brand Communications, which CEO Niall Fitzgerald introduced around the world, was a three-line whip, and basically every brand manager in Unilever had to use this system.' Not only did clients have to have a 'brand key' signed off internally before speaking with the ad agency about a potential brief, they also had to have completed a brand key of where they wanted to be in five years time, 'defining where you are today, where you want to get to, what's the process, what things do we need to change.' It sounds just like Stephen King's Planning

Cycle. And it is. Except it now existed in the domain of the client, not the ad agency.

Back at the big agencies, planning went global. And the networks which had offices sprouting up all over the map tried to redefine and codify their strategic planning processes, launching toolkits and training programmes across the agency and geographically diverse agency offices where planning also now existed. David Baker spent much of his time at JWT trying to move the agency from an advertising agency model to a communications agency model, recognising (as he would, being a media man) that media was exploding and there were multiple consumer touchpoints for engagement. In the 1980s at JWT, he launched 'Total Branding' designed 'to retain that level of brand custodianship and trust with clients . . . because in this century even though communications have changed so much, brands haven't fundamentally.'

'Total Branding' was an interesting description because it reflects what was going on culturally: namely, that communications were becoming more and more fragmented, involving more and more agencies, and even sometimes more and more clients. Marketing directors were now dealing with one agency for advertising, one agency for PR, another for the direct mail and customer relationship marketing, and soon, one for website and online . . . it went on and on. As Stephen King had always stated: '[A Brand] . . . has to be a coherent totality, not a lot of bits. The physical product, the pack and all the elements of communication – name, style, advertising, pricing, promotions, and so on – must be blended into a single brand personality.'

But brands were in danger (and perhaps still are) of disintegrating, bits starting to be represented and executed by different agencies, everyone becoming responsible for different parts. No matter how much analysis an ad agency planner did, it became increasingly difficult to do synthesis.

This is brought to life by Roderick White who tells about the call he received from JWT New York asking for help on the Kodak pitch in 1982. They had so much research data they didn't know what to do with it. In fact the client had had two or three different research agencies working to the same brief who had all analysed the results differently. Roderick managed to make the Southeast Asia research, the Latin American research and the Middle East research comparable, and only then started thinking about how to address the issue. They won that pitch.

It feels like the planning role, especially on the global stage, had become that of re-integrating data and insights from several locations and synthesising it to reach an overall understanding: planners as brand integrators.

Roderick's view is that New York never embraced planning with the same enthusiasm as London. The exception was at Chiat Day where it first took hold. We have already told the story of how Jane Newman was asked by Jay Chiat to start planning at Chiat Day. It was 1982 and he had recently returned from London and was in awe of CDP. He loved the work and the only thing that seemed different was planning, though 'he never knew what account planning was really,' says Jane. She took him up on the offer but not before writing a letter before she started, stating all the things the agency needed to practise in order for her to be hired: one of which was that the planners had to be part of the team and work closely with the creative department.

So she joined and says 'every other agency in the United States was floundering doing bad work, and here's Chiat who's winning every new business pitch, has clients that are totally loyal and happy and is doing brilliant work, every time out of the box. It was planning that drove that. So it was just a no brainer for America and Chiat Day's clients lapped it up, we hired as many planners as we could and then other agencies started following . . .'

Whilst Jane definitely was the first planner in America and received a lot of kudos for being so, she also credits the planners she hired. M.T. Rainey was hired for the Apple account: 'M.T. Rainey was hired to work on Apple, and she was very much a part of that "1984" TV commercial, working with Lee Clow who totally accepted planning, like John Webster had, because he could see it would help him do better creative work, not just by eliminating strategies which is one way, but also by giving him insight.'

Jane was incredibly successful exporting planning to the US, more successful than Doug Richardson later on. He moved to Ogilvy in New York, attempting to recreate the body of knowledge that had existed at J. Walter Thompson, but found that the culture was not nearly as receptive. He recounts gleefully what happened when Ogilvy's rule-based culture encountered a room full of ads. They gathered to discuss what makes a good and effective magazine ad: 'they'd done a deal with Gallup, where they had all the reading and rating scores of the top 20 and the bottom 20 ads, and they put all the top ones on one wall and the rubbish ones on another, and then they got all the creative directors in and said: "What is in them, get some laws out of this, we are going to look at these ads and see what made them work." And the first question I asked them was which of these two walls is the top 20. And I think out of the nine people there, seven picked the wrong wall – at which point we went home.'

It was a culture shock for a Brit planner. Doug again: 'You relied entirely for the decision-making on quantitative research and, you know, putting four ideas into research and doing day-after recall and all that kind of stuff, and it was an unbelievable process that squeezed anything out of it. The idea of brand in America didn't exist. It really didn't exist. And if you engaged people in conversation, they'd say, "Well no, Americans don't like brands they want to be sold to" . . . you invest hugely in getting the best product, you have phenomenal merchandising operation, then you demonstrate this super product, why wouldn't they buy it? And the emotional dimensions just didn't exist and so to try and persuade people that there was such thing as a "brand" was a major task.'

The States just seemed more set on a rational approach to advertising: planning as risk avoidance. So the British style of planning has never really taken off en masse, though James Best points out that we exported a lot of good planners to Goodby Silverstein. Advertising is not about emotional brand building in the US, it's about sales, and planners always struggled against the powerful account barons within the big agencies. Whereas in Europe and in Latin America planners struggled against the cult of the creative director. As if a throwback to Empire, planning did blossom in India, Australia and South Africa, suggesting that planning is a cultural rather than process-driven event.

Some time after having returned to London, Doug Richardson started to work with Tim Bell. In around 1987, they were at the top table of client corporations like the BBC, discussing and advising on communications strategy. Doug tried to persuade them that you should apply the same rules of advertising to the BBC – to think about what your core message is, and actually begin to use communications across a broad range of activities to engage and persuade people not just to inform them. A key part of the recommendations they made to the BBC was that they had totally screwed up their own branding with sub-brands and brand descriptors all over the place aimed at different audiences, and that the future strategy had to be about creating 'one BBC' and to use their own airwaves to run commercials. And they did.

Traditionally it would have been the ad agencies delivering that kind of expert advice, but now brand communications was in the hands of 'reputational' agencies in PR, branding, and design. Clients were multiplying relationships with different sorts of agencies – to design their packaging, their point-of-sale, their sales promotions. The national census had been linked to the postcode system allowing a marketer the ability to develop profiles down to 15 houses in a street. And lifestyle databases made it possible to target customers by mind-set and leisure interest. Marketers realised that their customer lists could be turned into customer databases and that CRM programmes could deliver sales more cost-effectively than using advertising to find new customers – loyalty programmes and loyalty card schemes began to pop up everywhere. Direct marketing programmes followed to recruit new customers, especially in financial services. Clients began to develop customer-related content, first through magazine publishing and then through mailing programmes. And the arrival of the internet as an effectively free communications channel, turned clients into media owners in their own right with branded content strategies. All of these developments required strategic thinkers as well as doers to stick the whole together. So planners multiplied across the expanding agency scene and inside client organisations as well.

As communications became even more fragmented, disregarding new kinds of media in favour of just TV and print felt more and more of an anomaly. Several new ad agencies sprang up to challenge the traditional model of the broadcast message. One of note was HHCL. Years before, CDP had wanted to engage the audience rather than tell them a message, and now HHCL wanted to go a step further, and encourage consumers to interact with the ads. Says Adam Lury, ex-BMP planner and HHCL founder: 'I wanted people who wanted to make really progressive advertising and to challenge the assumptions of BMP and the advertising industry as a whole. I'm a great fan of Madonna, she always used to say she wanted to fuck with people's minds. Advertising is a tool, it's got to have an impact to provoke, to disturb, to engage. It's engaging people, it's getting a response.'

In 1989 HHCL launched the telephone bank First Direct with a TV campaign, which aired two versions of the same ad simultaneously on each of the only two commercial TV stations the UK had. Charlotte Rampling appeared to tell viewers about the launch of a new bank which had no branches but would have people answering the phone. If you think that's a good idea, she said, stay on this channel. If you think it's a bad idea, switch channels now. In one you have a woman in a pink suit leaping about with a phone, and in the other a man in a blue suit saying this is a disaster. Only the former featured a phone number to call. It was an example of a new kind of agency – one that had spotted interactivity coming down the line and, in many ways, it is the ad that is the precursor to what would become everyday reality with digital communications.

'I used to talk about interactivity as the genie. When it's out it changes everything. But of course, that went right to the heart of what people in conventional advertising thought they were doing: controlling everything. Making these little mini sitcom or Hollywood films. They were fully in control of the message and the content. And you were allowed to be entertained or amused but you weren't allowed a voice in it,' explains Lury.

This kind of approach to a broader advertising canvas went beyond a lead-medium mindset and treated the whole world as media. And it was not long before the internet made everyone see the world as an interactive space, and advertising became just one of the many dots to join up amongst numerous digital dots that now make up our world. If anything, the challenge for this decade, and probably the next, is how to deal with *over*-communication.

Adam Lury had been an account man, as had Paul Feldwick – albeit by his own admission a hopeless one. And many of the planners from these years opted to switch into account management afterwards: John Bruce, Jim Williams and Jane Newman to name but a few. Dave Trott opines: 'The best planners were account men before they were planners and the best account men were media before account men.' This reminds us once again of the importance of cross-agency, cross-discipline, cross-media collaboration, and to treat planning not as a process, or a silo, but as a mindset which is held by all of us – about why you are doing what you are doing, and what evidence there is that suggests it will work. Perhaps the last word here goes to Geoff Howard-Spink, ex-BMP and agency founder with Frank Lowe: 'I can't stand the idea of planning as a cult, planning is a safe pair of hands to get things done.' Let's call it what it is.

The challengers: how the original models were challenged and changed

A surprising number of the planners we interviewed had stayed loyal to the agencies that had hired them, in some cases spending their entire careers there. They had also, therefore, stayed loyal to the founding planning philosophies of their agencies. But in this section we will focus on those who moved between the agencies, who have an outsider's perspective because they were able to compare the different planning styles between the two founding agencies. Or they decided to significantly change the model they had inherited.

Here is the list: Tony Mortemore, who worked at Pritchard Wood, then J. Walter Thompson and then CDP. John Siddall worked at J. Walter Thompson, then moved to CDP and then BMP. Jan Zajac, who began at BMP moved through CDP and then later went to J. Walter Thompson. Jack Krelle, who started at J. Walter Thompson and moved to CDP.

We have also incorporated feedback from a number of those who started planning departments or founded agencies and modified the model of planning they had been taught. Leslie Butterfield moved from BMP to establish a planning department at the Abbott Mead Vickers start-up before founding his own agency, Butterfield Day Devito Hockney. John Bartle started a planning department at TBWA before founding Bartle Bogle Hegarty. Geoff Howard-Spink became head of planning when he founded Lowe Howard-Spink. Adam Lury started up his own agency, Howell Henry Chaldecott Lury. We also have feedback from Dave Trott who left BMP to found Gold Greenlees Trott and took Barry Pritchard with him as planning director. All of these have clear ideas about how planning should be exercised and all were close enough to see first-hand how the BMP model of planning developed.

All of these are in some way critical of the agencies in which planning began. Movements need aficionados and disciples to perpetuate themselves. But we can learn much from the heretics. Doug Richardson even goes so far as to call planners the *thought police*, enforcing the philosophy of the agency.

Two of our interviewee challengers told us that CDP ought to be considered as an agency which used planning thinking, but did so in a way that was distinctive from BMP and J. Walter Thompson – and even superior. The stature of CDP's reputation as perhaps the British agency which produced a higher proportion of great advertising than any other, means that this claim does need further investigation.[57] Particularly as CDP was not known to be a planning agency.

Let's start with J. Walter Thompson, which Tony Mortemore describes as an agency devoted to service and which – via its aristocratic account supervisors – presented creative ideas to clients and whisked off the table anything which didn't suit them. Both Tony Mortemore and John Siddall describe themselves as grammar-school boys who were dazzled by the glamour and polish of the agency. But the other J. Walter Thompson planners came from similar backgrounds and don't mention this. The 1960s and 1970s were a time of social mobility when bright children could get into the top universities, or find their way into high status jobs without having to produce the right social credentials. The planning department at J. Walter Thompson was left-wing compared with the rest of the agency. Christine Gray tells of an exchange with Miles Cole-

57 Turn to our postscript where we resolve this question of whether CDP was a third pioneer of account planning.

brook who was managing director at the time. 'Planning at Thompsons was always regarded as the pinko lefty department. Miles Colebrook used to call it *brown bread corner*. We went to a seminar once and they served up a kind of fruit compote pudding, and Miles said "Ugh! account planners' breakfast." It did have that kind of reputation, although the only socialists I recall were me and Ev.'

Tony Mortemore describes what was an increasing impatience with the emphasis on process at J. Walter Thompson. Even in the early 1970s he didn't perceive much debate within the planning department about how advertising worked. It was a thoroughly intellectual environment. Speakers such as Edward de Bono and John Schlesinger would be invited in to address the department. But there wasn't a great deal of talking about planning. After all Stephen King had laid the principles down. 'My belief in planning was my belief in advertising. Advertising was just part of service. JWT was about service, doing everything nicely and beautifully, the notion of a great strategy, the T-Plan and how do we use Karl Popper? We were all told how to do it and we all did it. It was nothing to do with the dirtiness of advertising.' Which is why he found CDP such a revelation where there was constant discussion about how a piece of advertising worked in which anybody could participate. Not just the creative department as you might have thought with CDP.

He found the focus on process tiresome. Charles Channon, who years later was to run the IPA Effectiveness Awards, was brought in from the research agency BMRB to run creative services. 'Everything would have to go through Charles and his team. It was like quality control. So the planners wrote the briefs. Charles wasn't a planner. He was part of the creative department. You were within much more of a structure and you would have meetings with them but you would never relax. It was very formal. The creatives didn't present their work back to us. You were there. There would be a meeting but then everyone was there, so no small chats between the creatives and the planners.'

He began to resent the way clients were allowed to turn perfectly good work down without objection. 'It really was so genteel and gentlemanly. You did not argue with clients if they didn't like something. You said we will go away and think about that and come back with something else. CDP would argue.'

Jan Zajac remembers the sheer stability of the place. 'It was a different world. One of the guys had been working there for 17 years, which impressed me. To me that was mind boggling. People were working until retirement, which struck me too. It was a proper organisation. It tried to be as fair and as well-run as Unilever. You had a career and got stars at levels of success. Each star you got, the income and benefits changed. Very organised, very big. I worked on Kellogg's which was worth £25 million, which was bigger than the whole of TBWA at the time. But it comes with a price so if Kellogg's say, "Do this," you jump. You do it.'

He says bluntly that at JWT creativity wasn't the primary objective. 'JWT in its heyday built Andrex and Mr Kipling, not just as ads but institutions – so for them if they had a great creative person they probably didn't nurture them that much. And if they were good, they'd go off and get more money elsewhere. So it was almost an accident that JWT had any good creatives at all, because it wasn't seen as the be-all and end-all – the important thing was to get the marketing right. Ads like Kellogg's Cornflakes, where you've got the whole brand encapsulated in one commercial.'

Once he had been at J. Walter Thompson a while, John Siddall's deference evaporated. 'There were a whole set of drongos in the department, people who basically were not very good.' It was partly the pressure set up by the idea that the planning department was the intellectual hub of the agency.

Jan Zajac adds, 'Not all of the planners were that bright, maybe articulate, but not always thinkers. Quite a few of the account directors weren't going to give up that role and didn't like the idea that planning had relegated them to bag carrier status.'

Moving from JWT to CDP, Tony Mortemore was relieved by the plain speaking of a Geoff Howard-Spink or a Frank Lowe, who, if they didn't like what you were wearing, said so. 'It was great. It was like talking to real people. It was a class thing. You were dealing with ordinary people who were doing great work and enjoying themselves.' But what was touted as plain-speaking was an agency run along autocratic lines. If you want to make the best creative work then somebody has to impose testing standards, and ultimately one or two people have to make the key decisions. In the Postscript we give more reasons why we don't think that CDP represented a third, better school of planning, but in a nutshell it was because planning was put at the service of the creative product to the extent that a planner might be asked to rewrite a strategy to post-rationalise a great ad. That would have been anathema at J. Walter Thompson and BMP.

Turning to BMP, the Achilles' heel was the cycle of advertising development, which in theory could revolve endlessly until they found the right/best ad. John Siddall came to BMP after working at J. Walter Thompson and CDP. He says that the reliance on research results corrupted the planners so they simply reported what group respondents said. They didn't have to think. 'They used research far more literally, or they bent it under pressure from the creative department. They went around the creative research roundabout until you got a positive answer. Eventually the research would come right. You didn't have to, but there was an impatience within the agency and sometimes within the client, so yes, you could do another round of research and Chris Powell would say "That's the great strength of the agency: it's warts and all". But actually it wasn't like that. There came a point when you were under so much pressure to say "This is great", particularly if John Webster and Graham Collis had done it. I don't know what other people did. There was no sharing. I never knew what the others did.' Here is another difference from J. Walter Thompson that, once the planners were trained, there wasn't much reason for them meeting. They exercised the planning function within their account groups but knew little about what else was going on.

Dave Trott felt that the group discussions were being carried out with the wrong people, the majority being opinion followers. So Gold Greenlees Trott ex-BMP planner, Barry Pritchard would again set out to test the creative ideas with opinion formers – in a radical way. The video recorder was set up in the back of a van and driven round a series of pubs. Barry would stick his head round the door of the pub and observe who was leading the conversations in the pub. These he would pay cash to, to jump in the back of the van and view the concepts. This maverick strategy was used to develop the Holsten Pils campaign which required opinion formers to like it and talk about it. 'And suddenly all the work I was doing at BMP that was hitting the dirt, began to run at GGT, because instead of researching among opinion followers we were talking to opinion formers.' Research was being used as an aid to decision-making rather than some quasi-objective scientific process.

Leslie Butterfield thought he could do better. When he was given the chance to start a planning department at the start-up Abbott Mead Vickers, he was only 27. So he wrote down a list of the core principles he had learned at BMP as non-negotiables if he was going to join. The priority for him was saving time and wasting less creative resource by sharpening the briefing process. 'I really believe that the process at BMP did become wasteful. We went through the hoops too many times. That's not a big criticism because they were a first-class agency. I wanted to get the brief more right earlier, and then be more efficient with the creative development. I also figured that working with someone like David Abbott, I couldn't just use his kind of work as fodder in the way that creative sometimes got used at BMP. There were many tensions at BMP around that.' If the work had failed in research too often, then the planner and the original brief were put into the firing line. 'I thought this was something that I could address at Abbott Mead and we did address it. It worked very well.' When he started his own agency BDDH, he says that Derek Day wanted a much more rigorous process of briefing to get the right proposition, but more importantly the right support for the proposition.

At TBWA, John Bartle wanted to strike more of a balance between his experience of BMP planning as a marketing services manager at Cadbury and his perceptions of how planning was being done at J. Walter Thompson. So when he started the TBWA planning department, he didn't let his planners do their own groups. And he assigned planners to multiple accounts, not trying to keep the one-to-one ratio of one planner to every account person as there had been at BMP.

Geoff Howard-Spink has worked at an account handler at BMP and also at CDP where he came to be known as Frank Lowe's 'brain.' He takes a pragmatic view of planning as a spare pair of hands. What irritates him is the cult of planning. 'There was somehow or another this quasi-religious thing about it. And I always felt that that was just up itself. It's a business, you know. You could sense the whole thing of there is an account planning group, there are the account planning awards. Account handlers never felt any need to have an account handling group, or account handling awards. And that's in a way my hybrid: I suppose emotionally or philosophically, I was an account handler, the tools I used to do the job were planning tools.'

John Bartle recounts the story of when BBH won a string of Account Planning Group awards and how planning director Nick Kendall sent the awards back when he found that only the planner's name was inscribed upon them. 'I was completely against that, because I thought the whole thing is about collaboration. I got very concerned about the Account Planning Group becoming self-serving.'

Perhaps the most trenchant criticism comes from Adam Lury who worked as a planner at BMP through the 1980s. He was always unclear as to what the legacy of Stanley Pollitt actually was, besides a few bucolic stories. What were Stanley's planning principles? Nobody could tell him. The endless ferrying of creative work backwards and forwards had become worthy as if holding up the mirror to the consumer was sufficient. 'There were planners who would do 32 groups on a regional beer brand and they would write a 200 page qualitative research report. I couldn't make head or tail of that. I thought this is stupid. The level of thinking in the 200 page report wasn't a different way of looking at things. This was respect for the consumer which was basically holding up a mirror to them.'

What Lury points to is the fetishising of intellectualism. Martin Boase claimed in one year two per cent of all the graduates in the UK applied for a job at BMP. And that the equivalent of a board director's salary was spent by BMP each year, to identify and train the best graduate trainees. 'Most people in advertising around that time had a deeply internalised sense of shame. What George Orwell calls the "rattling of the stick in the swill bucket of capitalism". The notion was that they were doing something that wasn't very respectable, with minimal social value, and it was exploitative. But rather than deal with it they had just internalised it. And they found a whole lot of ways of expiating that. One option saying that's what is great about entertaining people making them laugh – the ads are the best thing on the telly. That allowed you to get out of asking that question. That was the positive side. On the negative side you didn't ask the big questions about what was really going on in advertising.'

Just as creatives fetishise creativity, so that no one else in the agency dares to call themselves creative, and organise regular and lavish ceremonies to hand awards to one another to compensate for the constant rejection of their work from day to day, so planners take refuge in the mechanics of creating advertising strategy. And the ultimate failure is that they connive to perpetuate legacy models of advertising which are about entertaining people. 'Advertising has missed the boat. It doesn't get what it's about. It is in thrall to creativity. And it thinks that creativity is about producing a clever idea that is invariably expressed in a 30-second film or a full-page press ad. And if you think like that the people who "come up with those ideas" are the most gifted and talented and special people in the industry, then you can never progress. You're not thinking.' Lury's argument is that, in stark opposition to the conventional model of reinforcing existing consumer experience, communications need – as Madonna memorably claimed – 'to fuck with people's minds'; to create social change with disruptive communications to particular audiences with their active participation.

Where to now?

In this section we have highlighted five questions that present themselves in planning today. Of course account planning is in transition – but when wasn't it? Perhaps if we look back, we can learn something from the past. We can revisit some of those principles that made planning the success it was in the later twentieth century, and use them to help define what planning should be in the future.

Talent: nature and nurture?

The first planners seemed to have had quite a lot of time: time to do things, to see people, to go for lunch, to discuss and debate and to hire and train other planners. Even at the very beginning – when both the JWT and BMP planning departments were only just emerging, and people often didn't even understand quite what a planner did – it was important to hire the right kind of people, those who could be moulded into planners and could themselves mould the culture of the agency to be one that valued thinking.

And 'the right kind of people' did not seem to mean just that they had the right skills, they also had to have the right kind of personality. Relevant skills were of course, required; but it was more a question of whether the person one was hiring was both interesting and interested in understanding other people. Ev Jenkins, for example, spent a lot of face-to-face time with consumers, doing her own research. She was getting under the skin of people's needs and motivations and hopes and fears by spending a lot of time in direct conversation with them – you needed people like that who could create rapport. Jim Williams and Leslie Butterfield, on the other hand, were doing AGB gains/loss analyses, which allowed them to know more about how consumers were behaving than most people at Cadbury – you also needed people like that who could get deep into the data and do the sums by hand.

Contrary to the myths surrounding the first planning hires in the UK, they were not all Oxbridge grads. Tony Mortemore didn't even go to university and reminisces: 'J. Walter Thompson was my substitute university.' Yes, the agencies wanted to hire the smartest people, but they didn't want academics, they wanted thinkers who could also just do things: do numbers, do analysis, do empathy. They were hiring people who wanted to not only understand how things in the world worked, but also how they could make them work better. In this sense, their blueprint for a planner is closer to that of the engineer.

That is probably not surprising given the type of person who was available on the job market around the late 1960s, early 1970s and the broader context of the space race, televised moon landings, and the development of a supersonic airliner. After the war, there were many talented physicists who were streaming out into the world or teaching others to do so in academia. And a generation of talented and ambitious 'engineers' were available to work in any problem-solving capacity in the commercial world. In some sense, that's what Stephen King and Stanley Pollitt were recruiting: problem-solvers. That being the case, potential planners weren't hired for their creativity but for their inventiveness in finding creative solutions to brand and business problems.

As Tony Brignull is quoted as saying: 'If you don't solve the creative problem for me, it's still here on the tip of my pen. I can't write because it's still there. I'm not being difficult, you need to get it away otherwise it will still be there. Your job is to get away the problem from the tip of my pen.' That's a great ad in itself, demonstrating the role of a planner.

Terry Prue explains: 'There was a sense in the early days that it was an important vocation . . . it was very much that this was about understanding marketing and understanding the real returns of advertising and the real consumer motivations behind it.'

We've found that there was little formal training but a lot of coaching and mentoring. Often younger planners were paired with more senior planners or worked closely with market research people. The training came from reading, understanding and involving oneself with consumer data and media data, on the job. In the main, one learnt along the way.

The most important skill to learn in the position of apprentice was, of course, how to deal with creative people: how to interpret insights and give feedback. Leslie Butterfield recalls: 'It had to be interpretative and constructive and helpful . . . the skill of managing expectations, de-briefing, explaining complex things to creative people who didn't necessarily think the same way you did.'

Butterfield goes on to explain that when he recruited for Interbrand, he still looked for the core skills that BMP were looking for when they recruited him all those years ago: 'Things like having a detective mentality, being inquisitive, knowing a breadth of craft skills in research and so on, but also a set of human skills over and above that, that are frankly innate rather than taught, which are to do with inquisitiveness.'

Perhaps not surprising then that by the mid-seventies at J. Walter Thompson, planners were arriving having done other things before. Ev Jenkins recalls that the planners were a very mixed bunch from different backgrounds with different ways of looking at the world, which made things more interesting if you wanted another point of view. Everyone had done something else beforehand. There was even an ex-vicar.

In addition to the apprenticeship nature of on the job training, there did seem to be an informal mentoring culture. Catherine Butler of J. Walter Thompson is mentioned by more than one of our interviewees as being an on-hand point of inspiration, whose brains other planners would regularly pick. Described by one interviewee as 'an Oxford bluestocking of formidable intellect', she wasn't allowed in front of clients because she could be so withering to them. Planners loved her but she had no rapport with the creative teams.

At J. Walter Thompson there were also market research experts. John Siddall told us that if he was planning research he would regularly seek out Tony Stead or Judie Lannon, pointing again to the fact that there was a lot of informal sharing and mentoring that went on outside of more formal departmental meetings.

But the main thing we learnt throughout all of our interviews was just how important 'conversation' was in making sure you were solving the right problem in a way that wasn't wrong. Planning was seen as a people business: people talking with people about other people. Jack Krelle goes so far as to ask: 'If, in the 1970s we all had time for lunch five times a week and still produced great ads, what are you doing wrong now?' Lunch of course, was a great facilitator of discussion and a time for problem-solving as a team. These days, it is spent in isolation with nothing but a Pret a Manger sandwich between the planner and their unfinished PowerPoint slides.

Planning enjoyed a kind of stature that came from the ability of the planners to articulate, argue and evidence their recommendations. And that, in turn, became honed through the discursive nature of the job. It again reminds us just how important 'conversation' was in terms of learning how to think things through properly. These conversations could be with colleagues over lunch, or with consumers in research, or with clients during both. But all the time, these conversations would be informing the planner with new insights, whilst at the same time, being used to test a communications hypothesis.

It's all a long way from how planners spend their time today. So much of that is about preparing presentation materials. If planners are not being chased by account handling to create a PowerPoint presentation, they are helping the client continually modify their own internal PowerPoint presentations. The very format of a 'presentation' sets up the whole idea of planning as a 'ta dah, here's the answer' bit of the process. And what the first-generation planners actually show us is how much of the great planning that was done, actually resided in the to-ing and fro-ing and talking through of ideas whilst testing them.

This suggests planning to be a much more iterative, collaborative, generative thing that it has turned out to be today. We think that what we have learned is that planning at its best is more symposium than system. Chat is seen as superfluous these days unless you can call it 'a meeting' and there is much less value placed on intellectual discussion in advertising today than then.

In general, one is left with the impression that the first-generation of planning was first and foremost about *people*: analysing them, understanding them, conversing with them, persuading them and just being surrounded by them. Somehow over time, planning has become more of a process. It has become more formal, perhaps more professional, certainly more prescribed. When Lee Godden completed her career as a planner, she moved into the HR department. Can anyone imagine a planner these days moving from an agency planning department into the agency's HR function? Today, we tend to think of the two as very separate, but 50 years ago, it was just about people; people who were interested in other people.

How can planners, or your own planning department if you lead one, encourage more conversation without it costing the agency time and money? How can lunch discussions become part of agency life once more, and how can the entire agency be encouraged to join in the problem-setting and the problem-solving, so that everyone's a planner, in that everyone is encouraged to think? Thinking and discussing, rather than writing and presenting, not only bonds an agency together, it unearths latent planning skills amongst those in the agency who aren't officially called planners.

Where to focus: upstream or downstream?

One trend that has been exerting pressure on planning – bending it out of shape from its original purpose – is that of a growing anti-intellectualism in the industry. At some point in the recent history of advertising, it became cool to be anti-intellectual. Ironically, what a lot of client businesses are now calling for is a lot more intellectual rigour, applied to their problem-solving. But intellectual rigour requires a bit of time and space to do more in-depth work and no one seems to have an appetite for anything but immediacy. So many clients and agency teams just want a short-term sound bite that will get them through the next quarter . . . or even just the next meeting.

And the explosion of social media and the courtship between it and TV, has meant that more of the focus has shifted away from effectiveness and towards engagement, or to put it another way: claiming that your advertising has had an effect on consumer engagement rather than consumer purchase seems to be enough. That of course is reflective in this era's need to be 'liked' above all else – whether one is a celebrity, a social media user, or a brand.

The problem is, vanity metrics on social media have, in part, become the proxy for a consumer's fiscal relationship with a brand – and there really is little appetite for wanting to understand what makes a person value one thing over another, to the extent that they will part with their hard-earned cash for it. It takes no time at all to share a You Tube clip on a social platform, but you would have to think twice if it cost money to do so. Engagement is easy to track and to measure, commercial effectiveness less so.

The first-generation planners' quest was really about just that: *how* does a specific piece of communication influence someone to do something even though it will cost them money. Not how does a specific piece of communication get a like on Facebook. *Encouraging likeability* would have been a small subset of what they were doing. And this distinction itself is not theoretical, because it is at the heart of how planning needs to evolve into the future. The first-generation of planners were working much more upstream, linking their communications solutions to clients' specific business problems, and creating long-term campaignability for brands. As Jan Zajac said: 'It was expected that any ad that came out of J. Walter Thompson would be an expression of the brand.' And in understanding exactly 'how' the communication was influencing a branded purchase, they could optimise that communication to positively affect that business. These days, many planners are working much more downstream, on wildly differing ad campaigns for the same brand, in different markets, creating something new every single year. Planners involved in that are, in the main, providing inspiration for the creative teams or post-rationalising the creative choices inherent in the communications strategies, rather than anticipating future effects or proving the business effects of past activity.

One might argue that the IPA Effectiveness Awards address this and showcase the very best and that rigorous planning around the commercial effects of communications still goes on. It does still go on, of course. But it is now treated as an add-on (something someone attempts to do every two years for the Awards) rather than the everyday 'business as usual' on an account. Paul Feldwick notes that about the time he was asked to be the IPA Effectiveness Awards Convenor of Judges, he was also becoming head of department at BMP, and he had many good people in the department who were always on the effectiveness case: Nigel Jones, Sarah Carter, and Louise Cook – who also hired in Les Binet and trained him. 'We had all the resources and were very dedicated to it,' he states.

Much of the difficulty in ongoing effectiveness understanding is driven by the ownership of the data. Increasingly it is the media agency or the client who has access to the data, not the creative agency, and often they will not willingly share it – making a creative agency planner's job virtually impossible.

But it is also a generational approach; junior planners often describe themselves as 'creative strategists' as if the creative product is somehow distinct from the commercial entity on whose behalf it is produced. But as with everything, it comes down to the structural decision to split media and creative agencies and is a legacy of that sad day. When ad agencies lost the 15% commission there was no slush fund to pay for planners to spend time on the 'thinking' bit of advertising. These days agencies think it is better to ensure that the production definitely happens no matter what the actual effect later on, because it is the only area where revenue can now be generated. Minimal money and minimal time are allocated to spend on working out 'how' a communication really works. Imagine if 15% of your client's media spend was once again focused on that task, how different would today's planning role be?

Many of the planners we interviewed talked about the importance of consumer research, particularly at BMP, where it was an inherent part of what planning was – a continual conversation with consumers about creative ideas. How odd it must seem to that generation to hear that it is very often the client inviting the agency planner to the groups – groups that the client has initiated, procured a researcher for, recruited respondents to . . . and all to discuss work *created* by the agency. It's an odd state of affairs, but once the client has their own insight department, market intelligence team, and head of research, of course the planners' role refocuses on the only thing they can now be seen to influence, the production.

One wonders how anyone can expect planners to influence communications' effectiveness these days, given their lack of access to the purchasing data, analytics or other quantitative consumer research. One of us posed a question on the subject to renowned marketer Byron Sharp, who has inherited the mantle of that great thinker Andrew Ehrenberg.[58] He responded with the tweet: 'I know of no pretest that has performed adequately in predicting sales performance of ads. Serious R&D needed.' In other words, more in-depth planning please.

58 We have already referenced Byron Sharp's book articulating Ehrenberg's thinking, *How brands grow*, OUP (2010).

Creative briefs: experimentation versus effectiveness

Any discussion about the role of effectiveness brings us to the brief. It is something that planners now seem to be bothered about all the time. What should it ask for? How many boxes should it have? Should there be a separate brand brief and task-based brief? Do we really need a proposition? Interestingly, the brief and its format, was something that the first-generation planners almost never talked about, and it certainly didn't seem to bother them at all.

What they said to us about the brief was largely very consistent across agency, account and individual planner, and it was that the creative brief didn't really matter as long as there had been constructive conversation: it was the *briefing*, not the brief, that held meaning.

There were of course templates like the T-Plan, but it wasn't necessarily prescriptive, rather a guide to help one's thinking. At J. Walter Thompson, the point of a creative brief was to capture the conversation about how the communications would contribute to the campaignability of the brand. It would include all kinds of marketing communications from packaging to vehicle livery.

Though it is fair to say that at Thompson's, there was more of a process. At one point, Charles Channon, who was head of creative services, would receive all of the briefs. Planners would write the briefs and they went to Charles, as part of a quality control system. That still happens at JWT today. The creatives didn't present their work back to planners, though planners were in attendance. There would be a formal, structured meeting in place of small informal chats between planners and creatives. One gets the impression from our interviewees that these were pretty angst-ridden.

At BMP, the creative brief would try to capture the way in which the creative execution would connect with the consumer. It was not a prescribed template and the reason for that was that it was not intended to be restrictive: box-filling encouraged inanity. For such a rigorous culture, the informality of the brief seems odd, but again it was a way of encouraging planners to think for themselves, to set up the problem in its own right. And it wasn't as if the overall model of how advertising works was not understood across the agency. Leslie Butterfield has his own take on this: 'It was a kind of "cuddle up to you" model of how advertising works and I think we always thought that advertising was something that could win people over through affection, through charm, through nudging, through cuddling . . . put your arm around the consumer, entertain them, involve them, engage them, persuade them, but do it gently, do it with charm, do it with panache, not a bang over the head. That was our model of how advertising was.'

One thing that our interviewees highlighted is the extent to which advertising is really about reinforcement, not recruitment.

We would venture to suggest that these agency planners understood this to be the case much more so than planners today. It's a difficult truth to handle because, whilst it suggests that advertising is not the automatic communications choice for launching something brand new, we know that the new business treadmill is dependent upon new emerging markets, supporting new brands with new product news. And further we know that clients have become increasingly expectant that the solution is always something new. When one airs a TV commercial today, everyone involved expects an immediate sales effect. And if that sales effect isn't seen in the eight weeks of rolling data that immediately follows, 99 times out of 100 the client will express their desire to can the advertising and start again with a 'different strategy'.

Over time briefs have become more focused on inspiring 'the idea' than the strategic job of defining 'the role' that advertising (or communications) should be playing in reaching the objectives that may have been set. This is a fundamental shift, because what it means is that the main reason now for planning to even exist in an agency, is to inspire the creative development process.

We saw that whilst that was important in the early days of BMP planning in particular, it was not the significant factor that made planning a success. What made planning such a success was the ability of planners to clearly and truthfully define the role for the advertising. Having done this, the creative teams and beyond were very clear about *how* their creative solution would appeal to their target consumer. Only then, did someone put pen to paper and write a brief. The power of the work which came out of the earliest departments, comes from the planners trying to find both creative ideas *and* advertising roles which were different, and which stood out or gave the brand disproportionate leverage. For that they didn't think that briefs were particularly important.

Our research also showed that JWT's T-Plan was really about targeting – and was designed to define customer response to the brand: it was not about what you put in, but about what a consumer took out. Perhaps this was not so surprising given how important the media department was in birthing account planning at Thompsons. A creative brief then, just wasn't a creative brief in the way we would think of it today.

*

Some of the creative briefs we uncovered throughout our interviews revealed the variety of approach. So much freedom did planners have in the early days that, as we have mentioned, Jack Krelle did a cartoon brief for Cornflakes that consisted of two cereal bowls, one containing a pair of slippers to depict Weetabix, the other containing an alarm clock to depict the wake-up call of Cornflakes.

James Best commented on how the introduction of a new creative briefing format became the easiest way for a new planning director to make their mark. With no appreciable improvement in the thinking or the quality of briefing.

We venture to suggest that whatever brief was used in the past, the intention was for it to be a contract about expected output. Today the brief seems more of a contract about the expected input.

And to make that point about the output even more forcefully, the planners' involvement did not end when the creative concept was approved. Planners would play an important role in the pre-production. Peter Dart, Thompson's then Unilever client, characterises the pre-production process with the planners present: 'We argued over every phrase, every line. You would have a session just to do the wardrobe. You'd have one session where you would choose the shirt, for instance, or what the mum would be wearing. What would be just the right colour, what sort of kitchen would it be? You would get into every single aspect of it. And no shortcuts like there are today, obviously.'

Krelle suggests that that sense of purpose around an execution never really leaves you and, rather tellingly, he describes the planners' role in directing execution as, 'you say, I think its look and feel is much more like this, rather than that; you can find words to talk about moods.'

There was a time when the planner, with their objectivity about the brand and insight about consumers, would not only brief the creative team but the media planners too. These days, the client tends to brief both the creative agency planner and media planner: another symbol of where the power and upstream objective-setting remit sits today – with the clients not the agencies. Perhaps the answer for today's planners is to follow a career on the client-side, rather than within the agency, if they want to do more business strategy and brand development per se.

Consumers: humanity versus technology

What was of paramount importance to both J. Walter Thompson and BMP was to understand consumer 'response'. And whilst J. Walter Thompson and BMP did not have a standard brief template for quite some time, they had a way of thinking about advertising that put 'response' at the heart of the communications.

As we've seen, BMP worked very hard at trying to understand what responses their creative concepts would generate, spending inordinate amounts of time with consumers in qualitative research.

And JWT in particular codified the 'response' approach. In Stephen King's 1987 version of the 'Advertising Planning Methods Manual', he writes on the need to set target responses: 'Views about responses underlie JWT's whole approach to advertising. Our belief is that it makes sense to plan all aspects of advertising from the point of view of the consumer, rather than the advertiser or the agency. That is, we should think not about what advertisements do to people, but about how people use and respond to advertisements. This viewpoint applies to the role for advertising, media selection, research and creative strategy. So we brief creative people not in terms of what we think they should put into their campaigns, but as what we would like the target group to get out of them – what we want people to think or do as a result of the advertising.'

And what is worthy of note is that, according to King and JWT, there were three possible types of response: rational, emotional and sensory.

In the 39-page, 1969 brief for Mr Kipling cakes, there were nine target responses set out as objectives for the creative strategy. These were:

> From the senses, we want people to go through a regular sequence of:
>
> i) top and outside of the cake – a home-made cake, uneven appearance
> ii) the cut piece of cake – light and moist texture
> iii) superb taste
>
> From the reason, we want people to believe:
>
> i) that these cakes are made by a specialist cake firm
> ii) that they are made by traditional methods to modern standards
> iii) that they contain good quality ingredients and the right total recipe, not just one 'magic ingredient' (like butter)
>
> From the emotions, we want people to feel:
>
> i) the nature of the brand: warm, friendly, personal, conscientious
> ii) the basic appeal: adult self-indulgence, a treat rather than a food
> iii) associations: all people who prefer high quality and traditional standards, in a modern setting.

The sensory aspect of response disappeared over time, and the convention became that a brand just needed to create a rational response (thinking) and an emotional response (feeling). Big FMCG brands built their brand-building models around this, and almost all of the literature presents brand management along this lines.

Perhaps it is time to revisit and reclaim the 'sensory' response, because in the world of service brands and brand experiences, sensory responses are the most important of all.

Take Apple as an example. The launch of iPhone was almost single-mindedly about the sensory response that the brand engendered in the consumer, so much so that the ads became aesthetically stylish product demonstrations that had people literally sensing the intuitive nature of the interface. Much of Apple communications' distinctiveness comes from the ability to create a sensory response, the Apple Store being the best example of this: carefully designed and orchestrated to create a sensory response – offsetting the thought that it all seems a little expensive.

The idea of a sensory response has come of age in the digital world. Where products and services are striving to become seamless, intuitive, instinctual, and immersive – the experiences they aim to deliver are sensory-first. We suggest it is high time for agency planners then to reclaim the dimension of a sensory response, alongside that of the rational and emotional, and begin once again to treat it as an important part of the brief.

The very idea of response connects the creative message with the media moment. And once the media agencies and creative agencies became separate entities, it made arriving at the right response and delivering it, that much harder for communications planners. That problem was not something that existed for the first generation of planners because media and creative were completely integrated within the same agency. Time and again those planners alluded to how imperative it was that creative and media were one and the same in the solution. But planners today have a much harder time connecting the two.

Connect them they must, though. The growth of social media and the need to produce 'branded content' has brought media and creative closer together again (albeit housed in separate buildings with separate planners). But the willingness to try to create advertising that is 'contextual', 'native' or 'earned' in media, shows that agencies are embracing the reintegration of the media and creative solution (if not the reintegration of the planning functions). It brings us a different kind of tension though and poses the question: what is it that planning should aim for – unlocking a deep-rooted universal human need, or uncovering a specific audience insight? Should we start with the brand and its role and meaning in people's lives, or should we start with a specific audience and find out what they are into? What should a planner focus on, in the hope of driving the best response – humanity or technology?

Whilst the answer is both, it isn't clear that one planner can do all of it. Can any individual planner, working across a portfolio of accounts or brands, really spend their time gaining deep human understanding through ethnography, or global surveys and trends forecasting – whilst at the same time analysing the user experiences of websites, mobile platforms, shopper marketing exit surveys, social media ecosystems and (if you're really lucky) till receipt data?

The first planners at JWT and BMP planned media schedules as well as the creative – these were actually technologically driven using the technology they had at the time (although the media landscape was a lot simpler compared to now). However, they still had a model of customer response that was qualitative. The dashboard didn't then, and should never really, take over. As planners we must always avoid the danger of limiting our understanding and explanation of human behaviour to personas, algorithms and reports. After all, that view of consumers as two-dimensional beings churned out from consumer surveys in the US, was what UK account planning was originally set up to challenge.

In a live twitter debate hosted by the IPA Strategy Group in July 2014, Tom White of AMV BBDO announced that his agency had found a new type of planner. He said: 'The most significant planning contribution to Doritos' social strategy wasn't an insight, a message, a media deployment or a creative brief. It was a person. A resource. A new type of planner. We call her Naomi. She's a fast turnaround, 24/7, always-on-call planner . . . We brought together social community management and planning – and "Naomi" was the result. Like any good planner she has a proper understanding of what's going to help her brand's business – so she knows that posting brand content and interacting with fans at times when our fan base would be attending gatherings or parties is particularly effective. But *unlike* a traditional planner, Naomi sits at the centre of a new organisational structure which means she has 24/7 access to Mac operators who can knock up any image request in a matter of minutes. She is plugged in to the planning team at AMV, has a hotline to the client in order to get fast approval and of course is connected to over 700,000 Doritos social media fans.'

This is admirable and the Doritos campaign was an industry-awarded success, but is Naomi really a new kind of planner? She sits at the heart of the organisational structure, yet her role is to pump out content in real-time. That is a very valuable service to a brand, but is it really 'planning'? This is the downside of putting too much store in having media drive the creative content, although presumably AMV would argue that the activity Naomi carried out, had positive effects on Doritos' sales. Perhaps this is the new face of 'response': real-time response, and we can add that to the list of types of response required from our communications – so that the list of considerations now reads: rational response, emotional response, sensory response, and real-time response. Our first-generation planners would have probably simply called that direct response.

What it demonstrates, though, is a real shift away from what we would call 'strategic planning' towards a new opportunistic, fleeting, tactical kind of planning that sits much more downstream. At the 2014 APG Conference on 'Big Thinking', Ben Malbon of Google, drew a distinction between 'Deliberate Planning' and 'Emergent Planning'. The latter has as its focus the audiences, technologies, interests of consumers, seen through a more tactical, newsworthy, opportunistic lens. It's the scrappy, messy, social, real-time planning one does when one is in a continual state of feedback and optimisation. And whilst there is no doubt that digital has transformed planning into a discipline that is more agile and adaptive than ever, the art of the long view (or 'Deliberate Planning') is afforded little credence or status today.

The first generation planners weren't looking for newspaper headlines and social media conversation about the content of their advertising, they were using advertising content to get people to buy one branded product over another. Yes they wanted to drive word of mouth too, but in addition to, not instead of, purchase. Times have changed and as a result the quest for, and communication of, universal human insights, seems to make up less and less of the planners role today – whilst more and more of their time is focused on delivering a momentarily engaging piece of entertainment. That's really Naomi's role. Let's just hope she has a twin, Nadia, who can concentrate on the other stuff.

What is planning for: consultancy or culture?

All of which brings us to the nub of the issue that the discipline is facing today, within advertising agencies at least, the burning question is: what is planning for?

Clients no longer need an extension to their marketing departments as they once did; they have insights teams, researchers, creative studios and increasingly their own planners. They procure the services of management consultants, qualitative researchers and media practitioners directly – it is no longer the role of the planner to pull the integrated strategy together, that now largely falls to the client.

So what are planners now for? We've seen just how important it was in the early days to create a culture of thinking and analysing, of understanding and expressing 'how' advertising influenced consumers. It was never the case that account men and creatives weren't already doing that, but it was the case that not everyone in the agency environment could do that. And planning became a kind of social engineering that encouraged a thinking, analysing, understanding, expressive environment for *everyone* in the agency. Of course not all planners knew what each other was working on exactly, but the conversational style, the iterative nature of creative development, the respect for data insights across the agency – created the possibility of cultural change that put the consumer, not the creative, at the heart of advertising. Both planning as consultancy and planning as culture are valid roles – and one can understand the shift, given that the latter can arguably only be sustained by the 15% commission system. As more and more agency work becomes project-based, freelancers now perpetuate the feeling that planning is the provision of consultancy rather than the establishment of a more enduring and directional culture.

When a planning department does work collaboratively and sees its role as having a cultural objective as described, it takes on a real importance within the agency that goes beyond individual accounts or individual briefs – it becomes the thing that keeps everything working well together across the agency, because satisfying the consumer, not internal politicking, is the mission. It becomes the compass for the agency, navigating the agency through uncertainties with a clear executable objective in sight.

However, increasingly what we have seen over the last 10–15 years is the rise of the consultant planner. Some planners attach themselves so closely to a client or account that they have no time or interest in investing in the social engineering aspects of a planning department. The agency then often has as its goal, not the long-term building of brands and strengthening of consumer relationships, but Cannes Lions and other awards glorifying specific creative executions, as if creative rather than a means to a commercial end, is the end in itself.

Who can blame them when they no longer have quite the standing with clients as they once did? As Peter Jones explains: 'An ultimate business understanding is very important. The client has got to have confidence in your judgement and the agency's judgement, which in the heyday at BMP, was a virtual total trust between the parties.' The problem comes when agencies stop taking the wider marketing tools into account. He continues: 'When I joined advertising we used to write the marketing plans and basically the clients looked entirely to the agency for their marketing thinking. By the time I left BMP, the clients had four or five different agencies and played tunes on those agencies, and the advertising agency was somewhat dismissive of the other ideas and just couldn't converse effectively with the marketing director any longer . . . they didn't understand the orchestra, they played their tune on their instrument.'

And it is very difficult in that multifaceted, multi-media, multi-agency world, to set yourself up as the goal-setter and course corrector for a brand, when there are other ways to achieve business results than through advertising alone. As Peter Dart puts it: 'There's so much tactical stuff and immediacy . . . and all these different agencies . . . and there is no one brand-centric person that holds all of it together the way it used to happen . . . you had that one guru, that Lee Godden person, who would be the conscience of the brand.'

And so things have come full circle. We are in a world in which the good brand managers and marketing directors have come into their own again, where they become disproportionately important to the brand's success. And the result of that, the authors feel, is that we are witnessing the disintegration of true planning as it was in the last third of the twentieth century.

Planning for the future

Planning today is being hit hard by two new circumstances: firstly, the trend for planners to become increasingly frustrated with the limitations that are imposed on their role by the agency in its quest to keep that important client happy; and secondly, the growing number of other companies and industries now searching for planners. These two trends together, present the planner with the choice of staying in an ad agency – where their analysis and ideation will be muted by account handlers desperate to chug along a familiar road – or leave and learn a host of new and intimidating skills in new industries where algorithms and big data are respected and admired. The limitations come mainly from the anti-intellectualism that now pervades agencies and the lack of willingness of agencies to really think originally. In the main, agencies provide their clients with familiarity, and it is now the neologistic 'innovation agencies' – fuelled by new technologies and data capture – that are really creating ground-breaking communications, new product development, new distribution strategies, and creating new business models with their clients. As a consequence they are more connected to the business effects of what they do, than advertising agencies can ever really hope to be.

Of course, there is an alternative perspective. And that is that digital was so disruptive to the advertising industry that we are back to square one. John Bartle takes up the point: 'Everything splintered. So we're back to square one – well before square one – nobody knows how anything works. So, if you're going into the industry now and you're 20 years old, you probably know more than anybody who's your boss, about how things work – you've got every chance to invent something and that's brilliant.'

But even then, there's one very important thing missing: fun. So many of the interviews for this study were full of humour, stories and events that were set over a liquid lunch, or just told with relish as those recounting incidents clearly did so with a sense of enjoyment at the time. After all, if advertising is supposed to be entertaining and the response we want from consumers is that they enjoy it, how can that spirit emerge from an industry, or a team, that is being crushed under the weight of so much procurement, client promiscuity and pressure? Jane Newman, when asked what she would like to ask the new generation of planners, said: 'Do you enjoy it, or is it just a means to an end? My feeling is that people are so weighted down by stuff that it is difficult to enjoy yourself.'

Perhaps part of the responsibility for that lack of fun lies with planners themselves though. Maybe they, and the agency, expect too much of them as individuals in 2016. And maybe it is time to redistribute the responsibility for planning to the rest of the agency too, rather than have it siloed in a department called 'planning' and become the preserve of only those with the title 'planner'. Maybe the way back for planning (in terms of gravitas and enjoyment) is to make planning an agency-wide priority as it once was in BMP and JWT at the time of its inception. John Bartle again: 'It's not about account planners. It's about planning disciplines and rigour, particularly in the strategic thinking. In BBH account planning runs through that agency in every piece of business, but you don't know who made the contribution? Who did the account planning? The pursuit of ownership is very dangerous.' We agree wholeheartedly and would like to see planning regain its sense of community, collaboration and the conversational style prevalent during the early days, when planning was an agency mindset more than a department.

Jeremy Bullmore captures the spirit: 'The big mistake was to assume that no planning was happening before planning . . . As Stephen used to say it was an attempt to organise what we did at our best anyway, to see that we did it more often. Because the best advertising has always been concerned with how people respond to it rather than what you shout at them. So look at the introduction of planning as undramatic, as a codification of what we did best anyway, so that more people could do it and do it more often.'

What we are witnessing today is the success of planning (or strategy as many industries outside advertising refer to it) as we encourage more people than ever to do planning, whether inside or outside of the ad agency walls. In effect, planning has outgrown the industry that gave birth to it. It means that what we see is a very bright, optimistic future for planning – not just planners – as it reaches beyond the boundaries of advertising, the industry to which it owes its origins. We think the planning pioneers should indeed be proud.

Appendix

In the original interviews we asked standard questions of the planners:

- What was your career high point?
- What do you wish you had done differently?
- Is digital and social marketing a whole new game or more of the same?
- What advice would you give to a young planner on their first day?
- What questions would you ask today's planners?
- Do you ever stop being a planner?
- What did you do next?
- Who was the best planner you ever worked with, and why?

What was your career high point?

For Paul Feldwick it was being asked to chair the IPA Effectiveness Awards and step into the rather large shoes of Simon Broadbent and Charles Channon.

For David Cowan it was the fateful decision to go into advertising and then to leap across to the start-up BMP, away from the safety of JWT.

For Christine Gray it was the day she realised she was a half-decent planner. JWT lost a pitch for the New Zealand Lamb account but the agency, Pritchard Wood, who retained the business tried to poach her on the recommendation of the client.

For Jan Zajac it was getting the job at BMP: 'I didn't realise what a lucky break that was.'

John Madell couldn't pick one: 'The thing about BMP was that we were arguably the best agency in London, if not in the world, and we knew it. So there was immense confidence and esprit de corps so we had, at that moment, a lot. I was terribly lucky to be there at that time.'

For Leslie Butterfield it was working on a campaign for HIV and convincing the client that it wasn't about AIDS but about HIV and controlling the spread of the disease. The agency lost the pitch but the idea – that it was about the size of friendship groups and the perceived risk – was kept and shaped the way the Health Education Authority approached the issue. So he was asked to make a presentation to the World Health Organisation that changed the way people thought about tackling the disease. 'I remember thinking that was an amazing transformation from one thing to something else entirely. So that was a moment I was particularly proud of, because it was a big issue.'

Peter Jones hesitates because he has done so many different things. 'I describe myself as a creative person in the fact that I have done a lot of different jobs. I sold quite a few different products including the "Group 6" bet; and my original analysis of horse trainers which became a yardstick in the horse racing world. And in some senses advertising seems quite narrow. But I was involved in the very embryonic stages of the Courage pitch for John Smith's bitter, which was originally pitched as Barnsley Bitter. But they closed the Barnsley brewery as soon as we had had the presentation. But – although the credit for taking it on goes to John McKnight and James Best who were the people who took it to market – my embryonic thinking was the need for Courage to have a northern beer but Courage thought that was a bad idea. That was one of the more pieces of more original analytical work that was done, based on lots of hard data and soft data done in Yorkshire, and other parts of the country.'

David Baker can't choose either. 'There's a few ads that I would put in my pile. There's a few advertising IPA Effectiveness Awards that I helped other people do that I can be quite proud of. I quite enjoyed parts of NatWest when I ran that. The trouble is I've worked on lots and lots.'

Ev Jenkins: 'I remember working quite early on with Stephen, on a pitch with St Ivel Gold and talking to him and then seeing it manifest itself in something that then just shot off. That kind of kicked it off for me, the kind of new awareness. You feel a bit privileged to be talking to, or listening to, people like Stephen King and Jeremy and Doug and the penny drops, and the early experiences were more attitude changing in terms of what to look for. You know there's got to be a little opportunity in there somewhere and just drag it out – I really enjoyed those early years.'

Jack Krelle doesn't see it like that: 'I don't think I had a career, you see, you are rather assuming that this is all somehow deliberate and that I think I'm a planner and I'm defined by my job, which sort of isn't true really. Just being myself really, and enjoying myself and . . . um, doing good things.'

For Doug Richardson it was simplifying a charity brief down to the absolute essentials: 'I did some work for a thing called the Windsor Group, which was in the top 30 charities. They were worried that charitable giving was in decline. And they wanted to run a campaign promoting the idea of giving and how you should care more. They gave me all the data they had. I was normally quite good at looking at numbers and seeing a pattern, but I mean, I spent three weeks doing nothing else than trying to make sense of these numbers and I couldn't find any pattern, I really couldn't. And that was pretty depressing. I thought well what could possibly cause this; that you couldn't really say that people in the north were more likely to give than the south, or whatever. It became obvious that the only reason it was a nightmare was because charities were asking for small change from everybody. So it wasn't that people were less caring, they just didn't know what to give. These charities weren't asking. So I went back to them, said, "Forget the generic campaign about making people care more. They care quite a lot already, why don't you ask them for a specific amount? And tell them what the money would do." I think that it sounds like a bloody obvious insight, but that at the time it felt quite fun to have thought that. It wasn't a matter of trying to make people more compassionate, or saying look at my poor dreadful people, care more about them than dogs – it was actually saying give us a fiver, give us 50 quid. Whatever. And we'll do this with it.'

For Tony Mortemore it was asking David Clifford if he could work on a beer, Whitbread, when he joined CDP and being told he could. What followed – the Heineken campaign that refreshed the parts that other beers didn't reach – is the stuff of legend. It changed the language of beer advertising.

What do you wish you had done differently?

Paul Feldwick is wistful that BMP is the only agency he ever worked for. He would love to have been in a start-up team. He even tells us that he came second. That Michael Hockney chose Leslie Butterfield over him to join the Butterfield Day start-up, but told Paul that if Leslie had said no that Paul would have been asked next!

David Cowan wishes he had been closer to the creative department. Which may have been because there was a divide between those who hadn't been to university (in the creative department) and the planners and account execs who had. 'I wish I had been much closer to the creative department – it wasn't much encouraged at BMP. Our job was to be the handmaidens and develop the work. Today the branding agencies use creative people to execute, but you have to control it otherwise it goes off the rails – the balance is what creates that great work. That's my regret; that I didn't try harder to step into their territory to give them the hook.'

Jan Zajac is candid that he wishes he had set up a Plan B for when he finished working in advertising. 'I should have realised from the day I walked in that this job has a limited shelf life unless you own the agency. In the advertising fallout of 1990, CDP fired a quarter of the people that day and I was one of them. You end up being a qualitative researcher but really I should have thought what I should be doing and planned a career with a longer life to it, but I never did that.

Most planners end up doing groups or in brand consultancy or headhunting but it's fairly limited.'

John Madell, who hasn't done at all badly for himself, wishes he had gone into investment banking instead!

Peter Jones is still haunted by the ones who were left behind when BMP started up. 'I would have fought harder to get two people into BMP earlier. Two people we left behind at Pritchard Wood were David Cowan and a guy called Tim Cox, who eventually became worldwide media director for BBDO. Tim went off to McCann. David went off to JWT.' Of course, David Cowan later joined BMP but clearly Peter still regrets leaving him, even though it appeared that Stanley got him placed at J. Walter Thompson which did his experience no harm at all.

David Baker wishes that he had taken the planning department closer to the BBH model than JWT. 'I think that planners can be better than JWT was at inventive creative strategies. At bringing them to life and giving them not only a strategic plot but a tangible strategic plot. My brain is more attuned to analytical and rational, which is what Stephen's was as well. The best balanced brain from that point of view and from a planning point of view was probably Jeremy.' And he would have radically simplified his Total Branding System. 'The only person who really knew the system inside out, was me – not a good thing!'

Jim Williams wouldn't have left BMP for SJIP. He didn't realise what he was giving up. 'It wasn't as much fun. It didn't produce as good work. No, I wouldn't have done that; but I have had some wonderful times latterly in Y&R in international advertising.'

Jane Newman would have found a way not to be promoted away from the front line. 'As you rise up in the organisation, you have to be careful where you tread. I was a good planner but not such a good account handler.'

Is digital and social marketing a whole new game or more of the same?

We were intrigued to find out what our first generation made of the impact of online advertising and in particular the way social media has become a mainstream communication form. Was this a whole new ball game or more of the same?

Paul Feldwick didn't see that there was much need for planners to change what they did. Even during his time working in advertising there were behaviour-based communications – namely direct response, which was measurable and simpler to develop than brand advertising. 'For me some are more interesting than others, and some more nuts and bolts: for example, with direct response you have known for a hundred years how to measure the response so you can try things out and optimise things. The important thing is to keep it in the wider context of what you do and not to overvalue the little bit that happens to be easily measurable. Or by getting it out of proportion when it may not be an important part of what you are trying to do. The interesting aspect of the planning job is keeping that overview of how those things fit together. At the end of the day it's all about the same business objectives; it comes together as part of the big picture and you need to keep a focus on what the real goals are. So 15,000 watched a TV spot on Channel 5, at three o'clock in the morning – these are not big numbers. It doesn't prove anything. So a sense of perspective is needed.'

David Cowan also thinks that you treat the new media in exactly the same way: 'We still ask the question "How does the communication create the effect?" It's such a shame that we treated the media department with such contempt, so they went off and set themselves up as independents and became king of the walk – it's just ridiculous.'

James Best hopes that it has made the job more interesting. 'If it helps planners to relate to a wider opportunity, to relate to members of the bigger world because there are so many ways they can get response and join with other people's thoughts, and join in with conversations. There seem to be some severe problems with it. So I haven't really got a clue. Planners seem to find it difficult to ground what they are doing in data – either they have too much and they don't have enough time to look at it properly, or it isn't very good data. Online is woefully lacking in demonstrating effectiveness. I don't understand why it is so difficult.' He points out that they had far more resources in the early days to analyse data and think about it – a better ratio between planners and account managers for a start. 'Clients were paying 15% commission and they got all this planning stuff thrown in as well. Not a bad deal at all.'

Christine Gray thinks it must be much more interesting: 'One of the most wonderful things about digital and digital advertising is that you can measure what people are doing, rather than what they are saying. It was every planners dream. To be able to match it with what people think they are doing, and rationalising it, must be absolutely knockout. I regret not having had that opportunity. Digital is different because it requires the customer to opt in. It must make enormous demands on the creative people to make sure that you wait to see what this creative is going to be about – it is very different from TV advertising. You had to go out or make a cup of tea to miss that.'

Jan Zajac's issue is with the fragmentation. It must be different if you can no longer talk to a mass audience with your advertising. 'Advertising was a great job to be in because it was powerful stuff. Now there's a million options for an advertiser to choose from and I guess it's why clients go digital now. I'm told that people spend half their budgets on digital, and I'm not aware of seeing any ads: too many channels and probably not enough money per channel to do any very interesting work. I can't see how you can do much more than announcements and maybe a website.'

David Baker thinks the planner's job has to be the same: 'I still believe fundamentally that brands have to have meaning. Therefore they have to have something at the heart of them that's got to be managed in total, and in the 60s and 70s an advertising execution on television was at the heart more often than not. There's got to be an idea at the heart of it. Even though you use all these different forms of digital, I still think that something has got to be there which is the magnet that everything else is attracted to, from a communications point of view. It's got to have a focus.'

Roderick White thinks it is more of the same. 'At the end of the day you still have the same sort of disciplines, it's who are we trying to influence and what do they think about what we are doing anyway, and how do we turn that round to our advantage. What is particularly difficult for planners – because they are supposed to know the answers quicker than everybody else – is that you get so much feedback so quickly that using it becomes very difficult. You can leap to the wrong conclusions and you have the pressures to do things about it, because you can change the message on the website or whatever so quickly, that it does actually become very reactive, and not very thought through. Somebody has to provide some sort of balance and that's a planner's job.'

Ev Jenkins thinks it's more of the same. 'If we start with a person, a target consumer, find out what they do and if they use social media and they use all the digital devices that you can use . . . I noticed actually, getting the bus from Crouch End to Finsbury Park, I just stood there and there were about 20 people on the bus and I think 17 of them were either on the phone, or they were plugged in, listening to music or whatever, and I thought they were all little bubbles on this bus and I think whatever they're doing, it's the role of qualitative research. My daughter is a qual researcher and she tells me where she goes, what she does and what they say, and I'm thinking it's tracking behaviour and attitudes, so whatever behaviour and attitudes change, I don't think it's different. It's over-complication honestly: if one target person is doing social media, watching television, shopping in Tesco, watching the pennies, worrying about the kids, worrying about how they can afford a holiday this year, all of those things – if one person can do all of that, then a planner can track all of that and it has to be tracked as a whole, and looked at as a whole; otherwise you start slicing people out and having committee meetings between the digital planner and social planner, I mean, I think it's stupid. I think somebody has to understand the total, not bits and pieces.'

Jack Krelle remembers going below-the-line when he moved from CDP to Aspect: 'It was fascinating, but more of the same. It's still media; it's just a different form of media. Any planner who is still dependent on above-the-line classic media would not really count as a planner. Your task is much more to understand the brand, understand the consumers, then what it is that you wish to consumers to know about the brand that you can in some way influence. So I mean it shouldn't matter at all. The planner should be more concerned about the architecture whatever materials they are building with.'

Doug Richardson would love it if planners could stay above all of it. 'The value of planning at its best – you need somebody that can stand outside the day-to-day and get a notion of what's really happening and what the real value of communications might be.'

Jane Newman thinks that it is much the same. 'I think how media works or how to reach people is very different. But it's still a communication and you still need to know the strategy behind it, so I can't imagine it would be that much different. You need to be current and up-to-date and know what's going on in the culture – but that was always the case.'

Jim Williams thinks it's the same job: 'The first thing I was introduced to at BMP when I joined was the media department. I was put in the media department for three months buying posters line by line. That really hasn't changed that much. It means we can dig more deeply or accurately hopefully. The media thing is very difficult. I think you have got to follow some approach which is inferential. We can't be accurate with mathematical solutions. It is like me doing my physics. Physics is an approximate science. Whereas mathematics is an exact science. We have to give more room for inferred solutions otherwise we complicate matters so much with all the variations.'

Tony Mortemore thinks all this focus on technology is overblown, the job is the same: 'Dear oh dear. Last week a guy said I have this new thing. And I said, God, it tells the time (because that was the biggest thing on it)!'

Catherine Simmonds thinks it's a big fuss over nothing. 'Advertising for hair products now has got those lunatic girls shushing their hair. I assume that effective advertising must be going on somewhere else. On social media perhaps, something that I don't understand at all. I don't want to sound all tufty dufty about it but I am astonished about how rarely I see a commercial on TV or an ad in a magazine that stops me in my tracks.'

So the majority view is that the planner needs to have the perspective and detachment to sit at the strategic level, above and beyond the executional and tactical.

What advice would you give to a young planner on their first day?

We asked them what advice they would give to a planner on their first day working in an advertising agency.

David Cowan tells you to build your skills. 'Analytical skills and knowledge. It has to be about data in the mix otherwise you're just another opinion.'

Christine Gray says not to take it too seriously.

Jan Zajac says get out now while you can! 'Especially now. In the 70s advertising was a sexy job. It's not anymore. I keep asking people – why is advertising creatively so terrible now? One guy said, it's because clients won't pay any repeat fees. Since 1990, there's been a huge backlash against creativity in advertising and while I was at Added Value, I could feel that, because I was working for marketing guys who resented ad agencies. They were glad they got their comeuppance.'

Peter Jones tells you to stick to the facts. 'Keep as firmly based in hard fact as you possibly can do. Because your credibility on the softer stuff depends on your mastery of the hard stuff. You can't be gainsaid on data if you know it inside out. If you have the right credentials to be a planner you'll be the only one who does know it inside out. And then you'll earn your spurs and will get acceptance on the softer aspects and just work hard at it. The only way to get on in life is to work very hard. I didn't have a lot of experience of doing qualitative research but I learned a lot from Creenagh [Lodge]. That needs an ability to listen rather than talk.'

Ev Jenkins tells you to go and do something else first. 'If you go straight from university to an ad agency and become a planner, I don't know what you bring to it. When I was at JWT, there was an ex-vicar who was a planner and he brought something else, a different way of looking at the world. When you went to pick his brains, there was a different slant. There were some people who had been researchers, they were a pretty mixed bunch. But everyone had done something before. Get a bit of experience.'

Lee Godden doesn't know what to suggest. 'You look at Christine and me and Ev and John Bruce and David Baker, we're all so different.'

Jane Newman says, 'Just have fun. Be honest and try and find the truth and work hard. Be first to arrive and last to leave, that's my philosophy.'

Jim Williams reminds us that it is all about finding the right strategy. 'Think. What exactly are you trying to do? Is it extending the target group or about becoming more competitive or maybe fostering relationships with consumers?'

John Madell thinks planners have to be even better at communicating. 'If they are going to stay in advertising they need to broaden their tools and their understanding of those tools. A client of mine went to one of those Marketing Society dinners and it was about how advertising works. A planning director stood up and apparently it was a load of babble. Gordon Brown of Millward Brown got up and gave a clear explanation of his model of how advertising worked. Planning has always operated in that area. If planning is too closely tied up with the solution, it's very difficult to move into strategy, clients think you're biased.'

What questions would you ask today's planners?

We also asked them if they had a question for planners today. Here's the list.

There was something of a challenge in the questions that were posed since the job is perceived to be a lot more difficult now and the creative output significantly worse.

James Best 'I would love to know what you stand for now. What's it about? Is your job more about co-ordination now? I am not quite sure. Were Stanley alive now he would accept defeat. There are lots of people called planners. It has survived, but it's not what he created and what this agency did even 20 years ago. I don't think it has overcome the dominance in advertising of glib solutions, client diktats and creative indulgence, and all the things planning was designed to stop.'

Christine Gray wants to know how do planners manage? 'Instead of press, posters, TV, radio, and cinema, there is so much to think about and to take into account, so much fragmentation and so much sophistication in the market. I don't know how you do it and I do admire you for doing it. What's the most number of accounts you work on? For us it can't have been more than five at the outside and two of them would be tiny which you would do something for, perhaps once a year. I wonder what planning you can bring if you have nine or ten accounts. How do you have time to think about it? Perhaps we thought about things too much, perhaps we did. Raymond Chandler talked about chess being the biggest waste of intellectual effort outside of an advertising agency – and I think he had the planning department in mind!'

Jan Zajac wants to know if you are curious. 'Do they want to know how things work? In a sense I was always a planner, at uni I had a nickname, which was "Twenty Questions" and I did, I wanted to know why people liked things. To me, that's what planners do.'

Leslie Butterfield wants to know if you know what an insight is and do you really understand the consumer you're talking to? 'Do you really have something that qualifies as an insight and I don't mean research findings, conclusions, observations or anecdotes – I mean true insight, which I think is rare. Are you really making the use of what is available to you now to deeply understand how your target customer is behaving? Because if you do, you can unlock some fascinating opportunities for brands and communications.'

Peter Jones wants to know what influence do you actually have on the final communication form. 'That output may be a 30-second commercial, it might be quite a complex econometric model, but the key thing is you've got to try to get inside the most important functions of the company. Then people look to you for help. If you're peripheral, they won't. The person who does the desk research, passes it on and never sees it again. You have to make yourself as central as you possibly can and make sure that you are asked for by name. And I would ask planners whether they do that in many different ways. There are many ways of skinning the cat. How many ways do you influence the overall product of the agency or the part where you had direct involvement?'

David Baker wants to know how you are getting your head around the many different kinds of communication. 'If you can crack that, you can use that to set brand strategy and brand communications, the role for advertising, the role for direct marketing and you can then be genuinely helpful. But I think unless you understand that, it's quite difficult to be practical.'

Roderick White wants to know what you see the job being about. 'That's a pig of a question, but that's really because the answer to it should reveal a whole mindset and at least suggest the sort of approach that they might then take to it.'

Ev Jenkins wants to know how culturally aware planners are today. 'Did you watch *Homeland*? I mean it would have to be something that would get them talking, that had nothing to do with advertising. I might ask them "What's your favourite ad and why?" but it would a broader cultural question than advertising. Because as a manager you have their CV, you kind of know roughly what people are like; it's a question of getting them to talk and seeing what kind of slant they've got on life.'

Jack Krelle wants to know where you are working and whether you like the people there. 'Are you enjoying yourself? I might find out from them what sort of planner they are. I would ask a much bigger question. If in the 70s we all had time for lunch, five or six times a week, and still produced great ads, what are you doing wrong now? It seems to me the whole industry undervalues itself. It's being put in the corner by cruel marketing folk and purchasing committees and all that kind of stuff, and not having time to have fun. While I know that the ad agencies did not make much money in the past, they don't make much more money now – they are still not anything like as profitable as research companies ought to be and media companies are. So why don't they find better ways to do it?

More of the CDP approach: "This is the answer if you don't like it, Fuck off." But you can only do that if you have a really good track record and a really good track record comes from serious autocracy and intellectual rigour of a worthy sort. I suspect that quite a lot of that has disappeared.'

Doug Richardson wants to hear planners talking about themselves and their lives. 'What interests them and what things they have done. One of the best planners I ever hired, her only job had been working in a plastic bucket factory in Runcorn. (Laughs) You know, you know, the fact that she was in my office, saying "Give us a job" was, I thought, fantastic.'

John Bruce wants to know if your job is as much fun as it was when he was working in advertising. 'It was fun. It was JWT in the 1970s. It was an exciting place. It seemed to be new. It was innovative. You were surrounded by bright people. We were at a formative age. We felt we were ahead of the game. There didn't seem to be the big issues of finance and making things pay. We were far more interested in finding a good solution than a quick solution. That was what Peter Cooper[59] and Stephen King had in common – it wasn't pragmatism.'

Lee Godden wants to know what other jobs did you think of doing.

Jane Newman wants to know how social media works. 'Doug Atkins was a planner here, then he went to America, he was at Wells, and we hired him from there. Now he works on dating at MatchUp.com. It's a big start-up, so I'd been talking to him

59 Founder of CRAM and one of the most influential qualitative researchers in the UK. John Bruce worked for him for a few years.

about it and got really fascinated and I'd like to know how planning responds to that.'

Tony Mortemore wants to know if you still enjoy it. 'Or is it just a means to an end? My feeling is that people are so weighted down by stuff it is difficult to enjoy yourself.'

Do you ever stop being a planner?

Paul Feldwick doesn't see himself as a planner any more – it's a job he used to do. Even though what he does now is strongly related. 'The job I did for 30 years has had a big influence on who I am now.'

David Cowan sees a strong strand of continuity in how he ran Forensics, a detective agency for marketers.

James Best sees his planning experience as a useful anti-bullshit tool. 'It pricks at your conscience if you aren't asking why? If you're not confident in the robustness of your argument. Understanding what's going on helps you structure arguments and presentations and helps you understand people better than otherwise. It constantly reminds you of how little you know and gives you a bit of humility.'

Christine doesn't think you ever stop being a planner. 'People who have worked in advertising still laugh at me and say we can tell you were a planner. What I do now is mostly related to voluntary medical research and there my background in understanding quant and qualitative research is enormously useful – I wouldn't be able to contribute without that background.'

Jan Zajac says once you have been taught how to do groups 'you know how to talk to people to find out why they do things. You carry it over into other fields. At Added Value for example, I did recruitment. Most people aren't very good at recruiting, the truth is people will tend to hire people like themselves only not as good. The recruitment process to me is about interviewing and I got those skills from research, to quickly sort out if someone's right for the job or not.'

John Madell has continued to apply his planning expertise to first market research and then his consultancy to grow businesses.

Leslie Butterfield wants to say he's moved on but comments that his partner would think he applies planning far too much to his private life! 'I think through and analyse situations from looking after my young children, through to how I should get my car serviced, through to, you know . . . whether we should buy a second home or not, with the same kind of attention to detail and rigor that I apply to my work life. I think part of it, as I said just now, is innate; it's that sort of detective mentality that's part of what you are. Honestly I think it's the best: it is and was the best job in advertising.'

Peter Jones has moved a long way from his planning roots. He grounds his experience more in the mental rigour he was taught at LSE than in the planning role at BMP.

Ev Jenkins considers that doing the job properly is time consuming. 'I quite enjoy it so I'll do it as long as it doesn't take over my life again, because doing it full time and being a mother of four kids is actually quite difficult. Especially when I was at Lowe because I was travelling so much. Mind you, the kids were always at dad's so it wasn't an issue; I couldn't have done it when they were young but again, all the travelling, it just seems stupid. Has nobody heard of Skype? People do take liberties with your time because they've got more time than you so they assume that you have a lot of time as well. Not people in the agency necessarily but clients. You know – can you be in Rotterdam by nine o'clock on Tuesday? Now, I would approach it rather differently and say – why? But I'd also say: can we Skype it rather than say, yeah I'll be at City Airport by six o'clock – it's stupid. So there is a lot of unnecessary face-to-facing with international clients.'

Jack Krelle, ever the contrarian, wants to argue that it's not about being a planner at all. 'It's about being Jack Krelle, I've got no idea. It's a bit like do you think being tall makes a difference? I don't know, I've never been short. If that's your mind set that's your mind set. I think it probably does. I think because we are rebuilding our cottage in the country, and I have used a bit of planning thinking: about execution, the feeling of it and what I wanted it to feel like . . .that influenced the way it was laid out, and I had to think about the progress and the timing as well, so yes probably.'

Doug Richardson is typically philosophical. 'I think you do. I'm asked enough to, to do planningy things that I can, that I can still do them. I think you carry on and you try and problem solve.'

John Bruce never stopped being a planner. 'I was certainly a planner all the time I worked in advertising even when I wasn't working in a planning department. Then in 1994 I was made redundant and I was 49. I did some freelancing and that was interesting, and I did some teaching of marketing and advertising at London City College. And that was fascinating because that was the first time I had gone back and thought about how you would teach it, and I found all these textbooks had been written but I had never read a textbook about it in my life. And therefore they liked having me because I could talk from real life.'

John Siddall is still applying his planning thinking in the Fine Cheese and Biscuit company he is running with his partner in Bath. 'If we start to think about what we are going to do this coming Christmas. We are sending it to people who have bought from us in the past so they are likely, because it is Christmas, to be sending a gift: that's 80 per cent of sales. We can talk about cheese but they know that. We have a very high churn rate. People think – I can't give them cheese again this year, so I need to give them socks instead. What we need to do is to find something they don't necessarily associate with the fine cheese company. So one of the ads is something unexpected. Trying to find a way to intrigue people so they buy a second time. Where could we be? That is pure planning cycle.'

Jane Newman doesn't think you ever stop. 'No. I think I was born one. I think a good planner has an innate curiosity, not wanting to accept what's obvious, all that stuff. But it only applies to work, I think. What else would I apply it to? Not really, the rest of my life is chaotic!'

Jim Williams: 'I am retired now. I do still think about it, I observe the world. Observe advertising. I must say I am rather disappointed with the advertising at the moment. When I watch advertising on the telly It's just crass. At least that's one thing they did at BMP and Y&R – everything that came out looked professional and beautiful. You wonder what they were thinking. I suppose I will always be a planner.'

Tony Mortemore thinks he'll always be a planner. 'No, no. I am doing the same thing. I find I have a certain focus on process and the travelling light of planning is quite interesting.' He misses working in advertising, 'I miss the repartee. People were bright. And sparked off each other. So it was like a perpetual *News Quiz*. You don't get that with people anymore.'

The theme of education comes through quite strongly, since a quarter of those we had spoken to went on to train planners in different parts of the world.

Paul Feldwick looks back on his time with DDB fondly. 'The training programmes and the global planning conferences were an absolute blast because, from all over the world, we got the most spectacularly clever and interesting people. If you got them together in a room lubricated with alcohol, the creative intellectual energy there was absolutely fantastic. My only frustration was that ultimately the agency as a whole didn't know what to do with it, so it was an underused resource.'

James Best, some years later carrying out a similar role, describes the different forms that account planning took in different parts of the world. 'There was the Anglo-Saxon style of planning in Australia and South Africa; the strength on the West Coast of the USA but where the rhetoric strays very close to sales territory; in Europe the idiosyncrasies of the mad genius planner and the resistance to rationality and careful building of evidence. The poet–planners of South America, the rational constructs and frameworks of Indian planners, and China being different again. It varies hugely – lightweight in most places, but genuinely culturally attuned and different. I had a global planning futures group and people from different parts of the world: we had a terrific time – we came up with some very good stuff, but I wonder how much of it was taken seriously by the network.'

Jim Williams worked for 20 years with Y&R Europe and travelled all over. 'It was fascinating because I would get to understand the similarities and differences in advertising cultures and consequently for cultures. The BAV (Brand Asset Valuator) is an international tool, so when you are recruiting for someone who is "maternal", what maternal means varies from country to country, there are different codes. That was fascinating and I had some good colleagues. There were a lot of local planners and a lot of them had copied what they saw in London and some of them were bloody good.'

Lee Godden and Judie Lannon both did stints as trainers and described these as the high points of their careers. It is a reminder that like many advertising skills they need to be passed on personally and there is a huge amount of mentoring and interaction.

What are you doing now?

Paul Feldwick is now consulting as well as teaching in a university in the west country. His interest is how to coach organisations to work better and get things done. So often organisations become dysfunctional and stuck. 'For me it's about improving the quality of the conversation; it's about liberating people to be able to work together more freely and that is the antithesis of the brainstorming session and the person with the flip chart. But it is about helping people to have conversations that are less inhibited by anxiety and are more constructive and creative and honest. The best planners have always done that.'

David Cowan has retired to a farmhouse on Dartmoor but he still works occasionally on what he calls detective work. 'Applying the ideas of planning to a much broader canvas. How do you grow a business? It's about detective work, understanding what is going on and trying to change it.' He's using his planning thinking to develop strategies for the stock market. But he won't tell us how he does it!

James Best consults – he still has an office at what is now Adam and Eve DDB, which he shares with Martin Boase and Chris Powell. When we spoke to him he was just looking at the proofs of a book about the life and work of John Webster. He is chair of the Code of Advertising Practice.

Christine Gray has been working on government committees relating to public health. She has spent some time working on the legislation around homeopathic medicines. 'Today if you buy a herbal medicine, on the patient information leaflet it says if you have any adverse effects you should fill in a yellow card or form. That is partly due to me. That is down to me, that's a little thing that I have done.' She got out of advertising after a brush with cancer, which she worked through. She suddenly thought: 'What on earth am I doing trying to persuade these customers to buy a phone from these terrible people? Why am I spending the rest of my life doing this when I have no idea how long I might have? And so I stopped.'

Jan Zajac is a painter working in Dorset – observing wryly he might have picked a part of the country less saturated with competitors.

John Madell is applying planning thinking to understanding what makes companies grow. 'Now I use consumer insights to develop growth strategies. There are elements but they have been developed on. The reason for that is that once planners stop doing their own focus groups, their contact with the world of research and consumer understanding moves from practitioner to commissioner and watcher. I think there is a fundamental difference. If you do it your mind is terribly active. You're always thinking can this be done better?' He also runs trips for fly fishermen round the world and has a trout stream of his own in the West Country.

Terry Prue has now retired from the research agency Hudson Payne and Iddiolls where he ran the quantitative division for many years. He is a governor in a local school.

Leslie Butterfield was Global Strategy Officer of Interbrand, the international brand consultancy, when we interviewed him. He now runs his own consultancy, Butterfield Harris.

Peter Jones continues to have fingers in all sorts of pies, not least horse racing. He runs a stud farm in Dorset where he trains race horses.

David Baker is retired and living in Kew.

Roderick White has used retirement to do a postgraduate degree in ancient history. He is back using basic and limited data sources to work out what would make a luxury product a best seller in 50BC.

Ev Jenkins still works as a very senior planner occasionally for various agencies. But she has started mentoring for the Kids Company.

Jack Krelle is consulting both in New York and in London. His partner is CEO of a bank in New York.

Doug Richardson was doing pieces of consulting around public relations. He died very suddenly in October 2013.

John Bruce is based in Bromley and works with a number of charities part-time. He says much of his work is about putting yourself in the other person's place, which is a lot of what planning is and finding a good solution rather than the quick solution.

John Siddall and his partner Anne Marie (former board director at BMP) runs the Fine Cheese Company in Bath and Artisan Biscuits in Ashbourne: www.finecheese.co.uk and www.artisanbiscuits.co.uk. He claims that his planning skills are ideally adaptive for running a business.

Lee Godden is a painter now travelling and painting in different parts of the world.

Jane Newman took her kids out of school and travelled the world with them. When her car broke down in Kenya she was rescued by a local tribe. She has since settled there and founded the Thorntree Project to improve literacy among the girls among Kenya's most remote tribes. Fundraising hand in hand with education. 'We just did a Girl Power programme. We researched it, we talked to the mothers and girls in the villages and school and found out what was going on. Then we analysed the exam results going back five years and the dropout rates of the girls and the declining exam results as soon as they get to class four – so actual behaviour and attitudes – and then we put the programme together. So yes, it was planning. I wasn't conscious I was doing it at the time.' In 2014 she was back in New York to be inducted into the Advertising Hall of Fame as the person who brought account planning to America. And yes, she's on the look out for sponsors: www.thorntreeproject.com.

Jim Williams is retired – he's suffering from Parkinson's now, but his mind is still as sharp as ever.

Tony Mortemore works in a local charity shop several days a week. And on Monday evenings he plays in a jazz band. As he says, planning is a lot like jazz. "After all the practising you have to go with your instincts and feel the music.'

David Clifford is retired and busy restoring a house above the Wye Valley.

Cathy Simmonds is retired and lives in Bath opposite a cheese shop run by John Siddall.

Let's give Christine Gray the last word. 'I'm quite ambivalent about my time in planning. I had the best time ever and I learned to think, which was a great bonus in life – but at the end of the day its not a job that contributes anything . It's a non-job. Life can go on without it. It doesn't look that different in the great scheme of things so I would say do it for 10 years then do something that *does* make a difference.'

Who was the best planner you ever worked with, and why?

This is the question we all wanted to hear and sometimes they wouldn't tell us. Partly because, as Jane Newman said, 'How can I answer that? Whoever I choose I'm going to piss off another 90, so I can't. They were all great.' But partly because as Tony Mortemore pointed out 'you don't see other planners working so how do I know how good they are?' But the reason we asked the question, apart from sheer curiosity, was to establish why that particular individual was nominated. What made them the best planner?

Paul Feldwick nominates Steve Harrison – who after he left BMP became a media buyer client-side. 'He was a very down-to-earth bloke. He was very bright. He had a degree from Cambridge, came from Leicester. He did a lot of the Courage work in the early days. He did the Honey Monster as well. He had a real rapport with people doing beer groups – it wasn't unique to him but he set the tone. You do the groups in the recruiter's house and when the group was over you would all go down the pub and then find out what they really thought. He just made himself part of that. Unlike a lot of planners even then, he was very numerate and scientifically-minded though his degree was in psychology. So he did have intellectual background to it as well. He later became a media man. He was quite a formative influence. He was one of the guys I worked quite closely with when I started in planning. John Siddall was another.'

David Cowan mentions Charlie Robertson, a later hire at BMP. 'What I was always looking for were people who had this analytical, causal way of thinking. They had to be numerate. They usually had some sort of sciency thing. And history was close to science because you are trying to find out why something happened. Charlie was an engineer so he had that side of it. He was also very creative and he was very interested in photography. He was quite a rounded person. I didn't stay long enough to see how Adam Morgan and Jon Steel progressed. I was on my way out by then.'

James Best named Ross Barr – one of the two grads hired after John, Jim, and James and who were trained by Jane. He became, with Chris Cowpe his fellow hire, joint planning director of BMP at the end of the 1970s. 'Extremely intelligent, thoughtful, a planner by profile. He could not be an account man. But successful at understanding brands and how people worked, and somehow quietly humorously on the nail. The planners are the quieter ones. They don't want the stress and excitement of chasing down client relationships. We were protected by our account people. We were not to be treated roughly. It was the account man who was to be treated roughly. We were the navigators, they were the pilots.' He tells a story about a presentation where Ross, following a loquacious contribution from the account man David Batterby, begins his contribution with the line 'Let me add bones to the flesh!'

'There are different models of planner. Paul Feldwick was a terrible account man and a bloody brilliant planner. David Cowan could have been a research scientist at Farnborough. Ross was a mathematician – the scientific mind was a really important ingredient. But we hired psychologists and artists. We hired scientists who didn't want to be scientists.'

Christine Gray nominates Catherine Butler. 'Stephen King obviously, but for me it was probably Catherine Butler – because she had a mighty mind, an amazing mind, extraordinary high standards. She wouldn't let go; she made you think. And she taught me how to think and she had insight – it wasn't just the quality of the thinking; it was the quality of the imagination. For me she was the great planner, she was my role model.'

Jan Zajac nominates Stanley Pollitt, 'because he was the one who said the way forward is to develop advertising with the help of insight, through consumers. I think that was the big breakthrough because before then, the creatives would say they were the arbiters of consumer taste. If he hadn't done that, the job wouldn't really exist. For JWT, that planning was fine, it wasn't revolutionary, it was another form of intellectualism, a lot of the account directors at JWT did their own planning anyway.'

John Madell can't choose. 'At BMP there was quite a spectrum of planning psychologies within us. David Cowan was always very analytical. Not only quantitative – a very sharp mind. So he would be positioned more at the quantitative end. Myself and Peter Jones were more interested in the business end of it. Jim Williams was like David, I think. Jane Newman was more qualitative and others would have fitted along that line so I think there was a bit of a range. And it was reflected by the work that was done for certain clients.'

Terry Prue nominates Ev Jenkins: 'I was always very much in awe of her, I always thought that her role within the agency was something I aspired to, but I don't think I ever quite got there. I think it's very difficult to be good at everything, you have responsibility but you don't have real power – you are an adviser, you are forever being an adviser to people, and I think that Ev was particularly successful at being able to push through her views.'

Leslie Butterfield nominates David Cowan. 'He certainly had more influence on my career and my thinking than probably anyone else. He didn't have the best man-management skills in the world, but he was a fantastic teacher. He was an inspiring thinker and he was a personable and brilliant man, so in terms of influence on me personally he would certainly be up there in terms of impact. But he is so purist that from a commercial point of view he might have been more successful if he had been less so. He was heavily involved with things like BT, which won Grand Prix at the IPA Effectiveness Awards, so he is probably top of my list in terms of planners I admire.'

Peter Jones mentions several, but puts James Best at the top because he avoided the extremes. 'James Best was one of the very best. He was a very rounded individual. He followed me on Courage. He did some excellent work and took Courage to places that I probably wouldn't have done. John Madell was very talented but a bit mercurial. Planners define themselves as well. Some went heavily down the qualitative route and I think lost the plot by doing that. Some went down the quantitative route and similarly lost the plot. And you can put the planners you know into those categories and there are relatively few that are balanced and down the middle.

'What I mean by well-rounded is you have got to have an eye on the ultimate solution. And an ultimate business understanding is very important. Which is what made James particularly good. You've got to be able to get on with clients which some researchers are not very good at doing. Because the client has got to have confidence in your judgement which in the heyday of BMP was a virtually total trust.'

David Baker nominates Jeremy Bullmore – someone who has never had planner as his job description. 'Jeremy I think. Stephen was very clever but I always thought that he was a person who was an academic who worked in advertising and that he could have worked in lots of other things, whereas Jeremy, I think, was more of an advertising natural. Do you know Robert Poynton? Is he still around? Well, I liked working with him. I learnt from him. He was more inventive and closer to the creative process than most of the other planners in JWT.'

Jeremy Bullmore also gets a citation from Ev Jenkins. 'Jeremy, I suppose. He and Stephen were very close and I think they even went to school together, I think their whole education was parallel, and Stephen was pretty creative and Jeremy was pretty thoughtful, so the two of them worked brilliantly well together. Stephen and Jeremy, and Doug as well, I have to say. Doug in a different kind of way, he was more practical in some respects. There was Catherine Butler – she was pretty scary, but when I got to know her, actually, picking her brains was really helpful.'

Roderick White also nominates Catherine Butler. 'I mean I worked initially for a lady called Catherine Butler. She was a formidably bright lady, and very, very logical and in many ways totally unfeminine with the way her mind works. She was extremely good actually, and I learnt an awful lot from her. I found myself working a lot with a guy called David Russell, who was different and he was much more of a sort of presenter's presenter. He was quite clever. I worked with him a lot over the years. I don't think there was anyone else in particular. There were a lot of really quite clever people around.'

Jack Krelle nominates Doug Richardson. 'Doug, I thought, had great planning insights. There was a chap called Simon at JWT who had a great insight once. He said that men don't drink coloured drinks. They drink brown drinks pretty much. If you see some drinking Campari, you are a bit worried, and anything else and it's pink shirt time. David Clifford was very good as well. At CDP, he worked well with the ethos there. His work on Fiat was very good.'

Doug Richardson mentions Ev and Christine. 'I think most of the planners we had were really very good indeed. You've met Ev Jenkins, who is tenacious and very persuasive, and extraordinarily down-to-earth and had passion about what she believed. She would always have a coherent argument. Someone like Christine Gray was a very insightful person. But others like John Bruce, or Terry Bullen or Bernie [Knox] had analytical strengths that could back up their case with structured argument. I don't think I ever had a single idea of what a planner was. It was about the individual always, rather than the model.'

John Bruce wants to talk about Ev Jenkins: 'Stephen King was remarkable for inventing account planning but he wasn't remarkable for being an incredibly good planner. For my top three, I would put Tony Stead in there, Ev Jenkins would be in there. Christine Gray? Perhaps. I worked with Ev in the same group for many years and what was fantastic was the way she built up a close relationship with the creative department and got them to think her way.'

Lee Godden comes out with a gem: Christine Gray, who she also claims was Stephen King's nomination. 'Christine. Stephen thought she was the best planner and I always thought she was. She sort of took all that information and had a lot of intellectual energy and she transformed it. Somebody has to listen to the heartbeat of the brand. Stephen's thesis was that it couldn't be done by the account people. Therefore there had to be another group of people who did it. I couldn't articulate it, I think you need quite a lot of curiosity. You've got to be comfortable with not being in the front line and not getting the medals, which is why I think girls are quite good at it.'

Jane Newman only told us who her favourite planner is on condition we don't tell you! What we can tell you is why: 'Their mind is amazing and they have a totally terrier mentality, keeping going and going until they get there. There it is. You're a catalyst for focusing on the end result and getting people to understand their role in that and how to work together.'

Jim Williams nominates Stanley Pollitt, 'because he understood what advertising was all about and he was passionate about ads. Too many account directors are passionate about clients. The work they produce is client-pleasing. Stanley would never present something to get the approval of the client. He thought deeply about how the advertising was going to work and he kept on pushing the people they had. At BMP in the beginning the people were just outstanding: the creative people, the planning people and the account management. They made advertising relatively easy.'

Tony Mortemore nominates Stephen King. 'He was right about the long-term. CDP was about campaigns, not ads. Stephen said if you build something the client has got an investment. It's not just about clever advertising. Woody [John Wood] would say a brand is something worth paying more for. And that was what Stephen fastened on to. I would rather have a BMW than a Ford, because it makes you feel better and there will be some reasons why that is true. That is what being in a consumer society is about.'

There is a postscript. Tony Stead was one of the first group heads at J. Walter Thompson – the one who came up with the name account planning. He has dementia now so his memories of planning at J. Walter Thompson are occasional and distant. But the mist parted and this was his nomination (which actually sounds like a mix of Catherine Butler and Ev): 'Ev Jenkins – she was so fierce she would tell the clients exactly what she thought of them. But if they listened she made them so much money.'

Postscript

The Rivals: two alternatives who claim to have started account planning

In this section we want to address two rivals claims to have started planning. Jeremy Bullmore mentioned an email he received from Stephen King a few days before his death, in which he was commenting on an imminent anniversary of the start of planning, saying he hoped that whatever was said there would be a round of 'who started what first?' It should be clear from this book how planning didn't start on a particular date, that the ideas which impelled planning went back to the early 1960s, and that two very different individuals, Stanley Pollitt and Stephen King, developed them for very different agencies. And that there was a measure of collaboration between them.

However, although in the 1970s account planning came to be widely imitated, there were rivals who claimed to have had the planning idea and implemented it even earlier than the 'official' start dates. So this postscript is intended to settle those claims.

David Brent – the Australian counter-intelligence expert who 'founded planning' in 1965

Let's start with David Brent – like Stephen King, in danger of being confused with a notorious, high-profile alter ego! David Brent claimed to have started planning in 1965 in Australia. This predates Stanley's Pritchard Wood experiment by a year and BMP and J. Walter Thompson by three years – so it needs to be investigated. In his view this predates anything happening in the UK.

You can read David Brent's own account on a website here.[60] From which you can also download a long paper detailing what he did when and with testimonies about how good it was. He was in the Australian army in counter-intelligence and did stints in Yugoslavia and also fighting the communist insurgency in Malaya in the late 1950s. He sees himself applying the principles of military intelligence and covert operations to marketing and advertising. During the 1960s he worked for Unilever and Reckitt & Coleman client-side, and also worked with several advertising agencies using the title marketing and research manager.

It is an interesting variation to apply military experience to marketing. After all, marketing is littered with the language of warfare, and David Brent seems better qualified than most to apply that. It is also true that until 1968 the term planning was not being used by anybody (not by David Brent either) so it isn't about what it was called but what it was. The central claim Brent makes is that he had the idea that it was customer response, not inputs, which was critical, before this idea took root in the UK. And he delivered this planning function in a Sydney agency in 1966. But from his own account he had to leave after 10 months because of 'adversarial elements in the agency ownership which were not conducive to the role proceeding smoothly'. He doesn't get back to the agency world until 1970, by which time planning is firmly established at BMP and JWT. It seems that during this brief spell he did indeed run home tests of TV commercials, which is indeed early. Brent doesn't seem to have been an easy person to work with. His account of what he did, and who he worked with,

60 http://www.originplan.com.

makes it clear he did not suffer fools gladly and that others would have found it difficult, if not impossible, to work with him. For example, just after joining an agency he tells a client that the commercial is not working – this is not how to win friends and influence people.

Critically he is not a team player. He builds no department – he trains nobody to do what he does. Which is why we regard this 1966 experiment as a one-off by a lone operator who failed to create a sustainable planning function. Using research alone isn't planning. There was lots of research being done in and around agencies during the 1960s. But JWT and BMP used research quite differently to understand the customer. If David Brent understood customer response as the foundation of account planning that is commendable, but he was not able to replicate himself in a department that survived him, as Stephen King and Stanley Pollitt managed to do.

CDP – the planning school that never was (account planning from 1964)

> *'Anyone could contribute to account planning at CDP – and our commissionaire frequently did.'*
>
> John Wood

We turn to the second rival claim by John Wood or 'Woody' as he was known.[61] He claimed that his agency Collett Dickenson Pearce was the first to use account planning. He joined in 1964 so that would predate the others by some years. What tantalises is that this is CDP – arguably the greatest creative agency the UK has ever produced. It had two golden ages, the first in the 1960s under the creative directorship of Colin Millward,

61 Taken from *Inside Collett Dickenson Pearce*, previously cited.

and then in the early 1970s led by Frank Lowe. Fiat (built by robots), Heineken (refreshes the parts), Hovis, Hamlet, Cinzano and the iconic advertising for Benson & Hedges cigarettes built around the gold box, are just a few examples of advertising which is still remembered. Their showreel is awesome and absurd – how could any agency be consistently this brilliant?

During the 1960s there was no planning department as such but John Wood and others played a significant role as senior consultants – arguably this is still different from the planning function founded by Stephen and Stanley. Does it represent a third school of planning? We don't think so. Brilliant, experienced, intuitive, advertising people have always worked in the higher echelons of agencies, but this isn't the same as the planning function.

Woody got the job at Collett Dickenson Pearce because he had debriefed some discussion groups about Benson & Hedges advertising ideas and told his client and agency audience to ignore the criticisms of the majority, and to focus on the opinions of a minority in the groups. Which was a radical way to interpret research. John Pearce secured him a job at CDP, from which point he took a role as a director, advising on strategy and research – despite the creative director Colin Millward telling Woody on his first day that the appointment was over his dead body. John Siddall, who worked at CDP in the early 1970s and also did stints at BMP and JWT, told us that he rated John Wood as the best mind he ever met. What he taught and practised was the pre-emptive generic and the brand discriminator.

In the section on brands we have already articulated John Wood's pre-emptive generic strategy. Jeremy Bullmore claimed that J. Walter Thompson used the same approach, calling it motivators and discriminators: 'If the brand left the motivations territory unoccupied we could go in there and take it over.'

The planning role, using research, was to identify the generic with which to pre-empt the market or to identify the discriminator which would challenge and undermine the generic if that is what the market leader was using – and to define it so forensically that the creatives would come up with creative so category redefining that it was unresearchable because it looked nothing like any other advertising in the marketplace. It was for this reason that CDP strenuously resisted creative pretesting of any kind. Though the truth was that they were made to do it by their clients more often than they liked to admit. The received wisdom was that brilliant award-winning advertising always performed badly in these tests but then went on to be a dazzling success. Ergo, pretesting advertising is a waste of time.

The myth of never pretesting advertising is as strongly attached to CDP as the myth of always pretesting advertising became attached to Boase Massimi Pollitt. And both myths served each agency well. To which CDP also added the rider that the client would be persuaded to sign off the advertising strategy before being shown a single idea – and was expected to buy the iconoclastic work that resulted. If the client rejected that idea – which as CDP claimed would be unresearchable – then CDP would fire the client. In reality this happened only once on Ford. Though firing such a major client sent shockwaves through the advertising industry.

A relevant example is CDP's long-running Cinzano campaign featuring Leonard Rossiter spilling the product over Joan Collins – which simply ridicules the lifestyle advertising of Martini, the market leader, by turning it into a comedy gag: how will Rossiter contrive to spill the Cinzano Bianco this time? Interestingly Campari's campaign by J. Walter Thompson follows much the same line, with Lorraine Chase as the chirpy cockney model who, when asked if she had wafted in from 'Paradise', replied 'Nah. Luton Airport.' The issue is whether the challenger brand successfully gathers the attention and trial of new customers or if they remember these as ads for Martini who is still the category leader. And the Martini brand is not dislodged or discredited.

Wood claimed not so much that there was a department but this way of thinking and working was planning and something everybody in the agency did. We would argue that this was not an early version of the planning function for the following reasons.

Firstly, the choice of which strategy to use was made by individuals and not by a designated department (or for that matter by everybody in the agency). In the 1960s that person was John Wood. Then David Clifford, who was recruited to head up the research department in the early 1970s (relaunched as the planning department at that time). Then Geoff Howard-Spink subsequently fulfilled that role working with Frank Lowe. Geoff Howard-Spink relates how he would be introduced to new clients more than once by Frank himself, as 'Frank's brain'. So the strategic choices were made by senior, very experienced people – as indeed they were made and continued to be made by agencies before the arrival of account planning and at agencies without a planning function. The planning department was operating as a halfway house running research projects to develop the propositions. But it was also post-rationalising strategies if the creative work bore little or no relation to the strategy that was initially set. The research/planning function was significant because only a desperate client would buy campaigns as expensive and extreme as CDP produced without any evidence. So the role of research and strategy was essential for CDP to break out of the limited circle of 'booze, fashion and fags' clients it attracted.[62] Packaged goods companies, with their increasing dependence on

62 The client list as summarised by CDP founder John Pearce – also from *Inside Collett Dickenson Pearce*, previously cited.

mass distribution through the supermarket chains, simply wouldn't tolerate the stance of the agency. And when they did break out with a client such as Birds Eye, this success was not sustained.

It did not help that Frank Lowe built up the myth of creativity at CDP to such a level you might think that no research or planning ever took place. But this way of developing advertising is more consistent with the way in which senior, clever, experienced advertising people persuaded clients to buy work they were nervous of running, using all means at their disposal. The radical ideas of Stephen King and Stanley Pollitt shifted the powerbase towards the evidence of relatively junior people working within account groups. And that idea of the account planner as the worker within the group was the idea which stuck. Which is not to say that there haven't been agencies deploying very senior planners as planning consultants. McCann Erickson followed that route. But the risk for this approach is that it reduces planning to a way of selling work, whether the work is right or not. It loses the connection to customer response. For that reason we are not going to unveil CDP as the lost school of planning, although great planning work was done by individuals at that agency. Planning is not the sole preserve of senior brilliant figures (as it had been in advertising agencies before 1968), but a way of forcing creative analytical thinking about customer response deep into the agency at junior levels and protecting this through mentoring and monitoring processes as happened respectively at BMP and J. Walter Thompson.

Timetable

This is a table which lists from 1960 to 1980 the major milestones in the development of account planning together with the development in the research and advertising industries, set against the current events and social change evident at the time.

	Industry events	Historical events
1960	CDP is founded. **Hobsons is sold out to Rosser Reeves and Ted Bates.** The International Passenger Survey launched.	The Pill is launched. **National Service ends.** The Lady Chatterley Trial begins. **The Beatles form in Liverpool.**
1961	Brunnings floats on the stock market 'to stop the American influx'. **Private Eye is published.**	Russia sends its first man into space. **The Berlin Wall is completed.** **Ban the Bomb demonstation begin.**
1962	D&AD is founded. **AGB is founded and starts TCA (a TV household consumption panel which later evolves into the Superpanel).** Schlackmans is founded. **The Moloney report recommends setting up Consumer Council to protect interests.** ASA self regulation is set up. **The Sunday Times launches its first colour supplement.** Jay Chiat founds Chiat Day.	Cuban Missile Crisis.

1963		**John F. Kennedy is assassinated.** France vetoes Britain's entry into the European Economic Community.
1964	Stephen King brings out the T Plan. **Jeremy Bullmore becomes Creative head of TV.** National Travel Survey starts. **Resale price maintenance abolished.**	**The Vietnam War starts.** Mary Quant launches her first boutique and the miniskirt (named after her favourite car!). **The US Surgeon General publishes a report linking smoking and poor health.**
1965		The Race Relations Act is passed. **Prescription charges are introduced.**
1966	Stanley Pollitt starts Pritchard Wood's Market Planning department. **Colour television is introduced on BBC1.**	Oil is discovered in the North Sea. **Barclaycard, the UK's first credit card, is launched.**
1967	Pirate radio stations are banned. The BBC launches Radio 1.	British Sterling is devalued. **British Parliament passes homosexual reform.**
1968	**BMP and JWT opens with their planning departments.** Campaign magazine is launched. BMRB launches TGI.	Theatre censorship ends. **Violent anti-Vietnam War demonstrations occur.** The Open University is founded.
1969	**BMP makes pretesting all advertising compulsory.** KMPH*, Bensons & Geers, Goss and CDP float on the stock market. **Commercial colour TV is launched.** Rupert Murdoch relaunches News of the World and the Sun Page Three.	**The UK voting age is lowered to 18.** Divorce law is liberalised. **The Death Penalty is abolished.** Concord makes its first flight. **Apollo 11 lands on the moon.**

1970	**Stephen King introduces the Planning Cycle at JWT.** Saatchi & Saatchi launches.	The Womens Liberation **Movement holds its first conference.** The launch of the Gay Liberation Front. **The Equal Pay Act is passed.**
1971	**JWT develops a decimalisation campaign.** Massimi leaves BMP and Webster becomes Creative Director. **Green opens the first media independent, MBS.**	Decimalisation is introduced.
1972	The CDP Planning department set up. **Frank Lowe moves to CDP.** The Sound Broadcasting Act approves licenses for 60 commercial radio stations. **The UK edition of Cosmopolitan magazine launches.**	**The US withdraws from Vietnam.** The Miners Strike and Dock Strike prompt State of Emergency.
1973	Millward Brown is launched. **LBC, the first commercial radio station in the UK, is launched.** The European Business readers survey is set up. **TBWA is founded.**	**The UK joins the European Economic Community.** VAT is introduced. **School leaving age is raised to 16.** The Arab-Israeli War triggers an oil crisis. **The price of crude oil soars.** The Green Party is formed.
1974		**The Three-Day Week is introduced to conserve electricity during the Miners' Strike.**
1975	The Historic Advertising Trust is set up. **Polls correctly forecast the referendum result.**	Inflation reaches 25%. **Referendum on EEC backs staying in.** Sex Discrimination Act is passed. **Government takes over British Leyland cars.**

1976	Saatchi & Saatchi buys Compton and becomes global network. **Martin Sorrell joins as FD.** The first JICRAR radio audience survey is done.	Unemployment tops 1.5 million; government abandons full employment policy.
1977		**More than 50% of new cars purchased are imported.** Punk arrives on the scene, including Sex Pistols, banned by the BBC. **National Front riots.**
1978	**Account Planning Group founded.** Saatchi & Saatchi win the Conservative Party advertising account.	The Winter of Discontent. ***The Times* and *The Sunday Times* are unable to print.**
1979	**Stanley Pollitt dies of a heart attack.** Saatchi & Saatchi becomes number one UK agency. **CACI launches Acorn Geodemographics.**	Mrs Thatcher forms a new Conservative government. **An ITV strike means commercial TV is down for 11 weeks; a contract for a second commercial**
1980	The IPA Advertising Effectiveness Awards are launched.	The Housing Act gives tenants the right to buy their houses. **The Employment Act restricts strikes and union riots.**

The board of Pritchard Wood and their wives at dinner.

The promotional launch photo of the directors of Boase Massimi Pollitt and their families. (© HAT Historic Advertising Trust)

Stanley Pollitt, father of account planning
at Pritchard Wood and Boase Massimi Pollitt.

John Bartle, research manager at Cadburys, before he left to start
planning departments at TBWA and Bartle Bogle Hegarty.
(© HAT Historic Advertising Trust)

Stanley Pollitt posing with the Boase Massimi Pollitt cricket team in the mid 1970s

'David and Sue Cowan at the races. 'Boase Massimi Pollitt was always a racing agency,' explained Martin Boase.

The Boase Massimi Pollitt planning department clowning around at the races in the 1970s.

A youthful Paul Feldwick - who got into the BMP planning department via account management

Leslie Butterfield at BMP before he left to start planning at AMV and then his own agency BDDH

Leslie Butterfield in a group of media planners at Boase Massimi Pollitt.

October 15th, 1968

To: Mr. J. Bruce

From: Stephen King (211)

Account Planning Department, etc.

Here are some papers to amplify our recent presentations and the pink memo about the reorganisation.

This collection deals with the Account Planning Department, the Research Department and the Information Services Department. It contains:

1. Notes for my own bit of the presentation on the reorganisation
2. Structure of departments
3. Allocation of accounts to Account Planners
4. Details about what the Account Planner's job is
5. The dividing line between the Account Planner's job and the Media Man's job (written by Robin Erskine).
6. The press release on the reorganisation.

We have found that one point in particular needs to be emphasized. That is that nearly all planning work is a group responsibility. The Account Planner's main job is working out creative strategy and media strategy, but it can only be done in partnership with the creative and media people and the rep.

I would be terribly pleased if you would pass on to me any complaints or suggestions about how this all works out in practice, and any comments you get from clients.

Facsimile of a memo to the new planning department from Stephen King before the department opened

Stephen King father of account planning at J Walter Thompson.
(© HAT Historic Advertising Trust)

Marking up a work schedule: an office scene from J Walter Thompson in the 1960s.
(© HAT Historic Advertising Trust)

A status meeting at J Walter Thompson in the 1960s.
(© HAT Historic Advertising Trust)

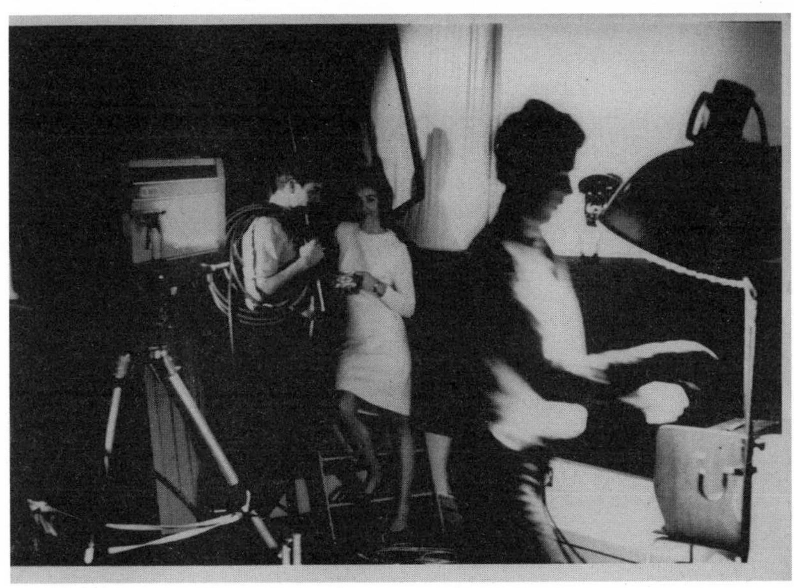

A TV shoot at J Walter Thompson in the 1960s.
(© HAT Historic Advertising Trust)

The reception area at J Walter Thompson in the 1960s.
(© HAT Historic Advertising Trust)

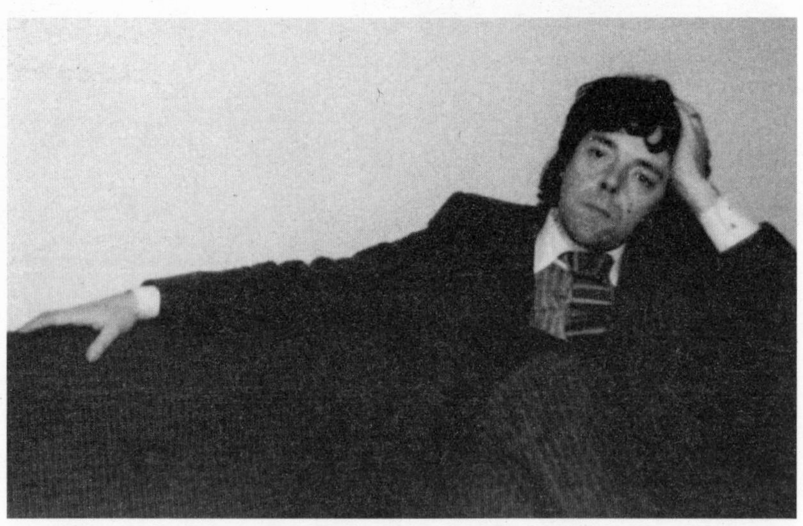

Doug Richardson, the 'zen planner', and first J Walter Thompson head of planning after Stephen King.

Ev Jenkins, the planner who knew how to take clients – and everybody else – along with her.

Terry Prue from J Walter Thompson consistently figured on IPA Awards-winning teams – and later on awards juries.

Account Planning - how we should go about it?

D.Richardson (J.W.T.)

"We are not satisfied with faith, in the sense of an inplausible hypothesis irrationally held: we demand to experience the 'evidence'."

R D Laing

D.Clifford (C.D.P.)

"The job of planning is to sell the ads first time around."

J.Bartle (T.B.W.A.)

"Account planning has put skilled data input into its proper perspective."

J.Williams (S.J.I.P.)

"The existence of planners is a sign of the tremendous importance the agency places on planning processes."

D.Cowley (F.C.B.)
CHAIRMAN

Account Planning Group second meeting.

6.30 Wednesday December 6th.
Ogilvy, Benson & Mather,
Brettenham House,
Lancaster Place, WC2.

1978.

Rare flyer from one of the first Account Planning Group meetings - if you have read the book the speakers will be familiar to you

Bibliography

Powers of Persuasion: The Inside Story of British Advertising 1951–2000, Winston Fletcher, Oxford University Press (2008)

Anatomy of Humbug: How to Think Differently about Advertising, Paul Feldwick, Troubador Publishing (January 2015)

The Art of Writing Advertising, Advertising Age NTC (1965)

Hidden Persuaders, Vance Packard, D. McKay Co. (1957)

The Book of Gossage, a collection of Gossage's advertising, published articles and homages by his admirers, Copy Workshop (2006)

Changing the world is the only fit work for a grown man (an eye witness account of the life and times of Howard Luck Gossage), Steve Harrison, Adworld Press (2012)

Sampling the Universe: The growth, development and influence of market research in Britain since 1945, Colin MacDonald, Stephen King, NTC (1996)

Ta-ra-ra-boom-de-ay – the dodgy business of popular music, Simon Napier-Bell, Unbound (2014)

Inside Collett Dickenson Pearce, John Salmon and John Ritchie, a 40th anniversary edition (2001)

House of Commons Library education report, Paul Bolton (2012)

1968: The year that rocked the world, Mark Kurlansky, Vintage Digital (2010)

Fifty in 40: The Unofficial History of JWT London 1945–1995, Tom Rayfield (1996)

Madison Avenue USA, Martin Mayer, Bodley Head (1958)

Behind the Scenes in Advertising, Jeremy Bullmore, Admap (1991)

How brands grow, Byron Sharp, OUP (2010)

Advertising Works 1981 IPA Effectiveness Awards, Ed. Simon Broadbent, IPA (1980)

Acknowledgements

We would like to extend our thanks to everyone who has helped make the book possible. Firstly, thank you to both our families: for their patience and support. Neither of us could have done this whilst juggling full-time jobs. John's wife, Karen, two years after the interviews were completed, sighed and said, 'You can always get back to work – just prioritise getting the book finished and published!' Thanks to everyone who pledged for the book, funding it even before we had written it – such faith. And a special note of thanks to our sponsors, J. Walter Thompson for their financial support, the APG for promoting the book throughout the planning community, and The History of Advertising Trust for their detective work in unearthing many of the photos from the era in question. The biggest thank you of course is reserved for all of our interviewees, and in particular Paul Feldwick who was an early supporter, Judie Lannon for providing as many names of Thompson planners as she could remember plus contact details too, and John Bartle for the precious foreword, and then his ongoing and invaluable help and advice. Everyone has been so generous in devoting their time, their stories and their connections so that we could bring this book into being. We hope you enjoy it.

Index

Supporters

Unbound is a new kind of publishing house. Our books are funded directly by readers. This was a very popular idea during the late eighteenth and early nineteenth centuries. Now we have revived it for the internet age. It allows authors to write the books they really want to write and readers to support the writing they would most like to see published.

The names listed below are of readers who have pledged their support and made this book happen. If you'd like to know more, visit: www.unbound.co.uk.

Phil Adams
Sean Adams
David Adamson
Laura Agostini
Enrique Henry Ahumada
António Albuquerque
James Allan
Burak Amirak
Audrey Anand
Simon Andrews
APG London
Emirhan Arat
Harriette Arellano-Setterington
Christine Asbury
Agatha Asch
Joanne Atkins
Kate Atkisson
Tara Austin
Mark Avnet
Vishal Badiani
Samantha Bagg
Kim Bailiff
Chris Baker
Jason Ballinger
Allyson Bancroft
Lee Bannister
Chris Barbee
Caroline Barfoot
Peter Barrett
Marius Bartsch
Merry Baskin
Elias Bassil
Peter Batchelor

Hugh Bateman
Christian Baujard
Charlotte Beckett
George Bell
Nick Bennett
James Best
Elias Betinakis
Fiona Blades
Nickie Bonn
Jo Booth
Sarah Booth
Jackie Boulter
Aldo Braccio
Tony Brandrick
Gerald Breatnach
Jack Brenman
Alvaro Bretel
Ligita Brodiņa
Aleksander Bromek
Mark Broughton-Foxall
Mark Brown
Pete Buckley
Ali Bucknall
Neal Burns
Jenny Buschhorn
Leslie Butterfield
Donald Cameron
Rob Campbell
Jane Cantellow
Josh Carlton
Andrew Catlin
Catalina Cernica
Julia Chalfen
Sanjay Chauhan, Atticus
Erica Chen
Kevin Chesters
Fung Cheung
Adrian Chiuhan
David Chriswick
Joanna Chrzanowska
Yusuf Chuku
John Clark
Claire Coady
David Cole
Colenso BBDO
Will Collin
Richard Colvile
Chris Cooper
Clive Cooper
Remi Couzelas
Jurandir Craveiro
John Crawford
Dan Cresta
Tom Curtis
Michael D'hooge
Jacolyn Daly
Daniel Marks London
Michael Davidson
Helen Davies
Vic Davies
Izabela de Fátima
Susan DeSimone
Matthew Desmier
Madonna Deverson, Ogilvy & Mather
Jesse Dienstag
Adriano Domingues
Michael Doody

Parrus Doshi
Robert Dougan
Danny Camprubi Douglas
Graham Drew
Angela Duffy
Kathleen Dunlop
Frank Durden
Mark Earls
Ian Edwards
Lauren Ellyatt
Michael Ellyatt
Craig Elston
Theo Erasmus
Tom Ewing
Matthias Eylers
Faris Faris
Richard Fearn
Paul Feldwick
Sonali Fenner
Justine Feron
Ricardo Amaral Filho
Eva Fischer
Kris Flemington
Al Flynn.
John Foenander
Sydney Follows
Tracey Follows
Leanne Forster
Jim Fraser
Falk Fuhrmann
Ken Fujioka
John Gamvros
Steven Garcia
Celia Garforth
Yelena Gaufman
Ian Gee
Matthew Gentile
Roddy Glen
Neil Godber
Roobin Golestan
Miguel H Gonzalez
Jan Gooding
Claire Goodman
Francis Goodwin
Esty Gorman
Brent Gosling
Chris Gough
Laurens Grainger
Robbie Greatrex
Simon Green
Andrew Griffiths
John Griffiths
James Gutteridge
Carolyn Hadlock
Carolyn Hall
Janette Hall
Gemma Hamilton
Mark Hancock
May Hanna
Naomi Hanson
Dr Mariann Hardey, thatdrmaz
Simon Harle
Ant Harris
John Harrison
Claire Hassid
Steve Hastings
Mark Hatwell

Espen Haugen
Emily Hayes
Ric Hayes
Lee Healy
Ally Heath
Matthew Heath
Daniel Hennessy
Caitriona Henry
Andreea Hirica
Nick Hirst
Rees Hitchcock
Omaid Hiwaizi
Jeremy Ho
Steve Hopkins
Tom Hopkins
Marc Horne
Gideon Hornung
Chris Huebner
Will Humphrey
Matt Hunt
Richard Huntington
Susan Imgrund
Elena Ionita
Andy Iverson
Dave Jackson
Sigrid Jakob
Gethin James
Lucy Jameson
Alexander Jaspers
Louisa Jean-Charles
Alex Jeffries
Hannah Jew
Ben Johannemann
Verity Johnston
Jourik Jourik
S K
Gareth Kay
Tim Keil
Richard Kelly
Jenny Kendall
Tiffany Kenyon
Molly Keyes
Dan Kieran
Annette King
Rowan Kisby
Maria Kivimaa
Phil Koesterer
David Kosmin
Hiro Kozaka
David Kratt
Candace Kuss
Jacqueline Lai
Catrina Law
Jon Leach
Heather LeFevre
Bex Lewis
Liana Liana
Madalina Lina
Dave Linabury
Paul Livingstone
Eduardo Lorenzi
Fiona Lovatt
Elizabeth Lynch
Gavin Mackie
Mimi Madell
Hanh Mai
Albéric Maillet
Caroline Marshall

Liudmila Matei
Craig Mawdsley
Paul McCall II
David McCann
Tim McEntaggart
Katie McLaughlin
Gordon McLean
Chris McNichols
Dee Mcpherson
Claire Meadows
Isabelle Meier
Jesus Melero
Jenni Mellor
Alessandro Mese
Jan Mikulin
Brian Millar
Laura Mills
Peter Minnium
Luis Miranda
John Mitchinson
Marco Moiso
Corentin Monot
Rebecca Moody
Beth Moore
Gareth Morris
Tom Morton
Ashley Moxey
Isaac Munoz, Ph.D
Fiona Murdock
Thomas Myring
Adib Nachabé
Jen Nagle
Sayed Naushad
Catherine Navarro-Harkin
Carlo Navato
Amanda Nenzen
Sarah Newman
James Nisbett
Marc Nohr
Melanie Norris
Matthew North
Fergus O'Carroll
Stephanie O'Donohoe
Patrick O'Hara
Michele O'Neill
Cressida O'Shea
Utymo Oliveira
Freddie Oomkens
Nicolas Orsoni-Durand
Gonzalo Gregori Osona
Anita Ozvald
Stefano Pace
Eric Pakurar
Fiona Parashar
Laurence Parkes
Dana Pascu
Simon Patterson
Matthew Pattman
Jamie Peate
Felix Pels
Claire Perry
Laurie Perry
Ewen Pettit
Stephen Phillips
Vu Nguyen Binh Phuong
Lara Piccoli
The Planning Practice LLC
Justin Pollard

Piers Pollock
Dominique Poncin
Jeremy Poole
Paul Porter
Ray Poynter
Tony & Pam Price
Eaon Pritchard
David prys-owen
Ainars Pudans
Renee Quan-Knowles
David Rabjohns
Tracey Rainey
Carol Reay
Tony Regan
Margaux Revol
Anton Reyniers
Sean Reynolds
Knut Riedel, Freelance Strategy Director, Germany
Nick Riedle
Tadas Rimkus
Simon Ringshall
Ketaki Rituraj
Toby Roberts
Charlie Robertson
Sheri Roder
Mike Ronkoske
Greg Rowland
Laurence Russ
Cristina Sánchez-Blanco
Hector Saracho
John Sargent
Julian Saunders
Johannes Schneider
Sunil Sekhar
Harry Sharman
George Shepherd
Margarida Silva
Toby Smeeton
Dawn Smith
Vera Sommer
Steven Son
Lilian Sor
Agustín Soriano
Mike Spencer
Liam Spinage
Andrew Stephenson
James Stevens
Kevin Sugrue
Jessica Summerfield
Kevin Sutherland
Lorraine Tabet-Curtis
Matt Tanter
Natasha Tauber
Gemma Teed
Phil Teer
Jestyn Thirkell-White
Leigh Thomas
Josh Tilley
Jimena Toledo
Kim Townend
Nigel Tribe
Dave Trott
Catalin Tudor
Nick Uzunov
Willem van der Horst
Joana Veiga
Miguel Velhinho

Nienke Vonsée
San Vu
Gillian Wakelam
Alex Walker-Sage
Paul Christopher Walton - The Artful Strategist
Judith Wardle
Helen Weavers
Daniel Weir
Sebastian Wendland
Colin Wheeler
Charlotte White
Simon White
Amy Whittaker
David Wilding
Cat Wiles
Charlotte Williams
David Williams
Denise Williams
Julia Williams
Oliver Williams
Paul Wilson
Emma Winter
Alex Wipperfürth
Kevin Wittevrongel
Chris Wojda
Ed Woodcock
Tom Woodnutt
John Wringe
Jan Zajac
Francesca Zedde

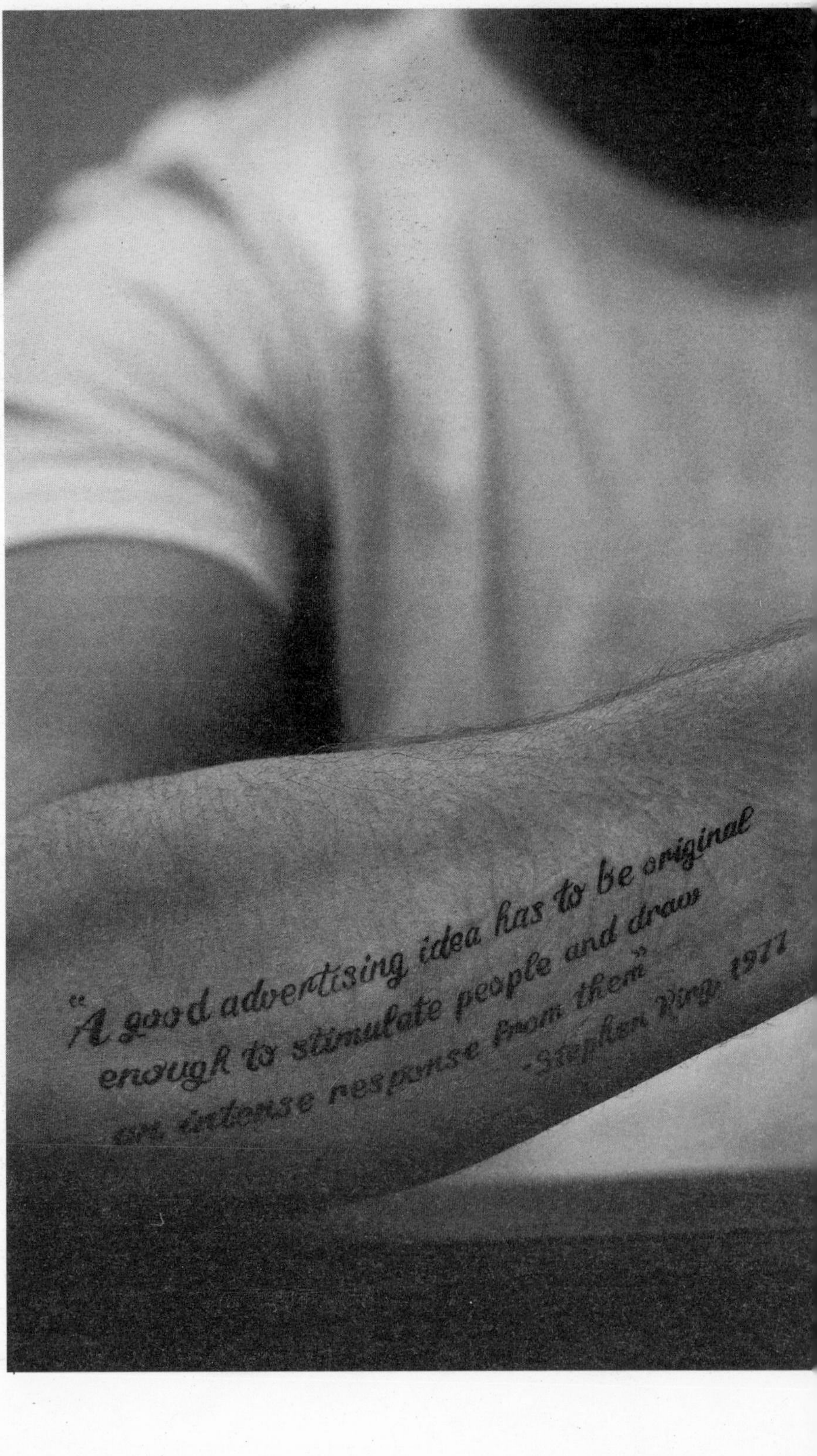

"A good advertising idea has to be original
enough to stimulate people and draw
an intense response from them"
-Stephen King, 1977